NEW RIGHTS
NEW ZEALAND

NEW RIGHTS NEW ZEALAND

Myths, Moralities and Markets.

Dolores Janiewski and Paul Morris

AUCKLAND
UNIVERSITY PRESS

First published 2005

Auckland University Press
University of Auckland
Private Bag 92019
Auckland
New Zealand
www.auckland.ac.nz/aup

ISBN 1 86940 345 2

Publication is assisted by the History Group, Ministry for Culture and Heritage.

Cover illustration: Dylan Horrocks
Printed by Astra Print Ltd, Wellington

Contents

List of Abbreviations

ACT	Association of Consumers and Taxpayers
AEI	American Enterprise Institute
AIPS	Australian Institute for Public Policy
ASI	Adam Smith Institute
CCC	Coalition of Concerned Citizens
CIS	Centre for Independent Studies
CNP	Council for National Policy
CPR	competitive privatising of risk
CPS	Centre for Policy Studies
CPSMU	Centre for Policy Studies, Monash University
DPB	Domestic Purposes Benefit
DSW	Ministry or Department of Social Welfare
ECA	Employment Contracts Act
EFTS	equivalent number of full-time students
FEE	Foundation for Economic Education
IEA	Institute of Economic Affairs, London
IEA-US	Institute for Educational Affairs
IMF	International Monetary Fund
IPA	Institute for Public Affairs
LEP	*Labour's Economic Package*
LEPF	*Labour's Economic Policy: A Framework*
LSE	London School of Economics
MCG	Ministerial Consultative Group
MMP	Mixed Member Proportional Representation
MPS	Mont Pelerin Society
NBR	*National Business Review*
NZBR	New Zealand Business Roundtable
NZVCC	New Zealand Vice-Chancellors' Committee
PTE	Private Training Establishment
SOE	state-owned enterprise
SPCS	Society for the Promotion of Community Standards
SPUC	Society for the Protection of the Unborn Child
SRS	Study Right Scheme
TVC	Traditional Values Coalition
UC	University of Chicago
UGC	University Grants Committee
UTTA	Universal Tertiary Tuition Allowance
WINZ	Work and Income New Zealand

Acknowledgements

The authors want to acknowledge with gratitude the Royal Society of New Zealand Marsden Fund which supported the research upon which this study is based. We thank the International Center for Advanced Studies at New York University, the Schlesinger Library, Victoria University of Wellington and its Faculty of Humanities and Social Sciences for additional funds that helped us complete this research. Just as crucially, we express our gratitude to Elizabeth Caffin of Auckland University Press. We thank the following cartoonists for their generosity in allowing us to reprint their work here: Bob Brockie, Dylan Horrocks, Ross P Kettle and Jim Urry. Brockie's work first appeared in the *National Business Review*, and Horrocks's cartoon in the *Listener*. We also thank Pennie Gapes, Aliki Kalliabetsos and our other colleagues in History and Religious Studies for their continued support. We thank our research associates, Jonathan Brookes and Andrew Gregg, whose first-class Masters theses are another product of the Marsden-funded research project of which we are proud. We thank Craig Turnbull, Scott Sheffield and Grant Morris, who took over some of the US History teaching so that Dolores could focus on research. We also thank Gordon MacKenzie, Sara O'Connell, Evald Subasic, Alice Miller, Rebecca Frost and Peter Fitzhugh who helped with this research. We recognise our debt to the archivists and librarians at the National Library, the Alexander Turnbull Library, the Lesbian and Gay Archives New Zealand, the Library of Congress, the British Library, the Bancroft Library at the University of California, Berkeley, the Hoover Institution Archives and the Victoria University of Wellington Library who helped us. Dolores owes a personal debt of thanks to Barry, Yvette, Maura and Steve. Paul thanks Mary.

Toto: Come with us. The prosperous land is just a short ways down this road!

Dorothy: Are you mad? I'd never follow the brainless, the gutless and the heartless – and that road's not going anywhere!

Introduction

What follows is our analysis of New Zealand's ideological encounter with the New Right in the 1980s and 1990s. By New Right we refer to an intellectual and political movement, sometimes called economic rationalism, market liberalism or neo-liberalism, that has promoted less government and more market over the last thirty years. This movement rejected the post-war consensus about the role of government that accepted Keynesian economics, the welfare state and other forms of state intervention in the economy. Instead, this New Right sought to revive public faith in *laissez-faire* capitalism, a belief in the unregulated free market, earlier discredited by the Great Depression, the vagaries of booms and slumps and the consequent widespread social distress. The demonstrated inadequacies of charities in protecting people also led to the development of government-sponsored welfare programmes to ensure social stability. Opposed to these economic and social interventions, New Right ideologues sought to restore the credibility and appeal of the market and argued for a minimal role for the state in economy and society.[1]

Partially self-generated but also derivative, our New Zealand New Right clearly shows the imprint of a transnational network of corporations, think tanks, political activists and hard-working ideologues. As the recipients of policies and visits from Australian, British and American New Right advocates, we heard much that was familiar in debates in the other three countries. We heard many of the same arguments, read the same books and listened to the same praise for the market and condemnation of the 'nanny' state. Social justice was either an empty slogan or a snare to lure the unwary into the foolish 'mirage' of earthly utopia. Only the stern discipline of the market legitimated the pursuit of self-interest, our individual betterment and future prosperity in the name of working for the 'common good'. Efficiency, personal responsibility and accountability featured as the new cardinal virtues of this market faith in all its temples of worship in New Zealand and elsewhere.

Our New Right resembled the New Rights emerging in other countries in the 1970s. A profound crisis of the state's ability to control inflation, rising unemployment, the end of cheap energy, the contesting of corporate profits from Third World producers and radical movements at home characterised the early 1970s for the United States, Britain, Australia and New Zealand. This shared environment of economic, political and ideological crisis challenged the existing Keynesian framework relying upon state intervention to manage the vicissitudes of the market cycle. The promise of market solutions to these problems gained traction within elite circles linked through the transnational New Right networks. This period fostered the growth of the New Right in all four countries as corporations and their intellectual comrades-in-arms seized the opportunity to promote the reduction of the role of government in the economy. This also entailed checking the power of the mobilised poor, workers, unions, feminists, racial minorities, indigenous peoples and environmentalists. In all four polities electoral successes translated New Right ideology into government policies.

In addition to these similarities, these four countries shared a British heritage, a common ideological lineage in the British imperial system with its emphasis on private property rights, the centrality of commercial enterprise and trade and institutions such as the joint-stock company and corporation. Strengthened military ties during and after World War II and the Cold War reinforced shared ideological commitments. The US ascendancy in the post-World War II era enhanced its influence on Australia and New Zealand, particularly with reference to its opposition to socialist central planning and its commitment to free enterprise. The expansion of the model of American free-market capitalism coupled with US corporate investment in Britain, Australia and New Zealand resulted in greater economic interdependence. Their common language meant increased interaction as modern communications spanned the globe. These interactions fostered the growth of the New Right networks that we discuss in this study.

Despite these shared factors, the rise of the New Right in these four countries as a response to crisis in the 1970s demonstrates the significance of pre-existing differences. There are evident divergences in the size, scale and composition of their economies. In New

Zealand, for example, the importance of the primary sector is far greater than that of the US or Britain. Likewise, our manufacturing sector is comparatively small, with Australia occupying the middle ground between us and the major industrial powers. These diverse economies have generated distinctive labour markets and patterns of unionisation. Class relationships and the role of trade unions, as a result, also varied, with Australia and Britain displaying greater union militancy while the US has relatively weak unions and New Zealand developed an arbitration system that regulated negotiations. All of these differences shaped the response of employers and workers to New Right reforms, with Australia showing the most moderate pace towards reforms of all four as its leaders negotiated an 'accord'. We, on the other hand, underwent the most drastic transformation from regulation to the Employment Contracts Act (ECA) while, in the US, unionisation continued its decline and, in Britain, New Right governments significantly reduced union power.

Politically, the four nations can be divided into two kinds. New Zealand and Britain had unitary, parliamentary governments and Australia and the US had federal systems. The federal structure necessarily entails more complex coalition-building to achieve electoral success and slows down radical and rapid structural change. These political differences partially explain how, but also when and to what extent, the same New Right programme attracted the political support essential to its implementation. In New Zealand the power of Cabinet, the small, interlocking business and political elites and the need to avoid resistance from the usual Labour constituencies both allowed and required New Right reformers to act in extreme haste to impose market reforms centrally and from above. By contrast, in Britain and the US the New Right policies formed an explicit part of election manifestos and party platforms of the Conservative and Republican parties that had historically been supported by businesses, big and small. This was the basis for a concerted campaign to persuade the electorate of the benefits of these proposals by building support for populist market capitalism. In New Zealand and, to a greater extent, in Australia, this kind of New Right populism became more visible in the late 1980s and 1990s, as the Liberals, the two National parties and New Zealand First sought support, often by attacks on beneficiaries, immigrants, refugees and criminals.

The US displays the largest, most vibrant and complex religious culture, a culture that mobilised in response to the challenges to the presence of religion in public life in the 1960s. The religious cultures of Britain and Australia are less dynamic, although Australia in more recent times is beginning to resemble the American case. New Zealand, on the other hand, has the smallest religiously active percentage of the population. These political, cultural and religious differences influence the uptake of New Right doctrines. The New Right coalition that developed most powerfully in the US never emerged here, where the religious and moral conservative right repeatedly lost, rather than won, its battles in the 1980s and 1990s. Our New Right focused on the market faith and the morality required for work, thrift and investment rather than on the sexual sins that excited so many in the US Market liberals assumed leadership positions in the Labour and National parties, but the religious right never managed to forge an alliance with a dominant political party during the fifteen years of the rise of the New Right. Even Margaret Thatcher's talk of 'Victorian values' and John Howard's 'market God' found only faint echoes in our political debates during the New Right ascendancy. The 'dependent poor' might be required to endure lectures about their conduct, but the rest of us objected to moral tutelage. If we could afford to pay the costs of our pleasures or our sins, we could avoid the public scolding or the censoriousness that seemed more prevalent where the heirs to the Puritans held forth. We thus proved less receptive to certain kinds of 'moral politics' than the US, Britain or Australia.

Ideologically, there are other telling differences. Views of the market, support for individualism, antagonism toward the state and the relative importance of equity and egalitarianism vary widely. Americans most stridently endorse the belief in individual autonomy, followed by Australians and then the British and us. Historically, American support for the market economy and opposition to state interference has been the strongest of these four societies. By contrast with the minimalist US welfare system, both Australia and New Zealand developed welfare states based on the universal provision of various services. Post-war Britain followed this pattern in building a broad-based welfare state while at the same time supporting a strong private sector. These differences are crucial to our understanding of the receptivity to the New Right transformational agenda and its scope. Our New Right needed to make the most radical transformation while also facing a public unaccustomed to the private provision of vital social services.

Just as important are the strengths of movements often oppositional to the New Right to which we refer as 'new rights' and 'social justice', occurring in parallel with the New Right's emergence in different polities. An analysis of US newspapers in the 1960s shows that the term 'New Right' often referred to the growing demand for equality for African Americans, for women, people with disabilities, gays and lesbians, prisoners, welfare recipients and other, formerly marginal or subordinated, groups. Over the course of the 1970s, the term 'New Right' increasingly referred to the mobilisation of groups advocating reduced government, free markets and limitations on the drive towards equality, in fact, resisting the advocates of 'new rights'. We will describe the interaction between these two ideological currents while recognising that, in some cases, market liberals displayed sympathy for some forms of individualist feminism, proponents of sexual freedom and entrepreneurial Maori. Indeed, in the New Zealand case, many of our New Right protagonists belonged to the generation that came of age in the late 1960s and 1970s. We may, therefore, have generated more examples of this sort of hybrid between the New Right and 'new rights' than elsewhere. Usually these ideological hybrids insisted that individual claimants for rights primarily sought self advancement, could purchase their own pleasures and adhered to the rules of the market.

The greater tendency, however, towards affirming notions of citizenship and 'social justice' among the proponents of 'new rights' usually resulted in conflicts with the New Right. This particularly occurred when the focus of reforms turned towards social welfare, public expenditure or efforts to promote greater equality through public policy. Our history thus argues for the importance of movements for 'new rights' and social justice as both a goad for New Right mobilisation and a check on the power and the potency of the New Right in achieving its goals.

We tell this history of our New Right with considerable attention directed to issues of morality that have usually been neglected because of the focus on elections, Treasury influence and public policies. We do so in order to make the important point that morality is not merely a reference to sexuality but also concerns the rules governing our conduct towards each other, the provision of health and education and how we view the relative importance of economic freedom, consumer choice and the rights of citizens. We also seek to uncover the religious imperatives often only partially disguised in the promulgation of New Right doctrines by self-identified missionaries and evangelists. In fact, all of us became the targets of moralising discourses during the New Right ascendancy. Welfare and education became *causae belli* in the political battleground of the ideological conflict between the New Right and 'new rights' advocates. The older social democratic and Keynesian consensus politics assumed that education, like health and welfare, constituted a 'public good'. The New Right just as forcibly insisted that these state-conducted enterprises were no such thing, but should be considered commodities like others to be bought and sold in the marketplace. This debate about the essential nature of the 'public good' raged over the fifteen years of our study as the Domestic Purposes Benefit (DPB), the dole, 'user pays', bulk funding, school vouchers, 'values', parental control and 'consumer choice' crowded onto the public agenda. Is the purpose of education to produce independent entrepreneurs or well-rounded, caring citizens? Is the purpose of welfare to enable full participation in community life or to supply a minimal safety net for the 'deserving poor'? Are these aims compatible? The process of cultural re-engineering was to start in the classroom, the welfare office, the streets, the bedroom and in our own notions of acceptable and unacceptable desires. During the 1980s and 1990s, the broader debates about growing the nation's economy to compete in the global world influenced these discussions.

The preferences of sexual consumers *vis-à-vis* the rights of sexual citizens constituted another recurring source of conflict during the same period. Is sexual orientation a right of citizens, a commodity to be sold or a sin to be punished by law for those displaying non-heterosexual preferences? In battles over ratifications of UN covenants, abortion, the decriminalisation of homosexuality and the legal recognition of sexual orientation as a human right we fought over this kind of moral terrain. While we brought over representatives of the British, US and Australian religious right to contribute to these debates, we also invited support from 'new rights' advocates from the same societies who taught us to speak the language of 'social justice' and 'human rights', fostering the growth of notions of sexual citizenship that continue to co-exist uneasily with notions of the sexual marketplace.

New Right organisations such as the New Zealand Business Roundtable (NZBR) and the Centre for Independent Studies (CIS) sought to teach us the market-appropriate answers to our social dilemmas. The CIS began in the mid-1970s in Australia and established a branch in New Zealand in the 1980s. In the mid-1980s the NZBR began its efforts to convert us to its members' faith in the market. Early in the 1990s it established the Education Forum to argue this case and attack 'false' notions of equality, cooperation and collectivism. These organisations published numerous reports urging us to adopt reforms intended to produce a more competitive, 'open' economy. Its spokesmen and imported lecturers combated ideas of 'public good' in order to prepare us to think of ourselves primarily as businessmen, consumers and taxpayers, rather than active and equal citizens in a participatory democracy. Public services, transformed into commodities to be purchased on the basis of unit cost and quality, became a part of the NZBR's efforts to privatise our values. The NZBR and other New Right advocates sought to inculcate enterprising virtues, teach us the joys of competition and the internalised discipline essential to success as self-actualising marketeers, consumers and entrepreneurs.

We begin this history with our analysis of the myths about our New Right experience that have shaped previous interpretations, pointing to the sources of these mythic versions of our past in Genesis, Exodus and other books of the Bible. In Genesis, the first book of the Bible, our first parents Adam and Eve, tempted by the Serpent, disobey God and eat the fruit of the Tree of Knowledge of Good and Evil. God ordered them to leave the Garden of Eden and earn their living by the sweat of their brow and, in the case of Eve, to give birth in increased pain and sorrow. This version of our past looks back to the Golden Age of the welfare state, the prosperous 1950s or the pre-European Maori past and puts the New Right in the position of the serpent that tempted Eve and Adam in the Garden of Eden. Exodus and the subsequent books in the Old Testament tell the story of the Israelites, enslaved in Egypt and then rescued by God, under the leadership of Moses and Aaron, who led them to the Promised Land. After many trials their long journey ultimately leads them into Israel, but Moses and Aaron have died *en route*. Moses is allowed to see the Promised Land but not to go there. Despite our ostensibly secular culture, we, often unconsciously, continue to draw from these mythic stories of origin and destiny to tell our history, even of the very recent past, as our first chapter will demonstrate.

As the second chapter acknowledges, we owe a debt to our predecessors who have written parts of the history that we now reinterpret. In our exegesis of the scholarship we point out where earlier authors have cogently described our New Right encounter before developing upon these interpretations in the rest of the book. In chapter three we widen the usual cast of characters beyond the Treasury, Roger Douglas, David Lange and Ruth Richardson to provide a series of vignettes of crucial actors in the New Right saga. Here we bring in Australian and New Zealand participants and introduce the stories of people who remain active in our public life into the present. These include such notable additions as Donna Awatere Huata, Jenny Shipley, Margaret Bazley, Don Brash, the current leader of the Opposition, and his office chief, Richard Long, John Stone, the former Australian Treasurer, and John Howard. This chapter draws parallels between our trans-Tasman neighbour and our own New Right experience while describing the earlier careers of still influential people.

The narrative then moves offshore to trace the New Right networks and the ideology that flowed through the circuits that connected us to developments and institutions in the US and Britain. Those countries' embrace of the New Right in the late 1970s and early 1980s undoubtedly influenced the reforms of both Australia and New Zealand in the mid-1980s. After discussing the New Right ascendancy in Reagan's America and Thatcher's Britain, we then analyse the moral vision of New Right prophets, beginning with Adam Smith before turning to Friedrich von Hayek, Milton Friedman, James Buchanan, Michael Novak and Robert Sirico. The New Rights of the US and Britain gave our New Right the example, vocabulary and specific policy reforms. The advocates of a morality compatible with the 'free' market provided the guidebook or code from which our New Right instructed us in market ethics.

The middle chapters trace the history of our New Right in the 1980s and 1990s as a political programme undertaken initially by the Fourth Labour Government in the 1980s and then by the National Government in the early 1990s. In view of the number of studies, particularly discussing the 1980s, we cover only the most crucial developments in this history of our New Right transformation. We next trace this history in three specific areas where the New Right and 'new rights' advocates were particularly active: education, sexuality and welfare. Here we show the differentiation between our New Right and other New Rights, primarily traceable to the strong and continuing resistance by proponents of what we call 'new rights' who enjoyed greater access to power and influence than in the US, Britain or Australia. These advocates of 'social justice' mobilised in parallel to the New Right, offering competing visions that opposed the New Right individualised morality and preference for market solutions. Out of that clash came our 'third way' approach that has largely defined government action over the last six years.

We then conclude this retracing of our New Right journey by pointing out that we continue to grapple with similar issues and debates six years after the official declaration of the death of 'neo-liberalism' and the 'third way' turn of our political fortunes. Much of this past maintains an institutional presence because we have not returned to the edenic garden of the welfare state and protected markets nor did we continue to march forward towards the New Right market utopia. Although New Right advocates such as the NZBR appear to have lost much of their earlier political influence, some of those who claimed Hayek as an inspiration may be on the verge of a return to power should the National Party win the 2005 election. Inspired by the successes of its American and Australian counterparts, the New Right-influenced National Party is attempting to persuade us to think of ourselves exclusively as taxpayers and consumers and promising us tax cuts and greater consumer power should it assume control of the Treasury benches once again.

Brash, the current leader of the National Party, and other members of the National caucus are well-connected members of the New Right transnational network. Their speeches, policies and criticisms resonate with the New Right policies of the 1980s and 1990s. In particular, the focus on welfare reform, condemnation of

Maori 'privilege' and 'political correctness', increased punishment for criminals, personal and corporate tax cuts and dramatic cuts in public spending all can be traced back to the 1980s and the 1990s. They claim that these policies will enhance market activity, encourage international competitiveness and create a moral system that rewards the hard-working and entrepreneurial amongst us while punishing the lazy, the feckless and the wicked. The contemporary debate over these proposals will replicate those found in this study.

Once again our New Right is facing off against the advocates of 'new rights' and 'social justice', hurling accusations of 'political correctness' against the proponents of equality and social inclusiveness. For example, Brash attended the Maxim Institute Forum on 'political correctness' in March 2004 with Peter Dunne and Richard Prebble along with other international campaigners against 'new rights'. Dunne seized the opportunity to denounce 'pink think' and defend 'family values'. Brash announced that he had deleted 'Pakeha' from his vocabulary in defence to the sensitivities of European New Zealanders, as a part of his campaign against 'racial privilege'. This was a recent episode in a crusade launched by the US New Right in the early 1990s that soon reached our shores, bringing terms like 'feminazi', 'welfarism' and, of course, 'political correctness'. From the British New Right we gained additions to this vocabulary of disparagement including 'nanny state'. This attack, often including the scapegoating of minorities – racial, class, gender – is one of the many rhetorical weapons of the New Right that promotes the market and undermines those who criticise neo-liberal economic reforms.

Also, as has been true in the US and Australia, we may be witnessing the revival of the fortunes of our religious right after a series of defeats over the last twenty-five years that we discuss in this history. The 2002 success of United Future, the appearance of the Destiny Party on our streets and the establishment of the Maxim Institute in recent years are signs that some of our New Right activists seek to emulate Australia and the US in fostering a resurgence of 'moral politics' focused on 'family values', education and welfare. The vocal presence of the Sensible Sentencing Trust is another example that points to the area of public policy in which we most closely resemble the United States: our reliance upon prisons to punish our criminals and the ethnic minority identity of our prisoners. As we will argue at the conclusion, the march towards the promised land of New Right visions may yet resume under the leadership of a new coalition of market liberals and moral conservatives. If enough of us express our willingness to resume that journey when we go to the polls, this history of the 1980s and 1990s will supply a road map for what we are likely to experience *en route* to the New Right Promised Land.

PART ONE

Genesis: Myths and Travellers' Tales

And out of the ground made the LORD God to grow every tree that is pleasant to the sight and good for food; the tree of life also in the midst of the garden and the tree of knowledge of good and evil. GENESIS 2:9

CHAPTER ONE

Garden of Eden or Pharaoh's Egypt?
New Zealand before 1984

And they burnt the city with fire and all that was therein: only the silver and the gold and the vessels of brass and of iron, they put into the treasury.
JOSHUA 6:24

The revolutionary's Utopia, which in appearance represents a complete break with the past, is always modelled on some image of the lost paradise, of a legendary Golden Age. All Utopias are fed from the sources of mythology; the social engineer's blueprints are merely revised editions of the ancient text. ARTHUR KOESTLER, *THE GOD THAT FAILED*[1]

'She'll be right' and 'do anything with a piece of number eight fencing wire' are the touchstones by which we understand ourselves as New Zealanders. We claim common sense as our supreme cultural virtue. Even as our national anthem proclaims 'God defend New Zealand', we pride ourselves on telling our stories unvarnished by religious or ideological gloss. 'Godzone' rarely refers to mythic origins but is more likely to be an ironic reference to our national secularity. While we rely on 'common sense' to account for almost everything, it is clearly not what we have actually used to explain the rise of the New Right in New Zealand. The 'right turn', initiated by the Fourth Labour Government in 1984 and continued by successive National and coalition governments until 1999, has provoked intense debate which has often been 'partisan, polarised and unhistorical'.[2] Those involved have relied upon myth to augment, if not totally displace, argument and history.

Surprisingly, given the apparently secular nature of New Zealand society, the Bible has been a major mythic source. New Zealand has no national church. Our attendance at religious worship is extremely low when compared with Australia or the United States and only a small minority of us has any education at all in scripture. When the story of the New Right transformation is told, however, we reach instinctively for the Bible. Myths are orienting stories telling us where we have been, where we are and where we are going. By invoking the known, myths enhance our sense of security because we already know our destiny. Biblical myths legitimate the present by re-narrating our past, providing a guide for the future. Myths simplify complex realities, suppressing ambiguities and erasing discordant details. The appeal of myth lies in this very two-dimensionality. But the repressed elements return in the form of alternative myths. This contest of biblical myths is evident in the rival accounts of the New Right.

The impact of rapid economic and political change in the 1970s and 1980s undermined our sense of security. This shock was intensified because a Labour Government introduced New Right reforms in 1984. The rewriting of biblical plots provided familiar frameworks to make sense of our profound cultural crisis. The two dominant versions of the origins of the New Right in New Zealand repeated the biblical stories of Zions lost and Zions yet to be found. One mythic current can be traced back to laments for a paradise lost, that is, a version of the Genesis narrative of Adam, Eve and the expulsion from the edenic garden. The other mythic source is Exodus, a story of liberation from oppression and the difficult journey towards the Promised Land. In the New Zealand case, the Exodus story preceded the retelling of Genesis, as one biblical myth generated another. New Right advocates utilised Exodus to tell of our liberation from serfdom. Their opponents turned to Genesis to defend our paradise, pre-1984 New Zealand. Biblical myths, part of the inheritance of all New Zealanders – Pakeha, Maori and Polynesian – explain the causes of our distress and offer consolation by plotting our way forward or backward to a better place.

Roger Douglas, leading instigator of New Zealand's New Right, the Moses of our Exodus story, began to use biblical themes in the 1978 campaign. Douglas established an informal think tank to promote the free market as the antidote to dependency in the house of bondage and the only way of funding Labour Party social welfare policies. He expanded his 1979 'Alternative Budget' into *There's*

Got to Be a Better Way!, published a year later. Here, Douglas contended that our country was the most regulated economy in the world, enslaving both individuals and businesses. We had lost our 'spirit' in the 'selfish pursuit of narrow interests'. Our dependency upon government had resulted in uncompetitive enterprises vying for political favour rather than efficiently meeting consumer demand.[3]

Our path to liberation entailed removing the evils of 'market distortions', inflation, balance-of-payment deficits and the other plagues afflicting New Zealand. Douglas intended to lead us from 'adversity and long-term decline' to our 'prosperous destiny' by means of a 20 per cent devaluation, an honest tax regime and the opening of 'fortress' New Zealand to the discipline of market forces. Declaring that we must 'trade or die', Douglas urged us to follow him towards the Promised Land of payroll tax, 'productivity' and prosperity.[4]

Exodus themes emerged still more fully when Douglas produced the 1983 economic statement before being anointed Shadow Minister of Finance. Adam Smith's 'invisible hand' – the market deity in this interpretation of Exodus – took a more dominant role as Douglas came under the influence of Treasury economists and other pro-market advisors. When Labour won the snap election in mid-1984, in this rendering of the 'burning bush' story, Douglas received the authority and power to lead us out of slavery. The Treasury briefing paper, *Economic Management*, and the Economic Summit Conference provided our marching orders. Designed to overcome deficit, economic deterioration, unemployment and excessive regulation, these market commandments outlined the path through the Red Sea of debt and currency devaluation to our promised freedom in the land.[5]

Completed the month of the Labour victory in 1984, Harvey Franklin's *Cul de Sac* stressed the importance of liberating us from the burdens of our past. Franklin added another mythic source to the Exodus story. Agreeing on the need to unleash 'market forces', Franklin predicted that Douglas's reforms might open 'Pandora's box' because New Zealand with 'its fixed ideas' and 'social divisions' might be unable to change. The welfare state had already created a 'rancorous, divisive society', which needed to be restructured in order to escape from the pharaonic Muldoonist state. Franklin and others considered this worth undertaking even if there was a high risk of never reaching the Promised Land.[6]

Unconvinced by the Exodus story, other commentators asked us to turn to Genesis for the correct interpretation of New Right reforms. In February 1985 Gordon Campbell characterised these reforms as 'Rogernomics'. Rather than portraying Douglas as Moses, this rhetorical weapon linked Douglas to Ronald Reagan at a time of friction between New Zealand and the United States. As the Genesis story unfolded, pre-1984 New Zealand became the Garden of Eden. Wolfgang Rosenberg's *The Magic Square* labelled the period from the founding of the welfare state to the late 1960s an 'economic miracle' and predicted disastrous results from the New Right reforms. The prophets of Rogernomics were zealots whose 'faith in the self-regulating powers of the economy for the benefit of all' had the 'fervour' of a 'religion'. We should return to our paradise lost rather than follow a misguided Moses into the desolate emptiness of a world stripped bare by market forces.[7]

Simon Collins and Brian Easton portrayed the capture of our government by an 'extreme form' of market liberalism as the serpent in the Garden. Collins depicted New Zealand before our fall into 'Rogernomics' as an enclosed, secure and safe space now being destroyed in an 'orgy of deregulation'. Douglas was a 'radical' who was 'reversing interventionist trends as old as Pakeha settlement' itself. Rather than leading us towards the Promised Land, this false prophet was taking us down an erroneous path towards greater inequality and the corrosion of our democracy.[8] Easton wrote a history of our 'intellectual colonisation' by monetarists and neoclassical economists based in the United States. He focused on a heretical cult of Treasury officials, including Roger Kerr, Bryce Wilkinson and Rob Cameron. Calling them 'the Group', he described these economists as worshipping the false god of the 'Chicago School'. Easton portrayed these heretics as 'so dominated by their theory that they tend to ignore contradicting evidence'.[9] In Easton's version of Genesis, the Tree of Knowledge of Good and Evil bore the poisoned fruit of ideology: neo-liberalism; monetarism; managerialism; privatisation; and public choice. The Treasury snake sought to persuade us to consume the forbidden fruit, but, having eaten it, we 'would surely' find ourselves naked and expelled from the Garden.

Bruce Jesson waxed nostalgically about the 'golden age of the historic compromise' before our paradise had been destroyed by the New Right reforms. When Chicago School acolytes took over Treasury, they succeeded in convincing the Labour Cabinet to blame the pharaoh's 'think big' for the evils that had blighted our land. Prominent members of Labour's left wing shared the antagonism to the heavy-handed Muldoonist state. Having been persuaded to eat the fruit of market liberalism, the Labour Cabinet, like the Treasury and NZBR, became greedy rather than wise. This tale described how we, having been betrayed by errant Adams and reptilian economists, found ourselves cursed and exiled from Eden. Jesson's narrative of the Labour Government's decline and fall became a lament for a paradise lost.[10]

By the 1990s, these rival mythical accounts had become a part of our cultural repertoire. Writing for the *National Business Review* (*NBR*), Chris Trotter deployed Genesis against Exodus as he wrote about the Fourth Labour Government. 'Toll gates' had blocked the road to the 'promised land' for the young, the unemployed, Maori and the elderly, but baby-boomers had achieved their dreams of power and prosperity. Incorporating a moral critique of the 'greedy', Trotter's version of the snake in the Garden included pensioners – 'an increasingly selfish and reckless generation' – who had grabbed generous superannuation for themselves at the cost of their children and grandchildren. David Novitz described a 'fragmented nation' gripped by the pervasive sense 'that we are lost'.[11] Despite wandering in the desert, we had yet to discover the direction to our Promised Land.

Ruth Richardson, the Minister of Finance in the National Government elected in 1990, followed Douglas, as Joshua did Moses. She blew the trumpet that made the walls of the welfare state 'tremble and tumble down'. Reading from Douglas's authorised translation of Exodus, Richardson portrayed 'Fortress New Zealand' as the 'most regulated economy', a 'choice-less' Egypt. The world's most protected and 'inflexible industrial relations system' had forced the slaves to labour on useless pyramid building rather than make it 'worthwhile to invest' in productive enterprises. After a promising start, the Labour Government had stalled the march forward and left us exposed to the ever-present danger of returning to the house of bondage where 'everything that is not forbidden is compulsory'.[12] So ran Ruth's sermon about our benighted past.

Issuing the new covenant in the 'mother of all budgets', Richardson described us as 'adrift' somewhere on a Red Sea that had yet to be crossed. Under her guidance, the boat would reach the shore and the march begin again. 'The 1990s will be New Zealand's decade' in which 'we discover the energy and self-confidence that we had of old'. Having briefly harkened back to the blissful 'life on the land' before the 'forty years' of welfare-state serfdom, Richardson proclaimed that we must soon reach the Promised Land, the 'true enterprise society' where 'we take on and beat the rest of the world' and finally 'think of ourselves as winners'. The rewritten 'Book of Ruth' redefined the relationship between workers and their bosses, slashed benefits to make toil rewarding and mandated market rule over all sectors of our national life. The 'tiger economies' of East Asia represented our enterprising ideal. Having escaped from the paternalistic 'collectivism' of the past and overcome its 'sapping of the spirit', we faced the challenge of completing our free-market 'renaissance' based on the 'initiative and enterprise of the individual'.[13]

Having moved from Treasury to his new position at the NZBR, Roger Kerr produced the chief executive's edition of the Bible, urging on the reform agenda and exhorting us to continue the journey. It was a collaborative effort by many of our corporate leaders. The apostles of the NZBR delineated the 'fatal delusion' and 'myths' of their opponents as they presented their textual truths. Kerr complained about the 'Marxian-Fabian vision' and reminded us to 'leap towards freedom, not shuffle'. He explained the difficulty in convincing us of the merits of reform by quoting from the *Book of Common Prayer* – 'We have left undone those things we ought to have done and we have done those things which we ought not to have done' – and therefore concluded that this explained why 'economic salvation has eluded us'. Instead of marching forward, we too willingly paused to take tea breaks or to purchase the products of 'snake oil' peddlers. Douglas Myers meditated on the barriers to our success, a long 'litany of shibboleths' inherited from the 'socialist bloc', 'command economy' of our 'fortress New Zealand' era. Alan Gibbs lamented that Marxism 'seems to be alive and well in New Zealand'. Asking what sort of country we wanted to be, Kerr, as God's scribe, listed the seven deadly sins that prevented us from having a 'culture of enterprise, excellence, tolerance and success'. Emphasising negative attitudes towards tall poppies, the United States and businessmen, the NZBR's biblical narrative concentrated on the difficulties of the ever-lengthening journey to the Promised Land.[14]

Colin James's *New Territory* allowed us to be 'free to choose' between the two versions of our New Right transformation. We had been 'burdened and blinkered' by two pasts. One was 'Godzone', our 'paradise lost'. The other was the hidebound society of Muldoon and the welfare state. Now we were moving into 'new and uncharted territory', the New Right's Promised Land. Our 'fall from grace' was also our journey towards a 'new sort of New Zealand' where we could become 'independent, self-reliant and outward-looking, bicultural and tolerant of diversity'. Arguing against the myth that a 'small cabal of usurpers' had taken control of the Fourth Labour Government, James's 'quiet revolution' can be considered a battle between two biblical myths narrating our past and predicting our future.[15]

Worried that we might prefer the 'old' New Zealand instead of the 'new', the NZBR published another chapter of their biblical epic in 1994. Douglas Myers offered us two future scenarios: 'fast forward' to reach 'East Asian levels of performance', or 'rewind' to 'fortress New Zealand' as advocated by the 'false prophets'. The gospel of Bob Matthew warned about a possible return to 'the Polish shipyard' if we followed the dangerously charismatic Winston Peters or sought to revive Muldoonist 'mediocrity'. Matthew wanted to lead us to the 'real world' where prosperity beckoned. Asking us to gird up our loins for the arduous journey, Kerr promised an 'economic miracle' if we discarded the remaining baggage of the interventionist legacy that burdened us. Miraculously, 'kiwis' could learn to 'fly' but a 'return to former bad habits' would turn us into a flightless 'endangered species' unable to move at the requisite speed.[16]

Countering the NZBR's Exodus, the authors of *A Leap into the Dark* issued jeremiads against the New Right. According to Susan St John, 'our political masters and their advisers who no longer believe in the traditional New Zealand values' had destroyed the welfare state. Referring to 'true believers in the values of competition, self-reliance, freedom, individualism, choice and market signals', she criticised New Right 'dogma' as trying to recreate the fantasy 'family of the past'. St John wanted the restoration of 'our traditional welfare state' to recreate an edenic New Zealand of 'fair play, justice, cooperation, community and equality'. Jane Kelsey featured two Rogers in her Garden story: Douglas as Eve and Kerr as the slithering snake. Tempted by the snake, Eve in turn tempts Adam, here David Lange and the Labour Cabinet. Kelsey argued for New Zealand's restoration as an autonomous nation, uncontaminated by malevolent external forces and able to maintain our own cultural identity. Both attacking the legitimacy of the New Zealand state and desiring its power to be restored, Kelsey described a paradoxical paradisial polity that exercised sovereignty and relinquished it at the same time, a utopian vision difficult to achieve anywhere except within the mythical Garden.[17]

For Andrew Sharp the destructive force in his retelling of Genesis was the uncritical reliance upon 'economic rationality'. Sharp objected to the imposition of 'abstract' models of justice and the 'free market'. We had become 'an unpleasant atomised consumer culture of possessive individualists', the very society Richardson had held up as a national ideal. Sharp narrated our transformation as a decline into ideological bondage turning New Zealand into an'arid desert'.[18] Describing a leap into the darkness of toil and trouble, Sharp reversed the Exodus journey. We had foolishly departed from the Promised Land only to wander in the wilderness.

Kelsey's *The New Zealand Experiment* added another Eve to the Garden story. This Eve was Richardson who pursued the 'liberal agenda with an evangelical fervour' turning her 'zeal' on beneficiaries. She allowed the 'invisible hands' of 'Rogernomics' to grip us just as tightly as they had before. Substituting tangata whenua for the Old Testament's 'chosen people' and Marx's proletariat, Kelsey located her Eden in the Maori past. She contemptuously rejected the 'social democratic ideal of the harmonious classless society based on the conformist, upwardly mobile, two-parent, consumption-oriented family unit, cosseted by a benevolent government'. In addition to Genesis, Kelsey adopted a 'turn around' rhetorical approach that linked the New Right with attributes usually associated with Marxists in anti-Communist diatribes. She deployed terms such as 'zealotry', 'ideology', 'enemies within', 'fellow travellers' and 'ruthlessness' to denounce the creators of a 'liberal reformer's paradise'. Kelsey's edenic Aotearoa alternated between a pre-European Maori culture and a future utopian New

Zealand, bicultural, pristine and protected from contaminating external influences.[19]

Easton adopted a similar strategy comparing New Right advocates to the totalitarian enemy they usually attacked as the 'Nanny state'. The 'Troika' of Douglas, Richard Prebble and David Caygill had mounted a 'blitzkrieg' reform offensive. Treasury 'philosopher kings' believed in a 'pure, flawless ideal of the market' that verged on ideological 'extremism'. Easton delightedly repeated Joseph Stiglitz's reference to 'market Bolsheviks', here directed against Douglas, Richardson and the Treasury. They used a 'peaceful version of Lenin's methods to make the opposite transition'. New Right reforms were the new 'permanent revolution'. Like Kelsey, Easton wrote about the 'religious zealotry' of New Right believers in 'ultimate truth', 'fundamentalist ideology' and their intolerance towards 'unbelievers'. Easton's nationalist critique of ideological 'imperialism' located evil as emanating from outside the New Zealand Eden.[20] The restoration of common sense and empirically based economics offered a way for us to escape from a fanatic monetarist cult that had seized power in our land.

Election years appeared to require another entry to the NZBR's recounting of the never-ending journey towards the Promised Land. Switching from birds to cars, the 1996 scriptural addition called upon us to move into the 'fast lane'. The process of reform must be accelerated. Aware, perhaps that we might object to speeding down the highway towards a destination unknown, the new chapter fleshed out details of our future. Importing a travelling evangelist of the New Right, the NZBR brought David Green to New Zealand. Proselytising on behalf of 'civil society', Green argued for virtue, independence and the 'moral order'. One of the 'industrious' characters in Charles Dickens's *Hard Times* was an admirable model for us. The Promised Land was entrepreneurial Britain before the 'corrosive effects of welfare' had degraded the 'moral sentiments' that the New Right Adam, the founding prophet of this creed, had extolled in *The Wealth of Nations*.[21]

Later NZBR commentators on Green's interpretation of the ideal society added the notion of 'Victorian values'. Including Friedrich von Hayek in their list of prophets, Green and his sympathisers warned against the 'fatal conceit' of thinking that we can remodel entire societies. Societies could not be 'born again' so it was best to look in the past to recover the values of 'bourgeois culture', a system of 'voluntary exchange developed historically in a particular moral setting' as the best way to insulate us from the 'tyranny' of the state. Myers affirmed the 'civil society' doctrine, condemned 'moral relativism and endorsed traditional values as the 'moral edifice' upon which 'civilisation had hitherto been based'. Warning of the danger of another 'dark age', Myers, like other contributors to the discussion of 'civil society', drew his blueprints for New Zealand's future from the British past.[22]

Interjecting himself into the debate, Donald Brash, Governor of the Reserve Bank, paid his own homage to Hayek in 1996 as he lectured at Green's home institution, the Institute of Economic Affairs (IEA) in London. Speaking about 'New Zealand's Remarkable Reforms', Brash identified pre-1984 New Zealand as an exemplar of Hayek's vision of 'serfdom'. Admittedly, New Zealand's version was 'bureaucratic' domination, not the 'police-state and concentration-camp variety' of totalitarianism that Hayek had predicted. Quoting Alexis de Tocqueville, Brash bemoaned the constraints of many small rules by which the 'will of man is not shattered but softened, bent and guided'. Not tyranny but enervation was the fate of those who allowed the government to become their 'shepherd'. In spite of evident successes, Brash lamented that New Zealanders had not yet been convinced of the need for additional privatisation and further market solutions. He quoted Lindsay Perigo describing New Zealand as a country 'reformed by Hayekians, run by pragmatists and populated by socialists'. We had yet to be converted into people who understood the requirements of a 'free society'. Although Brash's speech and Green's description of our future attracted critical comment, their arguments also found support from journalists and the NZBR faithful.[23]

The myths migrated into other media forms as they became increasingly established as the dominant 'paradigms of New Zealand national identity'. The duel between *Somebody Else's Country* and *Revolution* in 1996 translated Exodus and Genesis into traditional 'taking heads' documentaries. Unabashedly partisan, Alister Barry's *Somebody Else's Country* 'painted the conflict inherent' in the New Right transformation as 'part of an ongoing struggle between the forces of good and evil'. Likening the Douglas reforms to the Chilean coup, a military takeover that led to economic change being guided by Milton Friedman and his Chilean disciples, Barry named the Treasury, Douglas, Richardson, Jenny Shipley and the NZBR as villains. A 'loose coalition of Kiwis' occupied the heroes' position as they struggled against the 'New Right juggernaut'.[24]

Proclaiming 'it was our revolution', Ian Fraser, in *Revolution*, took his viewers on a tour of the 'feudal economy' of New Zealand during the Muldoon era when the Prime Minister 'decisively' used the 'levers of power' to 'control and regulate our lives'. The New Right reforms freed us from the 'heavy burden of the aging Muldoon generation' as 'we forged an independent identity'. Using the journey metaphor, Fraser described New Zealand as doing 'an about turn' and marching in a 'different direction'. Referring to the 'touchstones of Kiwi identity', Barry's depiction of a nation 'stolen from beneath our feet' contrasted with *Revolution*'s presentation of a 'new society'. In one documentary paradise had been stolen; in the other, a 'brave new free society' had been born.[25]

During the election year of 1999, the NZBR's rhetoric shrilly urged us to keep on speeding down the 'right track'. Rail metaphors came into play as though motor vehicles were no longer powerful enough to keep us moving forward. Fearing that the 'writing was on the wall' in the waning days of the Coalition Government, Myers warned that we had fallen asleep at the switch: 'New Zealand needs a loud wake-up call. The way we are going the whole country will soon be on Prozac. What is the way ahead?' Kerr asked, 'Why is New Zealand not doing better?'[26] He concluded that the New Right project might career off the rails unless we woke up. Having exhorted us to march, fly, drive and put our shoulders to the wheel, we had not yet reached the promised destination. Perhaps the problem was that the journey had not taken the forty biblical years to allow those of us who had known the welfare state to die out. The note of impatience with our sluggishness and ideological recalcitrance was unmistakable. Somewhere along the decade-and-a-half journey we had stopped listening to the commands to step up our pace. We had resisted the call to create a 'code of social responsibility' and we now appeared likely to vote the Coalition Government out of power. Time appeared to be running out for the New Right experiment and signs of panic appeared in the midst of the clamour for continued reforms.

Not seeming to notice the desperation of the NZBR's repeated use of Exodus, Jesson in his last book, *Only Their Purpose is Mad*, continued the scriptural battle, drawing upon Old and New Testaments. He lamented that the 'money men', the adherents of a 'political creed' espousing a 'dogmatic belief in the market', had destroyed the New Zealand he loved. Jesson mourned the disappearance of our 'unsophisticated, homely values', 'community spirit', 'mateship and belonging'. The prophets of 'acquisitive individualism' had successfully converted us to 'a culture of hedonism and avarice'. Kerr stalked 'the land preaching a free market, anti-state message'. The 'democratic institutions of the nation state', the welfare state and the 'full employment' economy had withered as the financial overlords took over. Although Jesson disliked the 'shallow culture' and the 'apolitical' conformity of pre-reform New Zealand, the 'material and spiritual poverty to which the New Right project has brought us' was far worse.[27] Both a temple defiled and a greed-polluted garden, New Zealand must be cleansed and the financial invaders repelled in order to bring us back to the Garden. Jesson would not live to see whether we had hearkened to his impassioned message.

The period from 1984 to 1999 was a time of heightened ideological crisis. Ideology always requires myth as its primary vehicle of communication. Myths are finally just that, orienting narratives, often of great rhetorical power and emotional appeal. In this case they framed the ideological debate between supporters of the New Zealand New Right and their opponents. As we have seen, the use of myth generated mythic responses. The clash of the myths of Genesis and Exodus operated at the surface level of rallying the troops and securing political and electoral support. By the 1999 election, paradise was long lost and the Promised Land ever further receding into the distance. After fifteen years, these myths had lost their credibility. We no longer felt consoled by the story of a past utopia because we understood that there was no way back to the Garden. We also remembered that Moses and the generation born into slavery never lived to see the Promised Land. The run-up to the 1999 election witnessed the 'final conflict' between these myths before their temporary storage in our political unconscious, waiting for us to need them again during the next period of prolonged ideological combat.

This chapter has traced the origins and appropriations of the revised editions of Genesis and Exodus. The importance of this account is to enable us to recognise the mythic dimensions of these stories, which reduce the complexity of historical events into their all-too-familiar plots. Myths use simple archetypes of good versus evil, paradise versus serfdom and true versus false prophets. Our history lies beneath these 'polarised' oppositions, only to be accessed by the interpretation of these myths. We need to read these stories from an 'ancient text' to uncover what has been concealed by their partial and fragmented versions of our recent past.[28] In the next chapter we undertake just such necessary 'exegesis'.

CHAPTER TWO

Exegesis:
Interpretations and Commentary

Myths may be used to cast light on past events or to conceal. RANGINUI WALKER, *NGA TAU TOHETOHE/ YEARS OF ANGER*[1]

And God spake all these words, saying, I am the LORD thy God, which have brought thee out of the land of Egypt, out of the house of bondage. EXODUS 20:1–2

Ranginui Walker's introduction to 'Myths Unmade', a chapter in *Nga Tau Tohetohe/Years of Anger*, shows that the work of exegesis is already under way. Like Professor Walker, we want to scape away the myths that conceal the past and corrode our collective memory. Scholars and perceptive commentators, including a number of those discussed in the previous chapter, have worked to rescue us from the 'endemic malady' that Ranginui Walker called 'historical amnesia'. We have an analogous aim: to shed 'light' on New Zealand's New Right.[2]

Dr Walker criticised our myth of a golden era of race relations. He challenged peace activists and anti-apartheid demonstrators to look as critically at New Zealand as they did the United States or South Africa. Elsewhere in his writings he calls for honest discussion. Referring to Christianity and the market as integral parts of a 'colonising' culture, he argued that the market is an historical creation rather than embedded in human nature as some of its proponents allege. 'Under capitalism' land became a 'commodity', an ideology in 'conflict' with the beliefs of tangata whenua who had opposed tribal lands being 'transformed to individual title'. As he correctly contended, laws, like myths, have been 'made and unmade' by human beings. Just as acutely, he pointed to the way the media disseminated myths about crime, gangs, activists and our history that make it difficult for us to understand our present and our past. Refusing to obey the injunction to 'forget the past', he exposed dominant myths.[3] His example will guide us in writing the history that is to follow.

Notwithstanding the rage expressed in Donna Awatere's *Maori Sovereignty*, it too offered a useful corrective to the mythic portrayal of the welfare state. In amongst the invocation of myths such as the Exodus, Awatere provided a withering critique of a settler state unwilling to relinquish its ties to its imperial ancestor. Rightly arguing the importance of culture, rather than race, despite her own inconsistent references to 'white' people, Awatere addressed issues that are ignored by nostalgic references to the pre-1984 past. Her writings in her later reincarnation as an ACT MP pointed to the unarguable fact that the New Right emphasis on 'choice' could appeal to Maori whose cultural aspirations had been submerged in a monocultural system.[4]

As the most prolific critics of the New Right, Jesson, Easton and Kelsey have exposed important parts of our recent history. Other commentators, particularly James and Jonathan Boston with other academic colleagues, have provided important insights from a more centrist position. New Right advocates have also highlighted important aspects of the historical situation in which they undertook the reformation of the New Zealand state and economy. These earlier analysts of our New Right past have clarified some significant parts of our history.

Not unsurprisingly, New Right proponents stressed the extent of the danger that we faced in 1984, the result in their view of years of avoiding necessary reforms in economic policy. The first issue highlighted by the reformers was the need for a consistent economic policy uncorrupted by the National Government's election 'bribes'. More important was the immediate foreign exchange and debt crisis of 1984 generated by the level of Muldoon's borrowing. Interviewed in 1999, Bernie Galvin insisted that there was no alternative to the devaluation of the dollar and the wholesale reform of the economy. He denied that there were alternative courses of action, such as the rescheduling of interest and debt payments, additional loans and so on. The reformers took the opportunity and ran with the 'crisis'. Following the devaluation of the dollar, New Zealand's 'protectionist state' was systemically taken apart in the light of the New Right strategy to open New Zealand to the world.

Douglas's analysis of the country inherited by the Labour Government in July 1984 was a nation in 'crisis' as 'a direct consequence of poor policy'. By the mid-1970s large-scale government borrowing and repeated failure to address productivity concerns had brought New Zealand to the brink of bankruptcy. The sheer weight of the centralism of a command economy had stifled economic growth and this coupled with the level of government involvement in business activities had distorted the domestic market and the markets for our goods overseas.

Critics – despite insisting that the exchange-rate crisis was either manufactured or overblown – agree that there were serious problems in the New Zealand economy and criticise the 'heavy-handed authoritarianism of Muldoon'. New Right advocates believe that business and political elites had rightly decided that market-based policies were 'inevitable' given the seriousness of our economic plight in 1984. New Right critics, like Kelsey, put 'apparently' before 'inevitable' even as they concede that our economy 'was in serious decline' due to its 'artificial foundation of agricultural products sold to protected markets'.[5] After Britain's decision to join the European Economic Community, even sceptics like Kelsey accept that some sort of economic reorientation had to occur.

Jesson traced the history of New Zealand's colonial relationship in a number of studies, lamenting our economic and intellectual dependence upon our colonial 'mother'. He described our 'golden age' of the 1950s as 'politically and intellectually moribund' and bewailed the 'prevailing pragmatism and thinness of political tradition' that made us particularly vulnerable to the importation of the ideas of the 'free market right'. Pointing to the 'long history' of pro-market thinking among New Zealand economists, Jesson explained our susceptibility to New Right experiments as due to our colonial history and the competitive, consumer culture that emerged more fully blown after World War II.[6]

Critics have insightfully begun to map the networks that connect important New Right advocates here to think tanks and organisations in other parts of the world. The process started in the late 1980s with a detailed examination of the NZBR and its economic connections.

Tracing what she characterised as a 'rigid ideology', Kelsey outlined the 'liberal path' that connected Douglas and Richardson to international circuits that disseminated pro-market beliefs. She wrote about 'technocrats' seizing power in what Jesson and Barry also called a 'coup' in the aftermath of the 1984 election. During this 'power shift', Labour and National ministers played 'frontmen' while the 'invisible hands of Rogernomics' linked groups like the Employers' Federation, the CIS, the NZBR and overseas interests in a powerful but largely invisible network of influence. Paul Harris and Linda Twiname focus on the NZBR tracing its connections to Britain, the United States and Australia. Jesson tracked the interactions between an Auckland-based cohort of Labour politicians, a 'right wing' of the National Party, adherents of market liberal ideas in Britain and the United States, ideological converts in the Treasury and business elites creating a powerful network committed to the New Right transformation of New Zealand.[7] Shorn of the hyperbole, these accounts offer much of value to our understanding of our recent past that we develop further in the chapters to follow.

Obviously approving such developments as the anti-nuclear stance, feminist initiatives, recognition of Maori grievances and homosexual law reform, New Right critics found it difficult to acknowledge that these changes might spring from the same reformist upsurge that they opposed. Kelsey advanced the notion of a 'three way-contradiction' and tended to portray Maori, feminists, gays, lesbians and the poor as victims of the New Right reforms rather than also beneficiaries and protagonists. Insisting that the New Zealand New Right embraced the 'moral conservatism' of its American counterpart, Kelsey avoided commenting on the actions of Richardson, Shipley and others in supporting sexual liberalism or that some Maori, feminists and others embraced the New Right. The curious career of Donna Awatere Huata does not appear in her analysis.

In addressing the coincidence of radical social movements and New Right reformers, Jesson portrays the radicals as 'highly individualistic', 'hostile' to 'authority', opposed to 'traditional moral codes' and biased 'against the state'. Their biculturalism was 'moralistic and individualistic' while their feminism lacked any concept of the marketplace. Portraying these movements as liberal, rather than socialist, Jesson's radicals resembled the New Right, making it easier for him to explain their common antagonism to an 'authoritarian system of political and social control'. Ignorance of economic affairs allowed them to fall victim to the New Right's aggressive assertion of the need for economic transformation.[8] Without sharing Kelsey's and Jesson's difficulties in trying to sort the actors into categories of 'good' and 'bad' reformers, we will build on their attempts to explain the synchronicity between social and economic reform.

Kelsey's *The New Zealand Experiment* built on her earlier model while extending the analysis into the National Government's period of New Right reforms. As she correctly understood, the New Right must be 'evaluated in its broader context' in terms of both chronology and the interaction between the global forces of economic change and the local experience. She drew our attention to the complexity of the process of 'embedding the new regime' and provided extensive and insightful detail into various aspects of the transformation of our economy and government. Her critical appraisal of the political and cultural deficits that produced both MMP and a language permeated by the 'catch-cries of liberal individualism' challenged the assumptions of 'economic fundamentalism'.[9]

Like those of other Keynesian economists, Easton's contributions to the history of the New Right have focused on Rogernomics, the Treasury/Reserve Bank 'group', the Cabinet 'troika' and an economic network connecting these protagonists to overseas influences. Primarily concerned with economic theory, Easton recognised the need for economic change, but disputed the necessity for a forced march to market freedom.[10] Preferring the slower pace and more pragmatic approach of Australia's Labor Government, Easton proposed a return to a corporatist consensus as a better alternative to New Right commercialisation. Agreeing with Easton on the importance of examining comparative examples of the New Right, we extend our analysis to Britain, the United States and Australia to determine whether speed matters when the destination is the same.

Simon Sheppard's *Broken Circle* offered a nuanced historical account of the Fourth Labour Government as riven by ideological and personal conflicts. Sheppard strongly suggested that rather than a unified New Right assault, incoherence, inexperience and economic ignorance weakened the Labour opposition to Roger Douglas, Richard Prebble and the other New Right proponents. Ironically interjecting the concept of 'staff capture' into an analysis of the Treasury's influence on the Government, Sheppard implicitly questioned the sincerity of New Right warnings about the dangers of 'provider capture' in the Treasury's *Economic Management* and *Government Management*. He quoted Lange's admiring description of a 'consistent, cohesive, intellectually convinced' Treasury group supporting a 'fire-breathing Minister' against an indecisive opposition. Including a biographical approach, Sheppard traced the evolution of the Lange–Douglas relationship from effective partnership to bitter divorce, while also noting that Douglas used financial resources to secure support from the Labour caucus. Ending with the 'fall' of the Labour Government, this truncated narrative fleshed out the internal complexity of the events but largely ignored the influences stemming from outside New Zealand.[11]

Deliberately steering between left and right with an acute sense of where the moving centre of New Zealand politics might be at the time of his writing, James's interpretations of the 'quiet revolution' sought to avoid taking sides. Like Jesson, James deplored our slowness to develop a 'distinctive independent culture'. He focused on the tensions between two generations as explaining the events of 1984 and after. A rising generation of radicals faced off against an ageing Canute – the World War II 'selfish' generation and Robert Muldoon. The new generation, including Maori, feminists, anti-apartheid and anti-nuclear activists, seized the opportunity to take control and lead us into 'new territory'. Rogernomics was a 'symptom' rather than a cause of our radical transformation.[12] Seeing no essential contradiction between social and economic reformers, James offered a generational rather than an ideological account for the events of the 1980s and 1990s.

Boston and his colleagues have published collections of essays detailing the Fourth Labour Government, National's 'Decent Society' and the Labour restoration in 1999. Agreeing with the claims of our 'relative economic decline' and 'mounting international indebtedness', these interpreters noted that structural unemployment, poverty, racial inequalities and low productivity were already evident before 1984. Recognising the need for change, they approved of the 'more market direction' deemed necessary to address these endemic problems. In their 1987 collection, the editors professed admiration for the 'political entrepreneur' challenging 'sacred cows' and initiating the 'politics of change'. Later contributions regretted the social consequences for beneficiaries and the working poor as the National Government shrank the welfare state.[13]

James Belich's *Paradise Reforged* offered the only sustained historical synthesis of this period. He argued that the developments in New Zealand from the early 1970s, including the rise of the New Right in the 1980s, are to be understood as 'decolonisation'. This explanation formed an essential part of his larger narrative schema that chronicles our changing colonial identity and relationship with Britain. Belich's stress was on Britain's entry into the European Economic Community and the consequent reduction of ties to the older Commonwealth. He argued that our decolonisation also resulted in emancipatory social movements for Maori, women and the generation freed from the claustrophobic conformity of our colonial past, the groups to which we refer when we write about advocates of 'new rights'.[14]

But what did the New Right get right? There is near unanimous agreement across the political spectrum that Muldoonist economics was unsustainable. It is also generally agreed that there was a need for greater 'openness' of our markets. Rising unemployment and inflation also resisted Keynesian remedies. From the mid-1970s the Australian experience significantly paralleled ours and 'less government and more market' ideologies echoed on both sides of the Tasman. That Margaret Thatcher came to power in 1979 with an overtly New Right programme and Ronald Reagan won the American presidency the following year with a similar programme enhanced the power and credibility of these ideas that challenged the 'Keynesian consensus'. The main proponents of the New Right here saw themselves engaged in an urgent campaign to save us from bankruptcy or worse. They followed these broader international trajectories by adopting and adapting them to create the specific programme of New Zealand reforms. The extent and speed of implementation here were unique.

Thanks to these predecessors, we have a more perceptive version of the origins and evolution of New Zealand's New Right. Clearly the welfare state and the golden age of the 1950s and 1960s was less than ideal from the vantage point of most Maori, many women and other groups who did not fit the conformist model. Nor was this pastoral idyll self-sustaining. It depended almost entirely on a protected market with Britain. Muldoon's attempts to ward off change only delayed the wrench of adjusting to Britain's departure into the European Economic Community. Much like our neighbours across the Tasman, we had to take account of new economic realities and respond in innovative ways.

Since we were not alone in this encounter with the New Right, it is safe to conclude that these events did not arise entirely from within New Zealand nor entirely from without. While almost everybody agreed that change was imperative, its pace and force was a matter of political choice and action. The economic theories embraced by the New Right had become increasingly powerful in three societies – Britain, Australia and the United States – to which New Zealand looked for inspiration and example. In tracing the routes of transmission and travel, we will go beyond the confines of the map briefly sketched by Kelsey, Easton, James, Jesson and others. Organisations like the NZBR and the CIS are part of transnational New Right networks. The OECD, the World Bank and the International Monetary Fund (IMF) are also transmission points. Entrepreneurial think tanks in Britain, the US and Australia significantly influenced New Zealand debates. Travelling evangelists and sacred books contributed to local conversions to New Right theology, but New Zealand congregations did their part by both embracing and rejecting the 'good news'. We will give these networks more careful scrutiny.

Alongside the New Right networks, we will detail other networks as yet largely unstudied. Certainly New Zealand 'culture wars' of the 1980s and 1990s reflected the impact of the transnational networks of identity politics. Religious conservatives, feminists, gays and lesbians, Maori and environmental and peace activists learned how to champion their causes, in part, with an imported vocabulary adapted to local circumstances. The events of 1981 brought issues of race and oppression into common currency. Threaded throughout Awatere's denunciation of 'white' culture was an overseas discourse utilising hegemony and other neo-Marxist notions. Readers of *Broadsheet* encountered American, Australian and British feminists. Lesbians and gays looked to America for inspiration. The decision to prevent the U.S.S. *Buchanan* from docking in New Zealand ports early in 1985 was not only a gesture of nationalism but also one of solidarity with a worldwide anti-nuclear movement assembled in the context of the 'second Cold War'. These networks are examined to explain why the tumultuous New Right era coincided with the liberating reforms that we call 'new rights' or 'social justice' in this analysis.

Just as importantly, we will portray the all-important moral dimensions of the New Right mission that aimed to reform character in the restructured welfare state to create an enterprise society. Indeed, at the heart of the debate between the New Right and its critics is a clash of two moral systems that we analyse in subsequent chapters. The defenders of the market confronted the advocates of 'social justice' as individual morality clashed with collective notions of responsibility. Whether expressed explicitly in religious terms or not, these moral frameworks help explain the reliance upon religiously derived myths by the New Right and their critics. Developing from what has been written by our predecessors, but going beyond them, we offer a new way to rethink our recent past.

CHAPTER THREE

Pilgrims, Pragmatists and Profiteers

*Wisdom and knowledge is granted unto thee; and
I will give thee riches and wealth and honour, such
as none of the kings have had that have been before
thee, neither shall there any after thee have the like.*
2 CHRONICLES 1:12

*The invisible hand is very reminiscent of the God of
fundamentalism: it has all the answers and makes
all the ultimate decisions . . . . Each fundamentalism
shares a desire to control individual behaviour, but
each strives to present itself as the path of self-
fulfilment . . . . There is a body of doctrine, and
there are demands made on believers, demands they
are under an obligation to fufil. The market, like the
Bible, is held to be inerrant . . . There's a clear sense
of salvation in each form of fundamentalism, and of
there being only one true way to reach it: a straight
and narrow path from which one must not deviate,
no matter what the temptations . . . ultimately
leading us to the promised land of self-fulfilment.*
STUART SIM, *FUNDAMENTALIST WORLD: THE NEW DARK
AGE OF DOGMA*[1]

This chapter develops our explanatory narrative of the rise of the New
Right in New Zealand. We people this chapter with a larger cast of
characters and a trans-Tasman plotline. So far the accounts discussed
have assumed the uniqueness of our New Right experience. These
critics described us as having been the unsuspecting subjects of a 'New
Zealand experiment' thrust into a 'test tube of total capitalism' and
bathed in the searing acid of market forces. Sympathisers emphasised
the uncommon daring and fortitude of far-sighted New Right
reformers who liberated us from 'fortress New Zealand'. Whether

we are depicted as victims or as unusually blessed, these versions offer us the pleasure of taking centre stage in our own New Right drama. Our interpretation requires that we make room for businessmen, lawyers, journalists, schoolteachers and for our nearest neighbours, whose history, as we report it, resembles our own.

This chapter expands beyond Douglas, Richardson and the Treasury economists to explicate the motivations of the three groups in Australia and New Zealand that we identity in the title: pilgrims, pragmatists and profiteers. By 'pilgrims' we refer to true believers or acolytes of the New Right faith in the market as the ideal instrument for economic decision-making. Pilgrim is a word that, in its French form, entered the New Right gazette through Mont Pelerin, the name of the place where Hayek first called together his disciples and started the pilgrimage towards market freedoms. 'Pragmatists' refers to politicians like Malcolm Fraser, Bob Hawke, Jim Bolger and Geoffrey Palmer who drew upon New Right policies because politically powerful elites adhered to those ideas. 'Profiteers' denotes those who benefited economically or personally from New Right reforms without necessarily believing or even knowing the details of Hayek's economic vision. These groups coalesced to exercise the power necessary to the implementation of the New Right vision, giving it the appearance of a consensus that made the mantra, TINA (there is no alternative), compelling. All of these people played crucial roles in the New Right ascendancy, but space has forced us to be selective. We trust that our readers can rely upon their own memories of the 1980s and 1990s, read the books previously discussed or take advantage of media databases to fill out this collective portrait.

Long before Don Brash became Reserve Bank Governor, he experienced a conversion to the new faith of market liberalism. After a youth spent as the son of a leading Presbyterian minister and a stint at the University of Canterbury studying with Wolfgang Rosenberg, a socialist economist, Brash enrolled at the Australian National University. He worked with W. Max Corden and Treasury official John Stone among other pro-market economists. Under their tutelage, he wrote a doctoral thesis assessing the favourable impact of American corporations on the Australian economy. He left Canberra convinced that free trade and investment produced positive outcomes. Brash's market-liberal faith grew more fervent during his years at the

World Bank between 1966 and 1971. Speaking to an IEA audience in 1996, Brash described the New Zealand he returned to in the 1970s as displaying 'the baleful logic of Hayek's *Road to Serfdom*'. Our version of the 'cradle-to-grave' welfare state had put us on the road to 'a sort of serfdom'. He conceded that we might not have developed 'the police state and concentration camp' predicted by Hayek in 1944, but that minor error in prediction did not prevent this fervent convert to market liberalism from celebrating the leading prophet of market liberalism. When he finally read Hayek in the 1990s Brash enjoyed the pleasant sensation of having his cherished beliefs confirmed.[2]

Other New Zealand converts shared Brash's assessment of the dismal state of our economy. Brash enthusiastically supported the efforts of a 'small but strategically influential team of civil servants, think-tankers, policy-makers and politicians around Roger Douglas' to rescue us from 'serfdom'. From his vantage point at the Kiwifruit Marketing Authority, Brash cheered on these efforts at ideological transformation, seeing the collapse of our 'mental defences against the intellectual counter-revolution' as a liberating event. Prophets like Hayek and pilgrims like Brash called upon us to march towards Mont Pelerin, the monetarist Mount Sinai, in order to receive our new commandments.

Following his meeting with Brash in the mid-1960s, the Australian John Stone took a similar route to Washington. Stone had entered the Treasury in 1954 after earning a degree at Oxford. He went to Washington to take up posts as Australia's executive director at both the IMF and the World Bank. He became Deputy Secretary of the Australian Treasury in 1971, the same year that Brash returned to New Zealand. Ultimately promoted to Secretary of the Treasury in 1979, Stone argued for the reform of the Australian state and economy until he resigned in 1984 after disagreements with the recently elected Labor Government. Moving into political life in the Australian Senate, he continued his activism as one of the leading 'dries' in the National Party and became the inaugural president of the anti-union H. R. Nicholls Society, enlisted in the anti-centralist Samuel Griffith Society and joined the Institute for Public Affairs (IPA) as a senior fellow.[3]

Stone advocated what Greg Whitwell called the 'Treasury Line' in a resurgence of pro-market economics among Australian officials, which culminated in the so-called 'Stone Age' of the early 1980s. Pessimism about the 'dramatic deterioration' of the Australian economy during the 1970s, the breakdown of the Bretton Woods currency exchange system and the accompanying political instability caused a loss of faith in Keynesian economic interventions. Instead of taking an optimistic, progressive view of human nature, the monetarist and public choice theories promoted in the 'Treasury Line' asserted that self-interested competitors could only be restrained through the punitive force of market discipline and the 'rule of law'. Governments must allow competitors to sink or swim while restraining spending and controlling the money supply to impose the same discipline on public officials and politicians. Stressing the need to combat an aggressive labour movement, Australian Treasury officials argued for the implementation of deflationary policies as prescribed by Friedman and the unleashing of market forces as advocated by Hayek. Under Stone's increasingly influential leadership, the Australian Treasury and Reserve Bank began to wage the 'monetarist' and Hayekian counter-revolution against Keynesian consensus economics.[4]

Douglas Myers grew up in a 'negative and uninspiring' New Zealand culture in the 1950s. A Cambridge University education convinced him that the 'stultifying' closed New Zealand economy needed to be transformed into a 'wealth-creating environment'. He returned from Britain to take a position at his family's brewery in the mid-1960s, enlisting in a battle against privilege that came from his position in a 'highly protected and regulated market'. A true believer that 'capitalism delivers wealth and freedom to all' and that 'collectivism' was a sure fire recipe for disaster, Myers joined the NZBR in the early 1980s to lobby for public policies that fulfilled his 'free-market dreams' and to wage war against 'economic irrationalists and other lost tribes wandering around in New Zealand'.[5] Myers became one of the most prominent businessmen associated with the NZBR.

Far away from Myers's uncomfortably privileged existence, the daughter of a former West Coast goldminer left school to work as a nurse. Margaret Bazley worked for twenty-five years as a nurse in psychiatric hospitals and became the matron of Sunnyside Hospital in the mid-1960s before moving into other management positions including the presidency of the Nurses' Association. Self-discipline and hard work led to her appointment as the first woman State Services Commissioner in 1984, two years before Roderick Deane enlisted in the same effort aimed at 'whipping the public service into shape'. Bazley's methods, labelled by admirers as a mixture of 'smart management practices and old-fashioned coercion', applied New Right theory to the 'shrinking' of the public service and to the encouragement of beneficiaries 'to be self-sufficient'. Given her own ethic of sturdy self-reliance, the DPB, a product of the one-term Kirk Labour Government, troubled her. It 'enabled single parents to have children' and created an intergenerational welfare culture. Known as a 'hatchet woman', among other less-than-flattering descriptions, Bazley received accolades from New Right reformers for being 'tougher than any man', for refraining from 'politically correct' tendencies and for her role as an 'unseen, effective achiever' in bringing efficiency to the public service.[6]

Hugh Morgan studied law at the University of Melbourne in the mid-1950s before launching a corporate career that resulted in his being 'singled out by friend and foe as a high priest of the Australian New Right'. The son of the then head of the Western Mining Corporation, Morgan pursued a legal career focused on labour relations before he moved into the mining industry himself in the mid-1960s. In 1976 he joined the Western Mining Corporation, beginning a climb up the executive ranks that culminated in appointments as Chief Executive Officer of the renamed WMC in 1990, to the Board of the Reserve Bank of Australia and as chair of the Australian group negotiating a free-trade agreement with the United States. Morgan participated in an Australian circle of market liberals who looked to the London-based IEA for ideological guidance and leadership. The group invited Antony Fisher, the founder of IEA, to Australia in 1976 to promote Hayekian ideas about market reforms.[7]

Morgan developed a particularly close ideological and professional association with Ray Evans, who graduated from the University of Melbourne in 1960 with an engineering degree, founded the Australian Council for Educational Standards and edited its journal advocating educational 'choice' in the early 1970s. Later Evans became Deputy Dean of the Deakin University School of Engineering before being recruited in 1982 into the Western

Mining Corporation, where he functioned as Morgan's assistant and co-founder of a number of pro-market activist groups. They became well known for asserting views that described the 'world of imposed equality' as a 'totalitarian nightmare', earning them the reputation of being among the 'self-interested extremists of the New Right' and, in the case of Morgan, of a 'firebrand'. From their Melbourne corporate base, Morgan and Evans established organisations promoting the monarchy and market solutions and, in particular, opposing aboriginal rights, environmental groups, trade unions and other representatives of the so-called 'Bolshevik Left'. Their views, characterised by Prime Minister Paul Keating as reflecting the 'the bigoted voice of the 19th century', circulated through an expanding network that connected the Hayek-founded Mont Pelerin Society (MPS), the IEA, the CIS, the IPA, the H. R. Nicholls Society, the Samuel Griffith Society, the Lavoisier Society, the Tasman Insititute, the Bennelong Society, *Quadrant* and the Business Council of Australia. Through his strategic position on the boards of many of these organisations, Morgan earned the title of 'ideological father of the New Right'.[8]

Greg Lindsay studied philosophy at Macquarie University in the early 1970s. Buying books from the Foundation for Economic Education (FEE) in New York, including Smith's *The Wealth of Nations*, Hayek's *Road to Serfdom* and Friedman's *Capitalism and Freedom*, Lindsay became an admirer of American market-liberal organisations like FEE. He also became acquainted with Ayn Rand and Robert Nozick, who shared his beliefs in individualism, free markets and personal liberty. In 1975 he travelled to the United States to meet the staff at FEE and to establish communication with the Institute for Humane Affairs, then located in Menlo Park, California. Returning to Australia, Lindsay organised seminars with conservative philosophers and economists at Macquarie University while planning an Australian version of FEE.

When Antony Fisher visited Australia in 1976, Lindsay sought his advice. Fisher approved of his plans and introduced him to other members of the IEA circle. Establishing his initial operation in a garden shed, Lindsay began the CIS. By 1978 he was able to hold a small conference criticising government intervention in the economy that attracted about 100 participants, including Padraic McGuinness of the *Australian Financial Review*. A flattering McGuinness column helped Lindsay gain support from Hugh Morgan, who 'did a financial whip around amongst mates for seed money for the CIS', garnering financial support from Australian corporate executives. Within two years Lindsay had attended his first MPS meeting in Hong Kong, met Friedman and Buchanan there, opened a CIS office in Sydney and added Hayek to its advisory board. As self-conscious 'change agents' determined to 'influence the general ideas environment', Lindsay and the CIS staff vigorously committed themselves, with the financial support of their corporate patrons, to the promotion of 'a free, open and prosperous Australian society'.[9]

Aware of the need to deal with the economic crisis that had secured an electoral victory in 1975 and interested in satisfying the major factions in the Liberal Party, Prime Minister Malcolm Fraser appointed David Kemp, a pro-market law and politics graduate from the University of Melbourne and Yale University, as his senior advisor. Kemp, a son of the founder of the IPA, wrote speeches for Fraser into which he inserted his Hayekian and Friedmanite views. Kemp eventually became director of the Prime Minister's Office before the Coalition defeat of 1983. Fraser also promoted Stone to the position of Secretary of the Treasury in 1979 and followed his advice to order cuts in government expenditure. At the same time, however, Fraser continued to subsidise Australian manufacturing, mining and farming in order to keep traditional supporters loyal to his party. Disdainful of this form of political opportunism and pandering to 'rent-seeking' special interests, Stone turned elsewhere for allies in his battle to reform the Australian economy and government. Despite continuing to work for Fraser, Kemp also proudly included himself among those Bob Hawke called 'political troglodytes and economic lunatics'. As part of the 'evil group of right-wing plotters', Kemp continued to fight against 'central regulation' with other members of the growing 'dry' faction of the Liberal Party.[10]

The pragmatic Fraser's deviations from pro-market orthodoxy strengthened the 'dry' opposition as the Liberal Party developed sharper ideological distinctions in the early 1980s. Treasurer in Fraser's Government and Deputy Leader of the Liberals, John Howard converted to 'dry economics' in the late 1970s and by 1983 was a 'radical liberal' and free-marketeer. Increasingly an opponent of Fraser, Howard became the leader of the dry faction of his party. Howard's Methodist upbringing, experience in the Young Liberals at the University of Sydney in the late 1950s and legal training made him a lifelong moral conservative. Politically ambitious, Howard developed a combination of 'gung-ho Adam Smith Liberal' ideology and a commitment to traditional values that allowed him to garner support from different Liberal factions and assume the party leadership in 1985.[11]

John Hyde, a West Australian wheat farmer, swam against the 'collectivist tide' during his years in the Australian Parliament between 1974 and 1983. Hyde joined a small group of Australian MPs seeking to curb the 'Corporate State' composed of marketing boards, quotas, tariffs, and financial and labour market regulation. Opposed to 'rent-seekers and bludgers', Hyde in 1978 started reading the publications of the CIS, which reinforced his market faith. He organised a ginger group of backbenchers, arguing that Fraser's protection of 'eastern' industry was subsidised by the West Australian taxpayer. Think tanks like Hyde's Australian Institute for Public Policy (AIPS) and the lobbying Business Council of Australia, both founded in 1983, became part of the ideological network agitating for market reforms.[12]

The parliamentary dries attracted support from conservative students, often Christian, who challenged the dominance of the left in Australian university politics. Baptist Peter Costello, Catholic Tony Abbott, Andrew Peacock, Eric Abetz, Michael Kroger and other young pro-market activists gravitated towards future careers in the Liberal Party. Costello, a graduate of Monash University, pursued a legal career in industrial and commercial law, winning victories over trade unions that brought him to the attention of Evans and Morgan. Simultaneously, he taught law and economics at his alma mater before embarking on a political career in the Liberal Party. The rise of young dries paralleled the increasingly vigorous 'Treasury Line' advocated by Stone and like-minded officials. Biding their time as they battled against the socially liberal wets and pragmatic politicians like Fraser, the political, organisational and bureaucratic core of the Australian New Right had coalesced by the early 1980s.[13]

Another New Zealander became an even more fervent apostle of market liberalism during his sojourn in Australia. Returning home, he propagated this faith with unrelenting zeal. Roger Kerr, the son of a 'very conservative' farmer who expressed 'a special dislike' for 'welfare layabouts', had initially studied French, mathematics and English in the 1960s at Canterbury with the intention of becoming a diplomat. He began studying economics part time at Victoria in 1968, with Deane as one of his tutors, and continued in Foreign Affairs until he joined the Treasury in 1976. Seconded to the Australian Treasury, Kerr met Fisher of the IEA and Lindsay. While Kerr was making these connections with the Australian New Right, Deane, his mentor, moved from Wellington to Washington to work at the IMF. Kerr quickly rose up the Treasury ranks, making common cause with Deane, who had returned from the IMF to take up a position as chief economist at the Reserve Bank in 1979, before becoming Deputy Governor. Kerr also worked closely with Graham Scott, Secretary of the Treasury, who had studied economics at Duke, Bryce Wilkinson, Doug Andrew and Rob Cameron. Convinced that 'fortress New Zealand' must be transformed, these ambitious young economists chafed under the restraints imposed by a traditional public service and a 'think big' Prime Minister deaf to their entreaties. Drafting *Economic Management* as the policy to be followed by the incoming government in 1984, Kerr and his colleagues awaited the outcome of the election, hoping for the opportunity to translate their pro-market ideas into practice. After two intense years of working closely on economic reforms with the new Minister of Finance, Kerr, enthusiastically recommended by Deane, moved to the NZBR to advocate on behalf of the leading corporates interested in speeding up the pace of our New Right transformation.[14]

John Fernyhough, a member of the Socialist Club at Victoria University College in the 1950s, took a law degree at Victoria and completed a doctorate at the University of Chicago (UC). He joined Russell McVeagh, a leading Auckland law firm, and in the early 1970s became involved in the takeover of the Union Steamship Company. Fernyhough became a successful investor and a self-described 'disciple of the New Right', as part of a risk-taking entrepreneurial circle that included Myers, Alan Gibbs, Deane and Peter Shirtcliffe. This circle argued for the urgent need to transform 'money-losing government departments into profitable organisations' which they themselves sometimes owned or operated. Intent on promoting better export incentives, the group moved rapidly in a free-market direction guided by 'powerful voices' in the OECD, the IMF, the World Bank, the Treasury, universities and governments. Credited with 'providing the intellectual and institutional fire-power' for what became known as Rogernomics, these 'visionaries' became the new power elite, wielding enormous commercial and political clout to 'effect change and push the free market'.[15]

Attracted to politics in his childhood, David Lange, a Methodist, paid his way through the University of Auckland law school by holiday employment in the Westfield freezing works and as a part-time public employee. Joining the Labour Party in the early 1960s, he made his first speech against US involvement in Vietnam. Going to London after he graduated in 1967, Lange attended the West London Mission, where he met anti-capitalist, Methodist preacher Donald Soper, who believed that the 'true Christian ethic' had 'properly to do with property and economics'. Journeying back to New Zealand via India with his English bride, Naomi, Lange took a postgraduate law degree before going into practice. He became known as a 'left-wing lawyer' acting on behalf of the 'less privileged' and doing volunteer work for the Council of Civil Liberties. Encouraged by his cousin, Michael Bassett, he entered Parliament in a by-election in 1976. Forming a close relationship with Douglas, Bassett, Jim Anderton and Richard Prebble, Lange became Leader of the opposition Labour Party in 1983 as a 'moderate' occupying the 'middle ground' but also as a 'left-wing' believer in the need for 'state protection from market forces' in health and education. His 'reluctance to go for the jugular' left him 'vulnerable' to those more 'power-hungry' and more skilled at building patronage networks. So long as the reform agenda focused on economic issues, Lange could maintain his position as a centrist and pragmatic leader; but his opposition to treating health and education as 'market goods' constituted a major philosophical difference with the reform-minded Douglas.[16]

Son and grandson of Labour MPs, Roger Douglas studied accountancy part time at the University of Auckland before entering Parliament in 1969. During the 1970s he took on increasing responsibilities for the family business, Red Seal health supplements, bringing him into closer contact with the Auckland business community. In the late 1970s, he visited IEA looking for answers to

New Zealand's economic difficulties. His experience as a businessman led him by 1980 to advocate the end of the protectionist tariff regime and the reduction of government intervention in the economy. His unorthodox proposals in *There's Got to be a Better Way!* resulted in his being removed from his position as Shadow Minister of Finance by Bill Rowling, the Labour Party leader. After Lange's rise to leadership, he regained this position in 1983. Douglas was involved in a number of groups each pressing in one way or another for economic reform. These included an economic discussion group with Treasury economist Doug Andrew, an Auckland business circle and a group of Auckland-based Labour MPs and activists convinced of the need for market solutions to the problems of the New Zealand economy. These groups linked Douglas to the transnational New Right, equipped him with a set of core pro-market economic convictions, provided a political support base in the Labour Party and helped him persuade the leading corporate executives to support the New Right reform agenda.[17]

A contemporary of Kerr and Lange, Geoffrey Palmer studied law at Victoria in the early 1960s. An active 'Young Nat' and editor of Victoria's student newspaper, he earned a postgraduate degree at UC in the late 1960s and taught at the University of Iowa before returning to New Zealand. His legal training, accentuated by his study of constitutional law at UC, convinced him of the dangers stemming from the 'unbridled power' of the state. While teaching law at Victoria he published *Unbridled Power*, a critique of New Zealand's unitary governmental structure. On the same day that this first appeared in print, Palmer was selected as Labour candidate for Christchurch Central for the 1979 by-election. He entered Parliament determined to remedy the 'defects of New Zealand's system of government'. A devotion to the 'rule of law' and an ability to 'stand firm on centre ground' between fractious social democrats and New Right advocates in the Labour Party earned him the reputation of being a 'smooth operator'. His considerable legal skills meant that, given the opportunity, he could translate proposals to 'rollback' the New Zealand state into legislation.[18]

In parallel to the growing influence of market liberalism in the Australian and New Zealand treasuries, increasing numbers of businessmen on both sides of the Tasman converted to the new faith.

Even those not particularly ideologically engaged, including the young and ambitious investment bankers Michael Fay and David Richwhite saw the benefits for their business that deregulation and commercialisation might bring. Fay acquired a law degree at Victoria in the early 1970s. He and his partner, Richwhite, made their first million through investment banking by 1979. Opening an office in Wellington in the early 1980s, they discovered that Muldoon was a 'pain in the neck' and looked for a change in the government to usher in a 'new era of opportunity'. Fay and Douglas 'talked the same language'. A 'monetary reformist experiment' was a 'godsend', enabling Fay and Richwhite to make new and powerful friends among industrialists and business interest groups. Close relationships with government ministers and the parliamentary staff secured appointments for businessmen like Fay and Richwhite in state-owned enterprises. Recruiting staff from Treasury offered additional sources of information and contacts that helped to amass fortunes for our 'new breed of young entrepreneurial people in the financial sector'. According to a former Treasury official, they quickly became the leaders of a merchant banking sector that was effectively 'running the country' through a 'symbiotic relationship between bankers, the government and Treasury'. In the ironic comment of a former associate, 'Fay and Richwhite had a monopoly of the free-enterprise system'. The sale of state assets enabled the firm to pick up the 'lion's share of this work' and often clip 'the ticket on both sides of a deal'.[19]

Mike Moore, the son of a widowed shopkeeper, and Bassett, a historian a decade older, grew up in similarly deprived conditions. They both entered Parliament in 1972. Three years later they experienced the bitterness of defeat losing their seats. Moore ended up on a dredge in Auckland Harbour while Bassett returned to Auckland University. Bassett's analysis of the reasons for Labour's defeat blames the welfare state for provoking animosities from wage earners. Moore decided that economic reform was just as urgently needed. When returned to Parliament in 1978, both departed from traditional Labour policies in a new openness to economic reform. Bassett became a part of the pro-market Auckland circle gathering around Douglas. Moore 'began to understand some of the views being expressed' by Douglas's group concerning 'our having been imprisoned by economic isolation'. He wanted to avoid the extremes of the 'command economy of the Soviets and the jungle of the Friedmanites' in order to achieve a 'negotiated style of economy'. While Bassett focused on the need for domestic reform, Moore concentrated on the removal of tariff barriers.[20]

Maori activist Donna Awatere (later Awatere Huata) journeyed to Cuba in the 1970s to see 'the best' health system 'in the world'. Disillusioned by the 'squalour' there and the 'privileged class' of party officials in Cuba, Albania and the Soviet Union, Awatere returned to New Zealand. She joined an Auckland study group to read *Das Kapital* in the late 1970s and 'apply the thinking to modern Maori life'. Reading Marx transformed these 'potential communists' into 'capitalist sympathisers' as they decided that 'Marxism' was not 'a creed that Maori will ever respond to'. Awatere's experience in owning her own business proved to her that profits were 'the incentive that drove people' and reinforced her doubts about the validity of socialism. Becoming convinced of the need for 'economic decolonisation', she came to see a 'vision of the future of Maoridom' with 'Maori being economically powerful'.[21]

Jim Bolger, son of an Irish immigrant worker, came to the National Party via Federated Farmers, serving under Muldoon as Minister of Transport. Bolger prided himself on not taking 'a rigid approach to economic policy' and distinguished himself from ideologues that spoke in 'slogans' and 'clichés'. He saw himself as a pragmatist opposed to those driven by economic 'dogma'. Persuaded of the benefits of some macroeconomic policies, such as the monetarist control of inflation, he favoured an approach based on the collective development of diverse 'social capital'. Nevertheless he forged a successful political alliance with those that he did see as dogmatists and ideologues.[22]

Growing up on a farm in a family of National supporters, Ruth Richardson believed in the importance of sturdy self-reliance and became an exemplar of Bolger's sloganeering ideologue. While a teenager she decided to pursue a political career. Attending law school in the early 1970s at the University of Canterbury, she gained an education that emphasised the importance of property rights. At university she developed a feminism of an individualist tenor and continued to be committed to the equity of women regarding property and employment. At Federated Farmers, Richardson argued for women's property rights and the urgent need for market reforms. She successfully pursued her political ambitions by seeking the National Party nomination for Selwyn in 1980. During the contest, she met Burton, a local National activist, and Jenny Shipley, a former teacher, who became her fervent supporters. A close political partnership developed during the campaign and after Richardson's election to Parliament in 1981. Burton's self-described 'extreme' right-wing views and Richardson's devotion to free enterprise combined well with Jenny's high regard for self-discipline, learned as the daughter of a Presbyterian clergyman. After Shipley's election in 1987, she and Richardson formed part of a growing New Right cohort in the National Party that wrested power away from the interventionists.[23]

In both New Zealand and Australia, parallel to the New Right political mobilisation, a private network emerged to promote the 'free-market agenda of privatisation, deregulation and fiscal stringency'. This network connected the IEA, the newly created Centre for Policy Studies (CPS), the Adam Smith Institute (ASI) and the Social Affairs Unit, all based in London, to like-minded think tanks in Australia and New Zealand. The Australian Foundation for Economic Education began in 1976, using FEE's name. Under the leadership of Dave and Rod Kemp, the IPA was transformed from a conservative organisation into a more dynamic New Right think tank. By the late 1970s an activist group of Wellington- and Auckland-based businessmen including Fay, Fernyhough, Richwhite, Ron Trotter and Harold Titter came together as a business executives' lunch club. From this group emerged the NZBR in the early 1980s. Michael Porter, educated at Stanford University and subsequently an advisor at the IMF, launched the Centre for Policy Studies at Monash University (CPSMU) in 1979. The CPSMU attracted corporate support from the Australian Mining Industry Council and Alcoa, the multinational aluminium company, to fund a large staff including Stone as a visiting professor. The corporate-funded Pacific Institute brought Herman Kahn, the founder of the Hudson Institute, to 'outline a range of alternative futures for Australia' in the late 1970s. Predictably, Kahn's *Will She Be Right?* argued for the model of market-oriented 'economic dynamism'.[24] By the early

1980s a set of institutions had formed the nucleus of a New Right network connecting New Zealand and Australia to Britain and the United States.

Travelling evangelists moved between the different centres of New Right activism. In the mid-1970s Friedman toured Australia and returned again in 1981 gaining converts for his monetarist 'counter-revolution' from Young Liberals, corporate executives and pro-market activists. Almost coinciding with Friedman's second visit, the AIPS invited Ralph Harris of the IEA to preside over an Australian summer school. Harris heralded the 'counter-revolution of market and monetary theory' as the answer for Australia. As part of his itinerary, Harris visited New Zealand to meet with interested activists.[25] Converting not only corporate executives but also journalists to the new economic thinking, these evangelists helped their disciples to assume positions of influence in the upper echelons of the public service in both Australia and New Zealand.

Early in the 1980s Hayekian-influenced academics, funded by Shell Oil, published *Australia at the Crossroads*. Wolfgang Kasper assured his readers that 'the nascent Libertarian Right' was rapidly gaining support from Australian business, the professions, economists and the media. He argued for the superiority of the market to 'central planning' and the importance of 'free choice'. The public knowledge of economic liberalisation was enhanced by support from *Quadrant*, a journal founded in 1956 with CIA backing as a 'counter-attraction' to 'the magnetic field of Communism'.[26]

In New Zealand journalistic colleagues labelled Richard Long a 'crusading conservative'. Opposed to the 'loony-tunes-policies' of the interventionist status quo, the veteran political journalist reported on the 'dying days of the Muldoon empire' from the parliamentary press gallery. He feuded with Muldoon and applauded 'influential bureaucrats' like Graham Scott, Kerr and Deane for undoing 'the hopeless tangle of regulation, debt and subsidy' strangling our 'precarious' economy. Long did not report in the *Dominion* about these bureaucrats 'privately promoting an alternative way, backed by influential business leaders'. Of the same generation as Myers, Kerr, Bazley and Deane, Long agreed on the need to break the 'shackles of an over-regulated, over-protected economy' as he became a leading proselytiser for the New Right during his rise up the journalistic ranks. He eventually became editor of the *Dominion*, where he produced editorial after editorial raging against trade unionists, the idle poor, economic wets, Maori activists and anyone questioning the need for nuclear ship visits.[27]

Market liberalism gained other advocates in the mainstream media in New Zealand and Australia. The *NBR* converted to market liberalism in the mid-1980s cheering on the reform agenda. The 'most influential organ for free market ideas' in Australia was the *Australian Financial Review*, edited by a succession of free-marketeers – Max Newton, Max Walsh and McGuinness. Columns by McGuinness, Terry McCrann, Alan Wood and Walsh popularised the arguments of Friedman and Hayek while writing approvingly of 'privatisation', the 'level playing field' and user pays. Stone, Hyde and Evans touted the British 'economic miracle' as the model for other societies in their regular appearances in the Australian press. *Quadrant* discussed 'the libertarian challenge to big government', asking provocatively 'Is Equality Morally Obnoxious?' Rupert Murdoch's *The Australian,* along with other newspapers owned by his News Corporation, disseminated proposals developed by the CIS and IPA and editorialised in the name of 'the ordinary Australian' who feels 'he is being over-governed, over-controlled and over-taxed'. Politicians, editors and journalists in Australia and New Zealand argued for New Right reforms in political debates, editorials, think-tank publications and business meetings. These heralds of the New Right turned pro-market policies into the conventional wisdom and derided critics as enemies of 'Western society', 'politically correct' and economically illiterate members of the 'chattering class'.[28] A steady drumbeat of pro-market commentary and a chorus of 'there is no alternative' echoed in the ears of radio and television viewers or marched their way into print in both Australia and New Zealand.

This chapter has delineated the significant parallels between Australia and New Zealand in the ways in which the New Right developed. These parallels included the founding prophets, their evangelists and their disciples. Although most existing studies have looked at New Zealand or Australia in isolation, this analysis has demonstrated the advantages of tracing the overlap of ideas, personnel and missionary strategies during the promotion of the New Right gospel. Pilgrimages to Washington, Wellington, Canberra,

Sydney, Melbourne and London, travelling evangelists from Britain and the US and the circulation of sacred texts converted key figures on both sides of the Tasman. By the early 1980s there were significant congregations of believers actively testifying on behalf of their new-found faith, preparing for the advent of electoral power. The New Right attracted two discrete generations of converts: a group born before 1945 and another group born in the post-war baby boom. The former narrowly focused on economic reform while the latter often espoused a broader programme of radical economic and social transformation that included some elements of 'new rights' approaches in regards to women's economic advancement, Maori entrepreneurship and sexual freedom. The New Right cast of players described in this chapter includes not only the usual economists, politicians and Treasury officials but also the media, lawyers, corporate executives, public servants and think-tank entrepreneurs in Australia and New Zealand. This full cast of true believers, pilgrims, fellow-travelling pragmatists and opportunistic profiteers acquired the power necessary to implement the New Right programme.

PART TWO

Exodus: Rescuing Us from Bondage

And the waters returned and covered the chariots and the horsemen and all the host of Pharaoh that came into the sea after them; there remained not so much as one of them. But the children of Israel walked upon dry land in the midst of the sea; and the waters were a wall unto them on their right hand and on their left. Thus the LORD saved Israel that day out of the hand of the Egyptians; and Israel saw the Egyptians dead upon the sea shore. EXODUS 14:28–30

And ye shall seek me and find me, when ye shall search for me with all your heart. And I will be found of you, saith the LORD: and I will turn away your captivity. JEREMIAH 29:13–4

CHAPTER FOUR

Leaving Egypt: The Right March on Washington and Westminster

If the LORD delight in us, then he will bring us into this land and give it us; a land which floweth with milk and honey. Only rebel not ye against the LORD, neither fear ye the people of the land . . . NUMBERS 14:8–9

So the people shouted when the priests blew with the trumpets: and it came to pass, when the people heard the sound of the trumpet and the people shouted with a great shout, that the wall fell down flat, so that the people went up into the city, every man straight before him and they took the city. JOSHUA 6:20

The previous chapter used Brash's speech to the IEA in 1996 to trace his conversion to market liberalism in Canberra and Washington. Like Brash, the pilgrims discussed thus far often experienced their intellectual epiphanies outside New Zealand. The locations for these individual conversion stories could sometimes be found in Washington or London. But it was not only New Zealanders who travelled to distant places to find enlightenment. Britons travelled to the US, market liberals journeyed to Switzerland and Americans flocked to the UC or New York in search of wisdom. Once converted to the faith in markets, they might return to their homes or embark on their own missions.

Evangelists crisscrossed the Atlantic or followed their own complex itineraries to Britain or within the United States seeking to convince their listeners to join their faith. These oracles and emissaries warned of a bleak future unless their policies were implemented. 'Madmen' like Keynes and his interventionist disciplines had deluded government officials and clouded the minds of the people. Motivated by righteous anger, these right-thinking evangelists preached the need for national renewal. Declaring their intentions to march on Washington and Westminster to drive the evildoers out of government, they urged New Zealanders and Australians to follow their example. When the New Right came to power in Britain in 1979 and Washington in 1981, these triumphs became testimonials to the correctness of their vision and the need for antipodeans to undertake a similar process of market reformation.

Two institutions – the UC and the London School of Economics (LSE) – emerged as centres for the revival of faith in market liberalism decades before their disciples achieved power in Washington, Westminster, Canberra or Wellington. Founded by John D. Rockefeller in 1892, the UC appointed Frank Knight and Jacob Viner in the 1920s. In the 1930s a circle formed around Knight and Viner. Aaron Director, Rose Director and Milton Friedman embraced the market faith with particular enthusiasm. Banished from the economics department after a bruising battle with an interventionist economist, Director started Law and Economics in the UC School of Law while his younger sister Rose married the energetic Friedman, who completed his Ph.D. at Columbia in 1946. Director's students, notably Judge Richard Posner and Robert Bork, the failed Reagan nominee for the Supreme Court, considered the law a vehicle to promote economic efficiency rather than the 'illusory' concept of social justice. Appointed by the UC in 1946, Friedman became the heir apparent of the 'Chicago School' while Rose became his occasional co-author and ideological comrade-in-arms. A revitalised economic theory called monetarism emerged from subsequent research. Committed to notions of the mutual interdependence of capitalism and freedom and the 'moral strength' of the 'free market', the members of the Chicago School defended 'individual freedom' from 'arrogant experts', 'grasping bureaucrats' and the 'tyranny of the state' to the eventual applause of admirers like George W. Bush who saw no conflict between their own exercise of power and their faith in the market.[1]

A diasporic community of Austrian economists nurtured another version of market liberalism, the so-called Austrian School. Ludwig von Mises arrived in New York as an exile from Nazi-controlled Austria to form part of a circle of market liberals in that city including

Henry Hazlitt, then the economics reporter for the *New York Times* and later a columnist for *Newsweek*. Fritz Machlup, Mises' former student, arrived in the US in 1933, but kept in touch with his mentor and other Austrians as he journeyed to various American universities, including Harvard, Columbia, Johns Hopkins, Stanford, Princeton and New York University, with occasional stints in Washington during the war and, later, at the US Treasury, from the mid-1960s to the late 1970s. At LSE in the 1930s, another Austrian exile, Friedrich von Hayek, girded up his own loins for an intellectual battle with interventionist economist John Maynard Keynes of Cambridge. Corresponding with other members of this cohort of exiled Austrians located in the US and Christchurch, New Zealand, Hayek expressed his frustration at the growing popularity of Keynesian economics. Turning to the public arena for support, in 1944 Hayek and his Christchurch-based colleague, Karl Popper, published *The Road to Serfdom* and *The Open Society and Its Enemies* respectively as defences of the market and free institutions against bureaucrats and interventionist economists. Covertly directed against the Soviet Union, the books overtly focused on Nazi Germany as the major threat to freedom. Once the wartime alliance with the Soviet Union had ended in the bitterness of the Cold War, their latent anti-Communism came to the surface together with their opposition to the New Deal and the British and the New Zealand welfare states.[2]

Published in March 1944 in Britain, *The Road to Serfdom* soon attracted admirers in both Britain and the US. A young science student active in Young Conservative circles, Margaret Thatcher, was favourably impressed. Machlup brought the book to the attention of Director at the UC. Similarly impressed, Director passed it on to Knight who persuaded the UC press to publish it in September 1944. A glowing review by Hazlitt in the *New York Times* brought *The Road to Serfdom* to the attention of Dewitt and Lila Wallace of *Reader's Digest*. Condensed by ex-leftist Max Eastman, *The Road to Serfdom* became a best-seller, crossing the Atlantic to attract a new group of British readers including RAF pilot Antony Fisher. Carefully illustrated with simple line drawings replete with Nazi signifiers but containing covert anti-Communist references, the book's appearance catapulted Hayek to fame. Visits to the US brought him into closer contact with the UC economists and market-liberal circles in New

York to which Hazlitt and Mises belonged, while also attracting the conservative foundation that would bring him eventually to teach at UC. The LSE network, the Austrian diaspora and the UC circle became part of an emerging transatlantic community of market liberals. In 1949, Mises' *Human Action*, published through another intervention by Machlup, strengthened the intellectual case for a focus on the individual as the only appropriate economic decision-maker instead of the interventionist state, economic planners or bureaucrats.[3]

In 1946 Leonard Read, a former manager of the Los Angeles Chamber of Commerce, established an organisation dedicated to the same fight against 'pagan stateism'. The William Volker Fund and corporate executives supported the new enterprise, FEE. Located just north of New York City, FEE promulgated the message of 'free market, private property and the moral principles which underlie these concerns'. Convinced by an executive of Southern California Edison that the New Deal was 'inefficient and morally bankrupt' and prone to 'fallacies' and 'fantasies', Read had joined a 'Christian-libertarian' enterprise called 'Spiritual Mobilization, Inc.' just before he established FEE. This Christian 'resistance movement' against the New Deal had deepened his faith in 'free enterprise' to the intensity of a 'religion' and strengthened his opposition to the 'social gospel'. Distributing the sacred texts of Smith, Mises and Hayek from Irvington, New York, FEE inspired one of its founding prophets, Hayek himself. During his 1946 visit to the US, Hayek met Read. Upon his return to London, Hayek solicited the necessary funds to follow Read's example, issuing a call for like-minded intellectuals to assemble at Mont Pelerin in Switzerland the following year.[4]

FEE attracted other converts to the same faith. Hazlitt was one of its founding members. When he shifted to *Newsweek* in 1946, he continued his propaganda efforts. F. A. (Floyd) Harper, a former Cornell marketing professor, joined the FEE staff on behalf of 'economic liberty'. He believed in the importance of the 'first personal singular', that is, 'self-ownership', as the source from 'which all other forms of property arise'. Similarly present at the creation, Mises shared Read's commitment to the 'freedom movement'. FEE's reputation, like its distribution network, spread far beyond New York eventually reaching Fisher in Britain and Greg Lindsay in Sydney. In the words of Gary North, the 'personal evangelism' of Read took readers on the road to 'unserfdom', ultimately inspiring the founding of the IEA and the CIS.[5]

Near FEE's headquarters, New York intellectuals opposed to Stalinism and concerned about Soviet anti-Semitism took a more circuitous route to the same ultimate destination: a faith in the unregulated market. Originally social democrats, socialists, trade unionists and ex-Communists, these New Yorkers wrote for *Partisan Review*, *New Leader* and *Commentary* rather than FEE's *Freeman*, *Human Events*, or *The American Mercury*. They excoriated the Soviet Union but did not oppose the 'collectivist' New Deal, the welfare state or trade unions. Despite these clear ideological differences with the FEE cadre, their political commitment to 'hard-line' anti-Stalinism, belief in the 'democratic, pluralistic, prosperous' nature of the US and their repudiation of 'ideology' eventually converted these intellectuals to a new faith, a hybrid of their past and present affiliations, called neoconservatism. Over the next three decades, they travelled the necessary ideological distance to form common cause with their conservative contemporaries. Neoconservative journals reached readers like the young university student Costello in Melbourne, who supplemented his reading of *Quadrant*, and British conservative Paul Johnson, with his reading of *Commentary*. Joined by welfare critics Charles Murray and Michael Novak in the 1980s, neoconservatives not only achieved significant influence in Washington but also undertook ideological missions to Wellington and Sydney as part of the market-liberal network.[6]

Two of the most important shrines to the market gods ironically originated with the Roosevelt administration and Keynes, the 'devil figure' of the New Right. At Bretton Woods, New Hampshire in 1944, Keynes and other delegates designed two institutions to manage the restored post-war global economy: the IMF and the World Bank. These planners of a new world order sought to create a free flow of goods, investment and labour while carefully regulating the exchange system to allow governments to manage their economic affairs. These institutions opened in Washington just as Soviet occupation of eastern Europe and the victory of Communists in the Chinese civil war dashed hopes of an open world economy. Through their later service at the IMF and World Bank, Stone and Brash learned to see the global economy from its market centre rather than the New Zealand and Australian periphery. Creatures of interventionist state power, these institutions, often staffed by Treasury officials from the US and elsewhere, served the same market gods worshipped by anti-statist thinkers like Hayek, Friedman and Machlup, who advised the Treasury during the period of Brash's and Stone's Washington sojourn. By the early 1980s, these bureaucrats had produced new market doctrines, the so-called 'Washington Consensus': a mix of fiscal stringency, privatisation, free trade, downsizing of governmental activities and other 'reforms' intended to rescue failed economies through integration into the global economy. Despite their New Deal, Keynesian and welfare state origins, the IMF and the World Bank preached the pro-market message New Right converts wanted to spread in the 1980s.[7]

An already existing organisation in Palo Alto renewed itself in the battle against the foreign and domestic proponents of the interventionist state. Founded by one of the most fervent opponents of the New Deal, the president whose electoral defeat resulted in Roosevelt's ascent to power, the Hoover Institution evolved into a research-oriented institution, supporting 'private enterprise', 'personal freedom' and the 'American system' limiting 'government intrusion into the lives of individuals'. Seeing no conflict between individual, economic and political freedom, the Hoover Institution dedicated itself to 'collecting knowledge', 'generating ideas' and 'disseminating' the products of its intellectual labour with the aim of becoming a 'prominent contributor to the world marketplace of ideas defining a free society'. Bringing together émigré intellectuals, conservative scholars, retired politicians and former public officials, Hoover became a new kind of organisation – a conservative think tank. Eventually including Richard V. Allen, Thomas Sowell, Friedman and other luminaries of the New Right, this ensemble of scholars sometimes sent missionaries to New Zealand or visited us by satellite with instructions about how to think on welfare, racial equality, markets and the 'rule of law'.[8]

Each element of the future transnational New Right built up its own strength before a fully developed coalition emerged. Hayek chose a place in Switzerland whose name, Pelerin, meant pilgrim in French for an initial meeting of free-market apostles. Aided by the Volker

Fund, ten American delegates – Friedman, Director, Read, Harper, Mises and Hazlitt among them – participated in 1947 in the formation of the MPS, which also attracted Popper and other members of Hayek's British and European network. The MPS manifesto drew upon a freshly minted Cold War vocabulary to describe the 'menace' to the 'essential conditions of human dignity and freedom' spreading across large areas of the world. The denial of 'all absolute moral standards', threats to private property and the market and a pervasive failure to enforce the 'rule of law' constituted dangers that must be combated by right-thinking individuals. Converts to a faith Hayek called 'neo-liberalism', the delegates created a network of like-minded believers convinced that the mildest form of state intervention led inevitably to serfdom, a secular version of damnation.[9]

After the founding moment, the incipient network widened its ideological reach over successive years. Not in attendance for the first seven years, Fisher forged strong links with key members of MPS. In 1953, Fisher journeyed to America to visit FEE. He not only saw the sort of institution he hoped to build but also learned about agricultural techniques from Harper's former colleagues at Cornell. Attending his first MPS meeting in 1954, Fisher intensified his efforts to develop a think tank in Britain, choosing Ralph Harris and Arthur Seldon as the directors of IEA. Seldon and Harris shared the MPS faith in the market as 'almost god-ordained'. Having successfully launched the IEA in 1955, they attended MPS four years later. Inspired by his success and invited by other MPS members to start similar institutions, Fisher functioned like a Hayekian circuit rider, helping to start the Fraser Institute in Vancouver, begetting the predecessor to the Manhattan Institute in New York, counselling the organisers of the Heritage Foundation in Washington and assisting at the birth of the CIS in Sydney. Eventually tiring of personal evangelism, Fisher founded the Atlas Economic Research Foundation to carry on the global missionary work. Emulating Fisher, Edwin Feulner, another member of MPS, crisscrossed the globe proselytising on behalf of the free market after he successfully built up Heritage as a central institution of the market-liberal network. Feulner's visit to the CIS in 1985 and the enrolment of New Zealand and Australian members in the MPS – Stone, Kerr and Richardson among them – led to a regional meeting in Christchurch in 1989 where free-marketeers mingled with

New Right politicians.[10] Funded by leading conservative foundations, Fisher and Feulner, Atlas and MPS helped to create a transnational network that encouraged the CIS, the NZBR and, more recently, the Maxim Institute, to pursue similar policies.

Just west of Los Angeles, in Santa Monica, Kahn worked at the Rand Corporation, another think tank, in the 1950s, creating 'hawkish conjectures' of Soviet military capabilities that justifyed enhanced military budgets, expanded intelligence services and increasing the influence of the military-industrial complex. A new priestly caste, the 'military intellectual', moved between Santa Monica and the Pentagon. In 1961 Kahn resigned from Rand to establish the Hudson Institute. A multipurpose think tank, Hudson blended market liberalism, technocracy and social conservatism. Kahn projected a future based upon 'economic man'. This market version of 'futurology' placed its faith in nuclear weapons and technology to solve the world's problems, particularly appealing to corporate executives and military contractors. Kahn eventually visited Australia to prognosticate about a future in which markets and the military offered the best ways to sustain economic growth.[11]

In 1954, William J. Baroody left a position at the US Chamber of Commerce to start a twenty-six-year career that transformed the American Enterprise Association into a well-funded research institute, the American Enterprise Institute (AEI). AEI reports soon appeared in the *Wall Street Journal* and featured prominently in major newspapers, news magazines and business publications. Lured by its burgeoning coffers and increasing influence, Friedman joined AEI as an advisor. New Right scholars, wealthy business heirs and corporate executives associated themselves with this institution built by a talent for promotion, fund-raising, alliance-building and the production of ideologically astute research. Luring Murray from the Manhattan Institute and hiring Novak, AEI became an intellectual New Right powerhouse that extended its influence as far as New Zealand and Australia.[12]

In 1955, in parallel to the founding of IEA, William F. Buckley Jr launched the *National Review* to pursue a 'fusion' strategy intent on building 'intellectual and moral unity' between different conservative organisations and ideological currents. Buckley and his patrons wanted to create an ideological consensus around core ideas about free enterprise, private property and a family structure that provided for the welfare of its members without relying upon the state. Buckley's religiously inflected version of free enterprise appealed to market liberals and moral conservatives. Aspiring Republican politicians, including then General Electric mouthpiece Ronald Reagan and George Bush, became an important part of *National Review*'s target readership. Five years later, Buckley sponsored the formation of the Young Americans for Freedom to create a 'New Right' adversary for the 'New Left' student movement also taking organisational shape at the same time. Growing out of a complex traffic in ideas that crossed the Atlantic in both directions, the *National Review*'s editorial staff set the political agenda for a New Right political coalition, while issues of the journal soon found their way to New Zealand and Australia to gain new supporters for the 'fusion' strategy.[13]

The mobilisation of conservative Christians paralleled the development of this network of New Right intellectuals and pro-market activists. Christian crusaders – Carl McIntire of the American Council of Christian Churches, Australian Fred Schwarz of the Christian Anti-Communist Crusade and Billy Hargis of the Christian Crusade – conducted moral and political campaigns. Schwarz's anti-Communism schools attracted the participation of Reagan, as personal links formed between religious and secular conservatives. Robert Welch, a corporate executive, a leader of the National Association of Manufacturers and a devout Baptist, created an only slightly more secular version of the same movement that combined 'Americanism', Christianity and anti-Communism with a strident advocacy of free enterprise. The resulting John Birch Society enlisted future contributors to the fully developed New Right, including oil-company owner Fred Koch, electronics manufacturers Lynde and Harry Bradley, *National Review* patron Roger Millikan and Read of FEE. These organisations unleashed a fervent anti-Communism equating governmental intervention in the economy, the United Nations and the New Deal with the totalitarian anti-Christ personified by the Soviet Union.[14]

Worried about the growth of 'extreme' anti-Communism like Welch's that attacked the reputations of leading Republicans, including Eisenhower, *National Review* advised its readers to avoid the excesses of the John Birch Society's leader. Identifying the Republican

Party as the most likely source of political support and having hopes for the future success of Arizona senator Barry Goldwater, Buckley denounced Welch. Accusations that Eisenhower and his brother were either traitors or Communist dupes could not be allowed to undermine the chance to develop a political coalition. Although Birch Society policies filtered their way into the mainstream New Right, the *National Review* carefully patrolled the ideological boundaries to prevent the label of 'extremist' from halting their successful march on Washington.[15]

Crucial to the success of the *National Review* strategy was the recruitment of attractive candidates. Goldwater, identified by William Rusher, the *National Review* publisher, as the most promising flag-bearer for the conservative movement, starred in a ghost-written biography, *Conscience of a Conservative*, by one of Buckley's brothers-in-law in 1960. Denied the presidential nomination in 1960, Goldwater became the object of a draft movement led by Rusher and Clifton White that succeeded in his becoming the Republican candidate in 1964. Baroody of AEI muscled into the Goldwater campaign, taking his first shot at achieving political power to implement his policy agenda, while Friedman signed on as economic advisor. Phyllis Schlafly, a former AEI employee, wrote *A Choice, Not an Echo* to rally conservative activists to the Goldwater cause.[16]

Despite a landslide victory for Lyndon Johnson, an energised group of conservative activists and wealthy supporters discovered a new candidate, Ronald Reagan. The response to Reagan's televised speech for Goldwater in October 1964 demonstrated an appeal beyond the narrow ideological coalition that failed to win the White House in 1964. Grooming Reagan for political office, wealthy California businessmen enabled the political neophyte to campaign credibly for the governorship of California in 1966. Calling for a 'moral crusade' to close the 'morality and decency gap', Reagan won the election, putting him on the road to the White House.[17] Although his conservative supporters could not prevent the nomination of Richard Nixon or Gerald Ford, they had found a determined campaigner willing to carry the conservative banner for the next two decades.

Just as Reagan began his meteoric political career, in 1965 the incipient neoconservative core coalesced around *Public Interest* under the editorial leadership of Irving Kristol and Daniel Bell.

The *New York Times* described the journal as 'expressing a trend in social thought' called the 'new right', presciently heralding the significance of the new journal. Kristol declared his editorial intention of presenting 'non-ideological analyses of such issues as poverty'. Soon derisively labelled 'neoconservatives' by socialist Michael Harrington, the advisor to Martin Luther King and the person most responsible for anti-poverty programmes, Kristol grudgingly adopted the term. Concerned about 'moral decline', neoconservatives joined other opponents of 'radical egalitarianism' in blaming poverty on the immoral behaviour of the poor. By the late 1970s, after six years as a regular contributor to the *Wall Street Journal*, Kristol joined ex-Treasury Secretary William E. Simon in establishing the Institute for Educational Affairs (IEA-US) and published *Two Cheers for Capitalism* as a testament to his new ideological affiliation. Norman Podhoretz, the neoconservative editor of *Commentary*, shared their opposition to the 'new class' in its 'struggle with the business community for status and power'. By the end of decade these neoconservatives and their like-minded spouses – Midge Decter and Gertrude Himmelfarb – along with the neoconservative editor of the *Wall Street Journal*, Robert Bartley, supported Reagan's candidacy.[18]

Simon, having been thwarted in his own presidential ambitions, formed the IEA-US as a part of a campaign to fight against 'statist ideas' by funding scholars and journalists 'who understand the relationship between political and economic liberty'. The IEA-US offered guidance to corporations to use philanthropy strategically to defend capitalist interests. Having helped to rewrite the rules of the international financial system in the early 1970s during his time as Secretary of the Treasury, former Wall Street financier Simon now prepared to defend capitalism in his private life. Strategically positioning himself at the Olin Foundation, he persuaded the Lynde and Harry Bradley Foundation, the J. M. Foundation and Smith Richardson Foundation to wage a concerted 'war of ideas' on behalf of free enterprise. The IEA-US funded a conservative student movement. Once graduated, these conservative acolytes staffed New Right journals, worked at think tanks or served on the staff of conservative senators like Jesse Helms.[19] Strategically positioned chairs in free enterprise and law and economics made inroads into prestigious universities through the adroit use of foundation money. Simultaneously, Simon and other conservative Catholics targeted the exponents of liberation theology and attacked Catholic bishops who criticised capitalism or nuclear war. Determined to win an ideological counter-offensive, Simon urged corporate leaders to follow his example.

Sensing the new political opportunities, a core group of Republican activists developed an organisational network sufficiently strong to persuade the Republican Party to adopt their moral, political and economic agenda. They established core New Right institutions – Heritage and the Free Congress Research and Education Foundation – as a Washington base for a grassroots 'moral' coalition to prod and push the Republican Party towards New Right reforms and moral conservatism. 'Hot button' social issues served as an ideological 'bridge' to connect moral conservatives from different faiths and regions. Grassroots activists found a 'perfect enemy' in gay rights activists and feminists, fighting battle after battle against gay rights legislation at the state and city level. Anti-feminist and anti-gay campaigns produced new organisations such as the Traditional Values Coalition (TVC) under the leadership of the Reverend Lou Sheldon, the Family Research Council led by Gary Bauer and the Moral Majority under the Reverend Jerry Falwell.[20] The Christian Right provided the grassroots base for an increasingly powerful political coalition.

Heritage set for itself a 'mission' to 'formulate and promote conservative public policies' based on free enterprise, limited government, individual freedom, 'traditional American values and a strong national defense'. It contended with the AEI for influence as part of a 'new breed of advocacy outfits' driven by ideological imperatives and funded by 'corporate largesse', spending substantial portions of their budgets on marketing ideas that served the interests of GM, Ford, Proctor & Gamble, Dow Chemical, Mobil Oil, Smith Kline, Chase Manhattan and other corporations. Feulner, the co-founder of Heritage with Paul Weyrich, built a broad support base and astutely moved the political agenda rightwards through close contacts with Republican legislators and their staff. Connected to IEA and MPS, Heritage attracted conservative politicians while providing an ideological platform for their campaigns. The IEA sent Stuart and

Eamon Butler to Washington to learn the skills of New Right policy formation at Heritage. Stuart stayed in Washington at Heritage while Eamon went back to London to establish the ASI as a British version of this activist think tank.[21]

In parallel to the growing influence of the US New Right in the Republican Party in the 1970s, Thatcher, standing on a New Right platform, defeated Edward Heath to become the leader of the British Conservative Party in February 1975. As leader of the Opposition from 1975 to 1979 she drew heavily and directly on the work of the CPS in developing Tory policies. In addition, her links with the IEA played a significant role in shaping her agenda as well as being the vehicle for her to meet Hayek, Friedman and other prominent New Right figures. Thatcher's embrace of New Right doctrines gave them a new political potency. Reagan, her future New Right soulmate, moved from the governorship of California to a seemingly perpetual campaign for the presidency during the 1970s that eventually gained traction as *détente* gave way to the 'Second Cold War'.

A dense collection of overlapping organisations translated the economic theories of Hayek, Friedman and Buchanan into morally appealing proposals appropriate to the regional socio-religious cultures of the United States and Britain while exporting this reform agenda to other parts of the globe. Building a powerful base in the Republican and Conservative parties, the New Right political coalition – market liberals, conservatives, neoconservatives and Christian conservatives – developed a policy programme. In the 1970s, the AEI, CPS, Heritage, Cato, IEA and Manhattan developed a policy agenda that attracted support from corporate executives and moral conservatives. Corporations generously funded these think tanks, particularly those opposed to regulation of their industries and the continuing battle over 'socialised medicine'. Oil and gas corporations, proprietary companies, pharmaceutical companies, tobacco, securities and commodities traders, defence contractors and chemical companies played particularly conspicuous roles.[22]

Media, including specifically New Right organs such as the Rupert Murdoch-backed *Weekly Standard*, *Commentary*, the *Wall Street Journal* edited by neoconservative Robert Bartley and *National Review* as well as the right-leaning mainstream press, played equally crucial roles in enhancing the circulation of the New Right message. In Britain Murdoch and his Canadian rival, Conrad Black, championed New Right causes in newspapers like *The Times* and the *Daily Telegraph* and, in the case of Murdoch, on the Fox News network in the US. Owner of influential Australian newspapers and partial owner of the Independent News Limited in New Zealand until its recent sale to Fairfax, Murdoch's ideological preferences shaped the choices of editors and editorial commentary. Specific corporations like Pfizer also launched their own form of news, establishing the Pfizer Forum to publish New Right essays and paying for Novak to lecture on the 'spirit' of the corporation. Urged on by the IEA-US, other corporations subsidised the work of New Right authors, helping to consolidate an ideological alliance between moral conservatives, market liberals and corporations that repaid their benefactors with research promoting the market agenda.[23]

Thatcher won the national election in 1979, campaigning under the slogan 'Who Governs Britain?', to become Britain's first woman prime minister and the first major New Right leader. Immediately, a neo-liberal New Right programme was begun, commencing with cuts in the levels of direct taxation followed by plans to privatise nationalised industries and apply monetarist principles to combat inflation by tightly controlling the money supply. Inflation was brought down from 27 per cent to 3 per cent but at the cost of massive increases in the number of unemployed, to over three million, and the generation of an economy in 'recession'. The 1981 budget went against Keynesian theory by increasing taxes during a recession, allowing for a cut in interest rates and fostering the beginning of an almost instant economic recovery. This apparently successful challenge to the then conventional economic orthodoxy bestowed a degree of legitimacy on New Right reformers and its impact was felt as far away as Australia and New Zealand.

The advent of Thatcherism in Britain and Reaganomics in the US after Reagan's victory in 1980 solidified the New Right support base while persuading the mainstream media to report a 'rightward' turn. The electoral turnout for Reagan enabled the Republicans to take over the Senate. The religious right now completed their triumphal march on Washington. Think tanks pushed for the implementation of policies reducing the role of the state for social welfare and other parts of the market liberal agenda. Heritage's *Mandate for Leadership* gave the Reagan administration a complete policy agenda for a process of New Right reform. Conservative Catholic Thomas Monaghan established the Acton Institute for Religion and Liberty to argue for the sanctified nature of the market economy. Well-subsidised authors provided key texts – Murray's *Losing Ground: American Social Policy, 1950–1980* and Lawrence Mead's *Beyond Entitlement: The Social Obligations of Citizenship* – as ideological ammunition that circulated through the New Right network and the mainstream media.[24] Reagan's re-election in 1984 and Thatcher's repeated victories appeared to give the New Right the official imprimatur on both sides of the Atlantic.

Other organisations marched on Washington and Westminster to pursue the same struggle against the interventionist state. State assets sales continued in the Second Thatcher Government from 1983 to 1987. The programme to transform Britain into an 'enterprise culture' of entrepreneurial individuals in a world where 'there is no such thing as society' also became more evident. New legislation to restrict the power of trade unions was enacted and market principles applied to more and more sectors of government activity and service provision. Public housing was offered for sale. The railways were privatised. The Conservatives won again in 1987 and Thatcher continued as Prime Minister until 1990. Her commitment to the New Right principles of market forces, competition and less government intervention in the economy, the 'Thatcher revolution', made Britain the model of the New Right for the US and later for New Zealand and Australia.

In Washington New Right organisations proliferated despite their supposed antagonism to the federal government. The Cato Institute, established by David Koch, son of a John Birch Society founder, and Edward Crane in 1977, drew for support on the Koch oil and gas fortune and an ideological legacy that claimed Thomas Jefferson as a 'market-liberal' visionary and shared the Hayekian opposition to 'socialism and government planning'. Originally based in San Francisco, Cato moved to Washington in 1981, sponsoring New Right intellectuals like Richard Epstein, a UC contributor to the field of Law and Economics who argued for 'limited government, individual liberty, free markets and peace'. Young New Zealand officials attended Cato workshops providing market solutions to social problems. After the death of Kahn in 1983, the Hudson

Institute moved to Indiana to develop an active presence in the midwest but also set up an office in Washington. The dual presence of Hudson and the Bradley Foundation transformed midwestern states into laboratories for New Right experiments in areas such as welfare reform, school vouchers and faith-based charities that eventually reached New Zealand and Australia through reports and visitors claiming success for these initiatives.[25]

Active clusters of New Right organisations, often religious right in orientation, developed in western states. Usually funded by the brewery fortune of the Coors family in the case of Colorado, these organisations included Focus on the Family, under the leadership of James Dobson, and more than two dozen other think tanks and organisations. In California campaigns to lower state taxes achieved the celebrated 1979 victory of Proposition 13, reducing state property taxes, mounted challenges to affirmative action for minorities at state universities, fought against gay-rights legislation, pushed for punitive measures against criminals and passed 'English only' language laws. Successes, trumpeted by the press and by other parts of the New Right network, inspired imitation in other states and other nations that received missionaries telling of these successful initiatives.

Regular meetings kept the New Right coalition marching to the same beat. Meetings of the Council for National Policy (CNP) set an agenda for the New Right movement while allowing compromises, negotiations and conflicts to be resolved in private. Meeting outside the public eye and without media scrutiny, the CNP enabled Christian Right leaders and market liberals to develop strategy, forge compromises and formulate political goals without being seen to have sacrificed immutable principles. Almost every major leader and organisation of the New Right attended the CNP's meetings: Feulner of Heritage, Schlafly of the Eagle Forum, Sirico of Acton, Dobson of Focus on the Family, Falwell of Moral Majority, Pat Robertson and Ralph Reed of the Christian Coalition, Rusher of *National Review* and Sheldon of the TVC. In Washington, AEI, Heritage and Free Congress performed similar maintenance functions both nationally and internationally, while Atlas and MPS primarily focused on the transnational network. Their British counterparts – IEA, ASI, CPS and the Institute for the Study of Civil Society (Civitas), an organisation that grew out of the IEA – tended both the British and transnational network. Each major think tank vied for recognition at 'the institutional center of the conservative movement' and for the support of politicians to translate their vision into legislative, judicial and political action. Thus connected, the New Right poured out a constantly replenished stream of policy advice that circulated across the globe, reaching Australia and New Zealand in the form of books, policies and visitors preaching the latest reform message.[26]

Writing in 1994, a year in which Republicans gained control of the House of Representatives, Congressman Richard Armey described the political transformation that the New Right had achieved in the US and Britain. Declaring that the 'foundation of statism has turned to dust', Armey predicted that a 'true Hayekian agenda' could now be implemented, ending the 'public school monopoly', ensuring a 'free market health-care system' and eliminating the 'family-destroying welfare dole'. History was now 'on the side of freedom' according to this Republican leader who celebrated the New Right's 'paradigm-shattering revolution'.[27]

Reports on our New Zealand New Right initiatives flowed back through the same circuits that carried success stories and cautionary tales about stalled reform projects in equal measure. Richardson, Douglas, Brash, Kerr and former National MP Maurice McTigue, a fellow at the Mercatus Center, moved around the New Right reform circuit as evangelists in their own right. Through their links the NZBR, CIS, IPA and the once vibrant Tasman Institute passed along reports of initiatives and shared the costs of bringing visitors from the US or Britain. Epstein, Sirico, Novak, Murray, Green, Sowell and Kenneth Minogue, among others, arrived in New Zealand and Australia on recurrent visits while they, in turn, welcomed New Zealand visitors to their home institutions. In no small measure, these evangelists contributed to a common vocabulary that criticised welfare 'dependency', denigrated 'political correctness', glorified markets and praised the virtues of the 'enterprise culture'. Even those of us who never left home could hear or read the same exhortations to free enterprise, limited government, individual freedom and 'traditional' values that echoed through the halls of AEI, FEE, IEA and ASI. Sometimes festooned with the portraits of prophets like Hayek and Friedman, these large and impressive buildings served as unsteepled places of worship for the acolytes of the market faith.

Milo's Week.

THE BUSINESS ROUNDTABLE IS RUNNING FOR PARLIAMENT...

NEXT: ROGERNOMICS...

CHAPTER FIVE

Revelation: Marketing Morality

*And judgment is turned away backward and
justice standeth afar off: for truth is fallen in the
street and equity cannot enter.* ISAIAH 59:14

*Not slothful in business; fervent in spirit; serving
the Lord.* ROMANS 12:11

During their journey to the Promised Land, the Israelites carried
an Ark of the Covenant containing the testimony, including the
tables of the law, that guided their moral conduct and gave them
directions for their journey through the wilderness. So, too, our
New Right marchers and pilgrims carried sacred texts with them on
their journey from political wilderness to power. These included the
founding documents of 'classical liberalism' written by Adam Smith
and published in the late 18th century. The contemporary New Right
sought to revive this classically liberal economic and moral vision
in the 1940s when Hayek published *The Road to Serfdom* and FEE
began to disseminate market liberal tracts. Hayek and his intellectual
allies engaged in a sustained attack on intellectuals and other 'second
hand dealers' in ideas who had been captured by 'socialism', an
ideology opposed to the free market and their moral vision. Rather
than merely criticising economic planning and the welfare state on the
grounds of economic inefficiency, Hayek and his disciples mounted a
moral challenge.[1] Their moral arguments reinforced and justified the
market in a polemic against the proponents of 'social justice' and 'new
rights' as the New Right expanded and developed its networks.

We will consider two discrete moral dimensions in the New Right
doctrines that influenced our policies, usually at second or third hand,
in the 1980s and 1990s. We examine the moral claims made by market
liberal prophets who trace their lineage back to Adam Smith, often
evoked by the New Right as its founding father. These include Hayek,

Friedman and Buchanan. We also explore the ideas of two Catholic New Right missionaries to New Zealand: Novak and Sirico. These New Right theologians reinterpreted religious doctrine to defend capitalism and the market in opposition to other religious thinkers who espoused a 'social justice' morality containing a more critical view of the capitalist economy and a more collective understanding of the moral economy.

The 'sacred text' of market liberalism, Smith's *The Wealth of Nations*, appeared in 1776.[2] The hugely influential, ponderous and lengthy work called for an end to the political management of the market by the state. Smith argued that the market, when given free rein, allowed the pursuit of self-interest to produce the collective good. A great deal of Smith scholarship concerns the relationship between *The Wealth of Nations* and his earlier work, *The Theory of Moral Sentiments* (1759), where he laid out his moral vision.[3] Notes made by students at his lectures at the University of Glasgow and Smith's sketch of his grand plan point to the conclusion that his belief in markets and defence of 'self-interest' formed only a part of his moral philosophy. Smith wanted to contribute to setting the moral agenda and promote market freedom at the same time.[4]

Through these two works Smith joined an extended debate between mercantilists and the proponents of free trade about the collective good, understood as justice, stability and prosperity. Smith contended that justice 'is the great pillar that upholds the whole edifice' and without it 'human society' will 'crumble into atoms'.[5] He intended to develop a model of justice appropriate to the new industrial and economic age, which he strongly contrasted with the classical models he had studied in his own university education. Complex relationships between people and transactions, often separate from family and locality, had emerged in contemporary society that meant that earlier theories of morality and economy must give way to more appropriate models. Smith sought a new basis for justice and social cohesion to reflect the new impersonal realities of modern social relations. He identified these as 'equality' under the law and in the marketplace. He wanted an inclusive economic and political society that translated the freedom from restraint, for example, not being a slave, into the ownership of the product of your own endeavours and the ability to manage this property without external regulation by a heavy-handed state.[6] Smith's new model of freedom privatised desires and passions and depoliticised individual morality. With morality privatised, Smith understood the market as producing moral outcomes at the individual level in terms of rewarding effort and enterprise. As a consequence, Smith's model removed morality from the collective or political level, while limiting the state to non-interference with market processes or outcomes but still retaining justice and benevolence at the core of his 'moral sentiments'.

Thus the author of *A Theory of Moral Sentiments* is a more complex moral philosopher than the pro-market caricature as the creator of the 'invisible hand' that often appears in New Right exegesis. Justice had a prominent place in his moral philosophy, as did 'benevolence'. Justice, Smith argued, was a virtue which could 'be extorted by force' when not freely dispensed, because its violation 'does real and positive hurt' to other people. Indeed, according to Smith, the 'happiness' of others is important even to the most 'selfish' man. As he argued, concern for the happiness of others could be expressed through the virtues of 'justice and beneficence; of which, the one restrains us from hurting, the other prompts us to promote that happiness'. He ascribed 'concern for our own happiness' to our 'selfish' instincts; while these other, more altruistic, virtues stemmed from 'our benevolent affections'.[7] Justice and altruism remained essential elements of Smith's moral vision, although his modern-day disciples often reject these virtues in their truncated version of his sacred text which, in the case of the Law and Economics school, excised justice almost entirely from the New Right conception of the law.

The version of market and morality developed by Hayek, Friedman, Buchanan and other New Right evangelists is an eviscerated version of Smith's 'moral sentiments'. Their New Right expurgation reduced human beings to isolated competitors, 'atomistic and estranged', who are 'possessively set against one another', in the words of one of their critics. They themselves identified this model as 'methodological individualism' and, in the words of Hayek, described the market as miraculously producing 'spontaneous order' from the individual decisions of numerous self-interested competitors vying in the marketplace. Only what Smith termed the 'selfish' instincts remained in this parsimonious version of 'man alone'.

Hayek's *The Road to Serfdom* pared down the moral complexities of Smith to self-interest alone. In his later book *Fatal Conceit*, he reduced Smith's critique of the 'selfish' instincts even further and turned it into an accusation launched against his 'social justice' opponents, whom he characterised as 'selfish' for their attempts to restrict 'the profits of others'. He reinterpreted European history to describe the development of moral rules to regulate property transactions that he called a 'new' moral code. He dismissed what Smith called 'moral sentiments' as 'innate morality' or the 'old' primitive moral code under which Hayek subsumed solidarity, altruism and other social virtues. He advocated their replacement by the 'evolved morality' of possessive virtues, in contrast to Smith's version that combined justice, benevolence and self-interest. Self-interest is all that is left of Smith's catalogue of virtues. The original sacred texts had been bowdlerised.

Hayek in a 1976 essay on Smith commented that the 'demand for social justice' was nothing but an 'atavism', a primitive return to the pre-historical context when the tribal leader redistributed goods.[8] He traced his own doctrines of 'unintended consequences' and the de-moralisation of politics to Smith. In his interpretation of Smith, the benefits of the markets do not arise because of our moral intentions but from the pursuit of our self-interest. In the last chapter of *The Fatal Conceit*, 'Religion and the Guardians of Tradition', Hayek argued that, in retrospect, we can see that over time an 'extended order' of acceptable 'traditions' developed as the market economy emerged and replaced the earlier communal societies. We live in the midst of these traditions and institutions built to support accumulation, participating in 'those spontaneous social forces through which the individual creates things greater than himself'. One of these emergent 'greater things' is the market. It was not planned – the notion that we can rationally plan for complex systems is the 'fatal conceit' – but evolved over time. Other parallel developments include moral dispositions, trust, property rights, the family and so on.

Hayek feared that socialist planning or even Keynesian economics eroded these 'natural' traditions. Religion and morality sustained the market system by being part of a linked archaic set of arrangements and institutions that are mutually reinforcing. This is not an argument for returning to God but one that claimed that religion is a part of our evolutionary inheritance. Religion by externalising morality tacitly recognised, according to Hayek, that human planning was of a different order from cross-generational traditional practices. Further, he contended that tampering with the market system had moral consequences as well as consequences for our creativity and our capability to establish a stable social order. This in part explains the compatibility of some forms of religious tradition with New Right doctrines. It also explains why so many of the New Right activists that we interviewed attended church irregularly but believed in the centrality of morality and religion to freedom and the free operation of the market. A market left to its own devices will not necessarily produce moral outcomes unless moral behaviours such as truth-telling, honesty and debt settlement are assured. Hayek and other New Right thinkers ignore the corroding power of market capitalism to undermine these same religious and moral traditions. De-politicised individual 'liberty', a negative liberty wielded against state interference, the liberty to enter the market and exercise individual power, is one of Smith's legacies that Hayek and his brethren do perpetuate.

Milton and Rose Friedman, as the intellectual partnership at the heart of the contemporary Chicago School, moved Hayek's doctrine still further in the direction of 'freedom' and away from any suggestion that social welfare or equality should be delivered by government actions. In 1962 Milton Friedman's *Capitalism and Freedom*, written with the assistance of his wife, conveyed the elements of his libertarian interpretation to an American audience. Based on lectures originally sponsored by the same fund that had supported FEE and MPS, Friedman's book acknowledged the inspiration of Hayek, Knight, Director and George J. Stigler, all colleagues at the UC. The Friedmans proposed limiting government's responsibilities to just the protection of 'our freedom both from the enemies outside our gates and from our fellow-citizens', in keeping with the 'new' Hayekian moral code of enforcing private contracts, fostering competitive markets and providing the necessary military defence against the 'evil men in the Kremlin'.[9]

A 'hermeneutics of suspicion' thus shaped the analysis, derived from the sense of estrangement of the individual from competitors, enemies and criminals, that was most strongly directed against government. Any use of government to 'accomplish jointly what we would find it more difficult or expensive to accomplish' individually was 'fraught with danger'. Inevitably, government action replaced 'progress by stagnation' because 'the invisible hand has been more potent for progress than the visible hand for retrogression'. Advocates of the 'doctrines pertaining to a free man', the Friedmans explained the 'advances of civilization' as entirely due to the 'initiative and drive of individuals co-operating through the free market'. The attainment of virtue was possible only in the 'free society', while the 'coercive power of the state' corrupted everyone despite the 'good intentions' of those who relied upon it.[10]

On the verge of a visit to Australia and almost twenty years after *Capitalism and Freedom*, the Friedmans published *Free to Choose* in association with a BBC documentary by the same title that soon arrived in New Zealand. Having gained in credibility from the receipt of the Nobel Prize for economics two years after Hayek received the honour, Milton and Rose Friedman continued their battle against New Deal liberalism and the welfare state. Now referring to the 'invisible hand' of government, they accused that hand of operating in 'precisely the opposite direction' from that recommended in Adam Smith's tribute to the benefits of the market. An 'individual who intends only to serve the public interest by fostering government intervention' actually promoted 'private interests'. They criticised the 'deadening effects of government control' and the 'new class' of bureaucrats who threatened to destroy the prosperity created by the free market.[11]

The Friedmans castigated the 'evils' of 'paternalistic' programmes that reduced the 'incentive to work, save and innovate' and, still more culpably, reduced the 'accumulation of capital'. After beginning with dire claims that 'we' were still 'speeding' down the 'road to serfdom', they concluded more hopefully. Written shortly after Thatcher's victory in Britain and the 'tax revolt' in the US, they predicted that 'the tide is turning' in public opinion toward 'economic freedom and limited government'. As the harbingers of the New Right, they now confidently looked towards the New Right version of the Promised Land, the 'freedom to choose'.[12] Words like choice, freedom and personal responsibility had become the major virtues of the Friedmanite moral economy while benevolence and justice disappeared.

Both Friedmans appeared virtually in Wellington, beamed in by live satellite link at the 2003 ACT Party conference. They argued a libertarian position maintaining that any government interventions beyond the minimal limit individual liberty, even extending this to taxes and social security contributions. Rose, in particular, made an exception for military force, however, arguing for an aggressive US response against Iraq and other enemies of freedom. Such force could extend the market, thus rendering it acceptable even if it enhanced state power. The Friedmans continue to define political liberty as 'intimately' linked to economic freedom and the latter to be a vital stage on the way to the former. Thus while the 'private enterprise exchange economy' or 'competitive capitalism' is morally neutral at the level of responses to the impersonal signals of demand and supply, it serves to 'decentralise' power and so acts as a 'check on political power'. Here again we find Smith's unintended consequences matched with the classical liberal notion of negative individual freedom.[13]

Buchanan, another product of the UC stable, offered a third prophetic vision for New Right seekers after enlightenment. Published with Gordon Tullock and appearing in the same year as *Capitalism and Freedom*, *The Calculus of Consent* deployed the economic tools of calculation to analyse the political organisation of a 'society of free men'. The authors translated 'methodological individualism' into a conception of politics premised on the notion of humans as 'choice-makers' and self-interested calculators. They applied the language of market liberalism that described people as motivated by 'utility-maximizing considerations' in their analysis of the 'politics of the good society'. A 'widespread adoption of Judeo-Christian morality' might be a 'necessary condition to the operation of any genuinely free society of individuals' but it must be tempered 'by an acceptance of the moral imperative of individualism, the rule of equal freedom'. Thus, they defined Christianity as a 'philosophy of individual' behaviour excluding any conception of 'social justice', social doctrines, or the Social Gospel. In the market, purely economic entities like corporations escaped any need to obey moral codes which bound only individual believers. Morality, and religion itself, became further individualised, privatised and separated from politics and economics in this version of the 'good society'.[14] Later developed into the 'public choice' school of economics, such ideas reappeared in our Treasury's own translations of the New Right sacred texts.

After Buchanan received the New Right version of sainthood, his own Nobel Prize for economics in 1986, he published a series of lectures devoted to 'Puritan ethics'. Once again transferring economic language to another area, he described his subject as the 'economic value of ethical norms' in the 1994 book, *Ethics and Economic Progress*. He paid homage to Smith, once again, declaring his intention to apply the distinction between 'productive' and 'unproductive' labour. Focused on 'menial servants', he asked his readers to apply the negative definition to the producers of 'many services, especially those that are supplied collectively or through governmental auspices'. The essays applauded the 'work ethic', arguing that 'working harder' can be and is, 'good' for all of us. Indeed, Buchanan believed that it was beneficial to 'feel guilty' for not working. Just as importantly, he adjured his readers to 'save more', updating his proverb to 'a dollar saved is a dollar earned' in deference to the declining value of the penny. He made even more explicit his religious zeal for the market by insisting upon paying 'the preacher' who taught the 'Puritan virtues'.[15]

Idleness, of course, was the vice that Buchanan and other exponents of market morality most vigorously condemned. He strenuously objected, moreover, to those 'moralists' who preached contrary doctrines about 'compassion', charity, protection of the wilderness or other 'unproductive' moral norms. Like government employees, these moralists inculcated vices rather than virtues, by teaching people to 'smell the roses' rather than work even harder, or to leave nature undeveloped. Thus Buchanan, like Hayek and Friedman, wrote a New Right version of Deuteronomy and Leviticus, preaching that capital accumulation and economic growth were the supreme moral imperatives.[16]

Novak, another New Right moralist, is a seasoned cold-war warrior. His advocacy of market capitalism links him to neoconservatives like Kristol. Originally a socialist theologian, the author of *A Theology of Radical Politics*, he experienced a second 'revelation' moving him 180 degrees to become a leading Catholic defender of capitalism.[17] The CIS sponsored Novak's second visit to

New Zealand and Australia in 1995. He gave lectures in Auckland, Wellington, Christchurch, Sydney, Canberra and Melbourne. The CIS published *In Praise of the Free Economy*, which includes 'Eight Arguments about the Morality of the Market' and 'Wealth and Virtue: The Moral Case for Capitalism' and its 'ten moral advantages' of capitalism.[18]

When we interviewed him in Washington in 2003, Novak had almost no recollection of his visit except for a negative local newspaper report. He did comment, though, that we suffered badly from the sin of envy. Rather than aspire to and celebrate material success, we showed resentment and avarice. In Novak's pro-market morality, the sin of envy, like the devil, usually 'masquerades' under 'some other name, such as equality'.[19] Novak thus continued Hayek's moral crusade against socialism and the welfare state as fostering vices rather than virtues.

In his books Novak claimed that the market generates moral outcomes by elevating the poor. Incentives teach them to 'smile and be helpful'. His indebtedness to the German social theorist Max Weber, who wrote *The Protestant Ethic and the Spirit of Capitalism*, was clearly evident in the titles of two of his books. In *The Spirit of Democratic Capitalism* and *The Catholic Ethic and the Spirit of Capitalism*, Novak argued that while Weber was right about the new 'spirit of capitalism', he wrongly identified it with the Calvinist Protestant tradition rather than Catholicism. Rather than an 'iron cage' of stultifying rationality, capitalism possessed a redemptive quality in that it nourished the sacred category of individual 'choice'. This choice is Smith and Hayek's individual 'liberty', the depoliticised freedom of the New Right. For Novak, the market economy directs 'our imperfections' to the common good. Novak concludes that capitalism depends upon democracy and morality for its sustainable existence, but is, at the same time, a necessary 'condition of democracy'.[20] Rounding out his works with a theology of the corporation, Novak deftly combined God and Mammon in a moral system that blessed profit-making and capital accumulation as a spiritual calling.

Although many of our pilgrims disclaimed direct knowledge of these texts and market moralists when interviewed, this New Right moral vision arrived on our shores encoded in economic policies,

Treasury documents, think-tank publications, documentaries like *Free to Choose* and the words of travelling evangelists. Seeking the imprimatur of the overseas expert, the NZBR and CIS frequently invited like-minded missionaries. Particularly effective were 'religious' visitors carrying their revealed laws aloft. They persuaded their co-religionists that capitalism is indeed compatible with their Christian faith and chided our churches for putting social justice ahead of consumer choice and freedom. They reassured us that the capitalist market system actually does deliver results that are moral. New Right prophets, secular and religious, disembarked to urge us to follow our New Right leaders. Epstein, the inheritor of Director's mantle at the UC, arrived for the first time in 1990 and gained credit for giving National the inspiration for the future Employment Contracts Act. Throughout the 1990s he returned six more times, advising us on the need to embed economic concepts like efficiency into our laws as he fostered the growth of UC-styled Law and Economics in New Zealand.[21] New Right visitors like Epstein redefined morality as individual liberty and economic freedom. Parallel to this privatisation of morality is the sanctification of economic growth as the 'heart of politics'.

Invited by the CIS and NZBR in 1993, Catholic priest Sirico, a one-time teenage evangelist, warned us about 'moral hazards' and objected to our confusing 'social justice' with 'socialism'. Described by an irreverent commentator as belonging to the 'Little Brothers of the Rich', Sirico told us that Pope John Paul II had condemned 'collectivism and its communist, socialist and welfare statist manifestations'. Insisting on absolute moral standards, Sirico's journal, *Religion and Liberty*, published the moral arguments of Epstein, among other commentators, arguing for the close affinities between markets and Christian morality. Like Novak's, Sirico's personal journey of faith took him from the left to being a right-wing theological commentator and a member of the MPS and to ordination as a Paulist priest. In Wellington Sirico spoke to the NZBR on the concept of subsidiarity, the Catholic doctrine that argues for the the primary exercise of power through the family and the church, with only limited resort to the central government. Sirico believes the 'magic of the marketplace' to be the answer to the 'most fundamental question of social theory', namely, how difference can be managed peacefully. For Sirico, the 'market has no moral compass' but requires for its successful operation that its participants be imbued with 'fundamental values', including the sanctity of the human person, private property and the honouring of contracts. The freedom to enter the market and act there of our own free will is the 'moral foundation of the market'. Since the market rewards risk-taking, enterprise and entrepreneurship, it becomes a moral instrument. Sirico, like Novak, came among us to preach a capitalist gospel and demand that we repent of socialist sins like envy.[22]

The 1970s and 1980s witnessed the resurgence not only of arguments in favour of capitalism but also the growth of evangelical and Pentecostal Christianity. According to Max Weber and also Buchanan, particular religious dispositions and practices are conducive to the development and growth of capitalism. Thatcher and Reagan's Christianity links morally conservative codes with the advocacy of unbridled market capitalism. The removal of the restraints on the market requires Christian virtues to check the excesses of the market. Lord Harris of the IEA argued that what was needed to ensure that market outcomes were moral was a code that included truth-telling and honesty. Although not a regular church-goer himself, he contended that traditional Christianity offered the most appropriate moral guidance. In a similar vein Robert Wheelan of Civitas recommended that the churches offered the necessary moral framework for the maintenance of a free society with a market economy.[23]

Local New Zealand acolytes of the market translated these doctrines into the Treasury's briefing papers, the NZBR's reports, speeches by prominent members, sympathetic editorials, columns and research affirming the market as the only correct way to organise our economy. They quoted Hayek, Friedman, Novak, Sirico and Buchanan. Australian, British, American and New Zealand voices sang 'hymns' set to the 'market's tune' with an occasional solo performance by a visiting Peruvian or Italian emissary to Australia and New Zealand.[24] Our policy-makers and politicians listened, even when they did not know the composers or fully understand the themes.

Our New Right reformers paid heed to Buchanan's call to 'pay the preacher' who inculcated market-oriented morality. Teachers, social workers and the staff of the ministries of Social Welfare and Education found themselves encouraged and sometimes required, to teach the virtues of work, thrift and prudence. The media, attuned to the amplified voices of the New Right, chimed in to 'beneficiary bash' or attack the 'cloth-capped' teachers' unions who dared to oppose bulk funding, vouchers or other reforms. Benevolence got a much less enthusiastic press, while justice was primarily defined as increasing the penalties for crime. Some of the more amenable of these 'preachers' learned to chant 'there is no alternative' to the market and the reforms designed to unleash market forces. Our students, the readers of our newspapers, our television viewers and our beneficiaries all received these sermons about the 'moral imperative of individualism' and the evils of dependency. We, who listened faithfully, redefined ourselves as competitors, consumers and taxpayers, subordinating our identities as 'free and equal citizens' embedded within a social system based on the 'principle of reciprocity'. Thus the New Right sought to silence the 'new rights' advocates and prevent incorrect 'moralists' from preaching 'unproductive' values. Subsequent chapters trace these efforts aimed at our moral rectification in regards to education, sexuality and welfare. They also trace the influences of New Right networks upon our public debates and their contestation by 'new rights' advocates.

CHAPTER SIX

Towards the Prosperous Land

*And Moses numbered them according to the word of
the LORD, as he was commanded.* NUMBERS 3:16

*And the people spoke against God and against
Moses, Wherefore have ye brought us up out of
Egypt to die in the wilderness? for there is no bread,
neither is there any water and our soul loatheth this
light bread.* NUMBERS 21:5

In the biblical narrative, Moses, the prophetic radical, sought to
transform his people from slaves to free men and women living under
the new 'law', secure, prosperous and independent. Moses, however,
was no orator and could not lead the people himself. He needed the
voice and popular appear of his elder brother, Aaron. It was Aaron
who pleaded with Pharaoh and rallied the Children of Israel. Douglas,
the New Right prophet in our version of Exodus, could not have
led Labour to electoral triumph in 1984 over Muldoon. Douglas's
mandate as a reformer depended upon the popularity and authority
of Lange. Our Moses carried on his reform offensive only so long as
he enjoyed Lange's confidence and cooperation. The biblical Jehovah
allowed Moses, after forty years of shepherding his people through
the wilderness, to see the holy land but not to enter therein. Our
Moses failed to achieve all the New Right reforms that he believed
necessary to bring us to the Prosperous Land.

Moses, the inspired prophet, also required Aaron and the Levite
lineage to produce the priests and the helpers who developed and
applied the new commandments. Our Moses relied on yet another
Aaron figure, Palmer, to develop the legislation to embody his
prophetic visions. Despite these important services, Palmer never
received full credit for his contributions to transforming New Right
ideology into law. This Aaron, like Lange, later distanced himself

from Moses and, in Douglas's view, betrayed the New Right vision, leading the people astray with a welfare state as the biblical golden calf. Palmer, however, in contrast to the biblical Aaron, outlasted our Moses, eventually replacing Lange as Prime Minister.

How are we to understand Douglas and his mission? Was it a question of waiting in the wings for the right moment to seize power and implement his New Right programme? The evidence does not support this intentionalist scenario of taking the opportunities as they arose to further an already existing plan. The alternative, a functionalist approach, is better supported by the evidence and Douglas's own assessment. The crisis engendered by Muldoon's failing command economy generated a desperate deregulatory response, which was most forcefully undertaken by Douglas but might well have been championed by another, and the plans changed as circumstances did. The Australian, American and British models already loomed large on our international horizons and the New Right think tanks and agencies had enlisted many influential New Zealand business people and government officials in their ranks long before Douglas became the Minister of Finance.

At the Fourth Labour Party Conference on the twentieth anniversary of the 1984 victory, Prebble, Douglas, Caygill, Palmer and many others reassembled to recall those heady days. Lange had not been invited and, after complaining about this, received an apology. The economic changes have come to define the major direction of that Labour Government and at the centre of that New Right direction was our own prophet, Moses. Douglas's revelation was less of a dramatic theophany at the burning bush and more a series of smaller piecemeal revelations. They can be traced though his 1980 alternative budget – *There's Got to Be a Better Way!* – via his February 1982 *Labour's Economic Policy: A Framework* (*LEPF*), *Labour's Economic Package* (*LEP*) and the Labour Party conference of 1983 to the 1984 election Manifesto and the sledge of reforms following the election itself.[1] The author of *There's Got to Be a Better Way!* was still heavily interventionist and favoured picking winners and a plethora of direct government controls. Already evident are some of his later themes, such as the proposed opening up of markets, reduction of government regulation and tax reform. None of this was surprising given the clearly failing centrally regulated economic policies of the National Government. Douglas's transformation to free-market liberalism was under way.

Douglas led his group in the Labour Party in an attempted coup to topple Rowling in 1981 as parliamentary leader and replace him with the younger and more dynamic Lange. The Labour Party increasingly supported the urgent need for economic reform, creating in part the momentum for Rowling to step down and Lange and Palmer to take charge in February 1983. Douglas attempted to bring together traditional Labour social policies of support for lower-income groups with the need for economic growth as the only possible funding of these programmes in *LEPF*. He advocated deregulation, business models for government departments, reduced government spending and competition within the private and public sectors to increase efficiencies. Here we are getting closer to the fully fledged market model but these proposals still had government making the decisions rather than bowing out and leaving these to demand and supply.

Even though there was wide agreement that economic change was necessary and urgently so, after a freeze on prices, wages, interest and exchange rates, there were evident tensions in the party. Douglas's faction with its New Right economic policies challenged other party members more suspicious of market solutions. Another faction subscribed to better interventionism, including fostering economic growth by targeting the 'right' sectors. In between, a middle group, while acknowledging the need for economic reform, displayed less faith in the market than Douglas's neo-liberal zealots. Douglas's group reworked *LEPF* into *LEP*, strengthening the New Right thrust for Labour's Policy Council at the end of 1983. Trade union representatives strongly opposed *LEP* amid fears that the consequences would have large and negative impacts on workers. They accused the Douglas faction of ignoring this. The 1984 Labour Manifesto walked the line between these different positions by affirming the positions of various constituencies. It, nevertheless, committed the party to economic growth as the priority and included anti-inflation policies, proposals for reducing unemployment and overseas debts, deregulation and a commitment to increase the competitiveness of New Zealand firms here and overseas.

What did Douglas believe at this time? He clearly believed economic growth required monetary reform but did not elaborate this belief very fully. After the election, the Labour Party's left accused him of having a New Right agenda hidden within the 1984 Manifesto, but it was just as likely that a brief and deliberately broad-brushed list of policy objectives obscured the detail of worked-out policy. Margaret Wilson attributes this winning, albeit compromised, 'something for everyone' document to the drafting skills of Palmer.[2] If Wilson is correct, then the Labour Manifesto gave Douglas scope for New Right implementation after the election.

We interviewed Douglas in 2002 and asked him about the intellectual sources of his evident 1983 change from interventionist to free-marketeer.[3] Curiously, he responded in the first-person plural as if he had always been and continued to be part of a group. It was not always clear who constituted this 'we'. He began by noting that his 'economic think tank', although it was short-lived, produced *LEP*. Douglas's own revelatory turning point was when he realised that 'economic policy was not just part but the very core of what governments were about'. It was not that political objectives were developed and then costed but that stability, 'security, prosperity, development, freedom and democracy itself' depended on having the right model of economic management. Specifically, he recalled the importance of the devaluation of the New Zealand dollar by 20 per cent and the control of inflation as the necessary kickstart for any economic reform. Displaying a proud anti-intellectualism, he claimed he had never read Smith, Hayek or Friedman's 'technical stuff' and that his 'ideological reading' consisted of summaries in business magazines, such as *Forbes*, and articles that his staff passed on to him. Douglas had visited the IEA in London and knew about its arguments for the benefits of the free market, in both the private and public sectors. When we pursued his IEA connections, he said that he had met Lord Harris and gave a Hayekian account of limited knowledge necessitating the failure of central planning and Smith's 'invisible hand' bringing together producers and consumers of required good and services.

Douglas also recalled tracking the Conservative reforms in Britain led by Thatcher and, in particular, her policies on inflation, government spending and privatisation. He claimed cognisance of the similarities and differences between Britain and New Zealand and where Thatcherite reforms were relevant and where they were not. When asked if he had been a monetarist at the time, he replied 'no, not really'. He told us that it was not his former Labour commitments to justice and equity that had changed in 1983. In fact, he characterised his part in the Fourth Labour Government as nothing but the 'dismantling of privilege'. What had changed was his new grasp of the mechanisms for effecting economic change and how it was to be paid for. This revelation arose out of his engagement with his advisors and 'think tank'.

Douglas and his ally, Prebble, celebrated their pragmatism and straight-talking, uncomplicated ways that made them highly dependent on their officials for anything beyond the broadest principles.[4] They thus failed to replicate Geoffrey Howe's successful 1981 British anti-inflationary budget based directly and explicitly on monetarist policies. The influences on Douglas included the Treasury official seconded to his office, Doug Andrew, Geoff Swier, another economist from the Labour Research Unit, historian Jim Holt and Auckland business associates. The biggest single influence, however, on his thinking on economic matters was the Australian Labor Government, he reported. 'We were fully briefed', 'watching them very closely' and 'guided by what they were doing'. Douglas's confidence in the direction of reforms was based on the Australian model. When we suggested that his policies had created new opportunities for privilege, he did not deny this but asked us to view these as part of the broad 'package of reforms'. He outlined his position in 1983 as a version of the theory of 'comparative advantage', familiar to all first-year economic students, often in the guise of Richard Lipsey's 'guns and butter' analogy.[5] Douglas saw the end of interventionist market distortions as allowing New Zealand to play to its strengths internally and externally. He recognised that this would drive non-competitive businesses out of the market and that this in turn would clear the path for new entrepreneurs and enterprises.

Douglas also recollected that the decision to move fast and on a number of fronts at once was a conscious one, as 'it would be the one chance we got'. The election victory on 14 July 1984 was followed immediately by a financial and constitutional crisis. The foreign exchange market was closed on 15 July 1984 and, in spite of the objections of the former Prime Minister, the New Zealand dollar was devalued by 20 per cent on 18 July 1984. The Australians had devalued by 10 per cent in March 1983, with generally beneficial results, and the direct government support of the dollar had cost more than half a billion from the announcement of the election until the election itself. The move from crisis devaluation to the floating of the New Zealand dollar on the 4 March 1985 provided an interesting case study of the creation of a competitive market from a protectionist situation. In October and November 1984 Douglas removed the regulations that had restricted New Zealanders and New Zealand companies from borrowing overseas capital and the limits on foreign investments in New Zealand. His officials amended banking regulations to allow New Zealand banks to deal directly overseas without going through the Reserve Bank. These moves prepared the way for a free-floating currency with its values were determined by the market rather than by regulation and the direction of the Minister of Finance.

A few days after the devaluation of the dollar, Douglas became Minister of Finance with Caygill and Prebble as his associate ministers. The Cabinet Policy Committee responsible for the Government's high-level strategy and objectives included them, together with Lange, Palmer, Russell Marshall, Stan Rodger and Colin Moyle. *Economic Management*, the brief to the incoming government by Treasury, soon arrived. In contrast to the merely suggestive Manifesto, it explicitly recommended that the state's trading activities be subject to market forces. It also blamed past government economic policy directly, particularly for the failure to recognise the realities of the markets in which New Zealand businesses had to operate and the huge costs of protectionism. Treasury trenchantly criticised government inability to view the economy as an interrelated whole. These partial views meant that attempts to tackle specific issues tended to fail, promoting further inefficiencies and increases in government expenditure. The Treasury unequivocally promoted the universal application of market disciplines.

Inspired by Australian Prime Minister Hawke's Summit Conference of 1983, the Government's Economic Summit, held from 12 to 14 September 1984, focused on our economic plight and discussed possible remedies. Chaired by Lange, it brought together more than 200 representatives of government, trade unions, employers and the New Zealand business sector. Sir Ron Trotter chaired the Conference

Steering Committee, which had produced *A Briefing on the New Zealand Economy* as the core document for the summit. It contended that our economic woes could be traced to our own failure to adapt to 'the changing world scene' and that the vagaries of 'world trade' were at best a partial explanation. More than a hundred papers addressed the issues raised in this briefing. In our interview, Douglas portrayed the significance of the summit as guaranteeing the necessary 'buy-in' for what was to follow in the budget. The conference participants struggled with the challenge of using our considerable resource base in the most productive ways and ensuring the social inclusion of the most economically marginalised. The summit aimed to achieve a consensus on the way forward and issued a statement to that effect.[6]

Building on the Treasury's *Economic Management*, the summit statement began by claiming a unitary view of the economy and aimed to foster investment into the most productive areas, to promote lifelong education and training, to create the conditions for full employment and price stability, reduce overseas debt, work towards greater income equity and develop an incentive-based tax regime. The Treasury proposed that government, management and the unions become public-relations vehicles for 'selling' this programme to us. The Economic Summit was followed by the Maori Economic Development Summit in October and the Employment Summit in March 1985. Douglas and other Labour MPs interpreted these summits as secure mandate for the New Right reforms.

Douglas presented his first budget in November 1984 and gave notice of five related bills. The document had been drafted by Swier and promised to cut the existing deficit in half. The Minister of Finance reported his first concern was to simplify and rationalise the tax system. He introduced a new indirect tax, the Goods and Services Tax (GST) on almost everything, effective from April 1986 (later delayed until October 1986 at the rate of 10 per cent). He modelled the justification and outline of the GST operation on the British Value Added Tax. With immediate effect Douglas removed the exemptions for life insurance, superannuation and mortgage interest contributions and made fringe benefits taxable from April 1985. He announced tax rises on beer, wine and spirits and an average 46 per cent hike in road-user charges and a new surcharge on additional income for pensioners.

Douglas's second concern was with low-income earners and his new 'family care' programme increased rebates for the poorest families and improved some welfare benefits. Douglas's third focus was on the reduction and elimination of the extensive system of incentives and subsidies. This applied primarily to farmers. Finally, he markedly raised the cost of the electricity supplied by the state to reflect actual production and distribution costs rather than to continue to subsidise specific industries and sectors. This first budget set the New Right agenda of the Fourth Labour Government with the emphasis on taxing consumption, removing 'market distortions' generated by subsidies, tariffs and incentives and the remodelling of government 'businesses' as commercial enterprises.

Between the first budget and the second, produced in June 1985, Finance and Social Welfare jointly set up a Budget '85 Taskforce to review personal tax and social security benefits, issuing a call for public submissions. In the second budget, Douglas introduced new monitoring procedures for government department spending, efficiency measures for state-owned businesses and 'market rates' for government services. He announced extra funding for employment training directed at lowering unemployment figures and for defence, education, health and housing. Later he announced rises in the fringe benefit tax and company tax rates and new procedures for taxing share dividends and overseas income while cutting the top rate of income tax from 66 per cent to 48 per cent. A new system of 'family support' replaced 'family care' by bringing in a tax benefit system for welfare recipients as all benefits now became liable for tax. To contribute to this effort, the Department of Social Welfare published *Benefits, Taxes and the 1985 Budget: A Review and Summary* making clear Douglas's goal of addressing taxes and benefits together within his conception of economic management.

Douglas presented his *Economic Statement* in December 1985, detailing the next phase of his reforms. He signalled new targets for public sector efficiencies, a review of industrial and labour relations, the commercialisation of state-owned enterprises (SOEs) and the removal of hundreds of tariffs on imported goods. Douglas also addressed the difficulties facing farmers in the newly deregulated agricultural sector by extending depreciation periods and setting up a Committee on Livestock Taxation headed by Brash, who had also chaired the GST Advisory Panel. Douglas continued to cut sales taxes for most goods.

In May 1986, the Government published its *Statement on Government Expenditure Reform*, introducing 'corporate structures' to electricity, coal and mines, the Post Office and civil aviation. These 'businesses' now faced the requirement to make 'profits' and lost their former protections and privileges, forcing them to compete in the marketplace in terms of costs, tax liabilities and raising finance. The 1986 Budget further streamlined the tax system. Douglas extended the deregulation programme by announcing tighter financial controls of the producer boards and the dismantling of 'think big' projects. In April 1987 the corporatisation programme accelerated, with SOE legislation creating nine public corporations.

In time for the 1987 election, Douglas forecast his first anticipated budget surplus, claiming success in controlling direct public spending and with the removal of subsidies and the readjusted inflation and exchange rates. The largest single and most significant component of this surplus was the revenue gained from the one-off sale of public assets. He invited the public to invest in SOEs and announced further asset sales. After the election and the stock-market crash Douglas's *Economic Statement* proposed a single low tax rate, the so-called 'flat tax', from 1988 and a company tax rate set at the same level as personal income tax and internationally competitive. In another part of the package he advocated additional rebates for low earners, giving a 'minimal family income', and increases in the level of deductions for childcare. In addition, he made superannuation funds fully taxable and established a set of interim arrangements to bridge the gap between old and new tax regimes. In line with his economic principles, Douglas mandated competition in the telecommunications sector and the review of professional and occupational organisations to eliminate monopolies. Finally, he insisted upon a review of local government. These radical proposals threatened government revenue and alarmed New Right critics in the Labour Party and the New Zealand public.

These New Right proposals so horrified Lange that he unilaterally announced the indefinite deferral of the flat tax and the 'minimal family income' in late January 1988. During the first week in February both Lange and Douglas claimed majority caucus and party support. Douglas presented a *Revised Economic Package* leaving income tax at 24 per cent and 33 per cent and company tax at 28 per cent and including a number of other measures. The July budget largely confirmed these measures. In November 1988 Lange, after a rancorous exchange over asset sales, dismissed Prebble, the Minister of SOEs and less than six weeks later replaced Douglas with Caygill as Minister of Finance after a row over the speed and direction of economic policy. When caucus voted to restore Douglas to Cabinet, Lange resigned in August 1989. Palmer became Prime Minister and the pace of economic change slowed to a crawl. Without the driving force of Douglas's New Right vision, the riven Labour Government lost the 1990 election and would not return to power until 1999. The newly elected National Government continued the New Right march towards the land of prosperity.

In this chapter we have focused on the enactment of the New Right economic programme into law and policy. Some areas of government remained relatively protected from this reformist onslaught. Although Douglas frequently discussed the need to reform the labour market, industrial relations remained relatively unscathed because of the influence of trade unions within the Labour Party. This reprieve occurred despite the failure to establish a tripartite system of negotiations about employment conditions between government, employers and unions, as successfully developed in Australia. Douglas had little time for these negotiations and his commitment to a free labour market doomed them. The NZBR, under the leadership of Kerr, turned to National to deregulate the labour market, a major goal of the New Right.

In only four years the impact of New Right reforms had effectively transformed the public service and our economy. Close links between the business community and the government and the widespread use of private-sector expertise restructured the formerly public sector, producing such new members of the business elite as Rod Deane and Alan Gibbs. Markets appeared where there previously had been none and Trotter, Deane, Gibbs, Fay, Richwhite and Fernyhough benefited. The tariff, incentive and subsidy culture of forty years almost entirely disappeared.

The same period witnessed the creation of a new corporate lobby system. Trotter served as the first chair of the NZBR and Kerr moved from Treasury to become its executive director in 1986. The members of the NZBR insisted that market reforms benefited us all, but clearly some of us gained far more than others. In the past lobbying had related to particular licences, subsidies or contracts, but the NZBR lobbied on behalf of profit, growth, less government, more market and lower corporate tax rather than for specific favours. Although when we interviewed him recently Douglas gave us the impression that he had major disagreements with the NZBR, there was a considerable overlap in agenda both generally and in relation to legislative details and direction during 'Rogernomics'. A generation of SOE millionaires, often prominent members of the NZBR, enhanced the influence of the corporate class over government policy and direction.

Reforms occurred on a number of fronts simultaneously at variable speeds. The simplest of economic faiths in universal market solutions held this programme together. In practice, these reforms created major social disruptions and imposed heavy human costs in unemployment, insecurity and increasing disparities in wealth because of the priority given to competition and market forces over 'full employment' and equity. These reforms resembled those that occurred in Australia, the US and Britain. New Zealand attracted higher levels of overseas investment than it had before 1984, until the lion's share of the New Zealand stock market was owned overseas.

At the time and in the aftermath of 'Rogernomics', it became clear that there were a variety of economic policy options, even in relation to asset sales. When asked if he would change anything about his actions while in government in the 1980s, Sir Roger Douglas said no, but then added that he only wished that he had acted more quickly to reform the labour market, welfare and education. He remains as certain and confident as ever and continues to believe that the successful performance of today's New Zealand economy should be credited to his reforms.[7] There were, however, alternative strategies that might have produced better and less divisive results. The 'privatisation' of the railways, power companies, Air New Zealand and the Bank of New Zealand have all had spectacularly poor results. Telecom, as another example, has only recently been forced to allow competitors an approximation of a 'level playing field'. The massive increases in unemployment and the numbers of beneficiaries point to the human cost of the direction and the speed of this radical economic transformation. The reformers' commitment to New Right ideology inured them to this form of 'collateral damage'.

The New Right programme was considerably more than a technocratic reduction of government spending and regulation. It was fundamentally an expression of a faith that the market can and does operate to increase productivity, promote growth and reward enterprise equitably. The New Right and its 'new rights' and social justice opponents differ just as much on the nature of the constituent elements that make up our society and how it fundamentally operates. For the advocates of social justice and 'new rights', the economy should be regulated to maintain our human dignity and promote our collective well-being. The proponents of the New Right insist that the market will always deliver better or purer outcomes than the distortions caused by any government interventions. Individual consumers and entrepreneurs populate the New Right world, operating in a competitive market of winners and losers where only prudence requires a minimal safety net. According to this faith, government policy must respect market rules in order to lead us on the road to prosperity. Their social justice and 'new rights' critics urge the extension of the principle of equality into the distribution of income, wealth and power as fundamental to an expanded notion of citizenship and their notion of the good society. Their ideal of an active welfare that promotes relative economic and social equality clearly contrasts with the New Right insistence that such an activist model of government constitutes one of the 'seven deadly economic sins'.[8] Precisely the same conflict that had doomed the Labour Government would reccur when National and Richardson moved to occupy the 'commanding heights'.

PART THREE

Leviticus: Encoding the Law of the Market

But whoso looketh into the perfect law of liberty and continueth therein, he being not a forgetful hearer, but a doer of the work, this man shall be blessed in his deed. If any man among you seem to be religious and bridleth not his tongue, but deceiveth his own heart, this man's religion is vain. Pure religion and undefiled before God and the Father is this, To visit the fatherless and widows in their affliction and to keep himself unspotted from the world. JAMES 1:25–27

CHAPTER SEVEN

From Decency to Deuteronomy:
Jim's Gospel, Ruth's Book and Jenny's Code

Then said Boaz unto Ruth, Hearest thou not, my daughter? Go not to glean in another field, neither go from hence, but abide here fast by my maidens: Let thine eyes be on the field that they do reap and go thou after them. RUTH 2:8–9

Now therefore hearken, O Israel, unto the statutes and unto the judgments, which I teach you, for to do them, that ye may live and go in and possess the land which the LORD God of your fathers giveth you. Ye shall not add unto the word which I command you, neither shall ye diminish ought from it, that ye may keep the commandments of the LORD your God which I command you. DEUTERONOMY 4:1–2

As the Labour Government fragmented into warring factions, the National caucus struggled to overcome its own divisions between Muldoon loyalists, New Right true believers and pragmatists. The stock-market crash and the open split between Lange and Douglas opened the way for National MPs like Philip Burdon to woo the corporate community now bereft of its Moses figure and looking for a 'post-Rogernomics vision'. The NZBR and CIS favoured the 'hard liners' now engaged in a battle with the 'moderates' for dominance in the caucus and future Cabinet. Richardson, 'tutored by Treasury' and 'the NZBR' and her 'admiring acolytes' – Shipley, McTigue, Simon Upton, Maurice Williamson, Doug Kidd, John Falloon, John Luxton – members of the National's 'triumphalist New Right', preached the 'doctrine of undiluted Friedmanism'. The pragmatists, including Burdon, Don McKinnon, Paul East, Wyatt Creech, Warren Kyd and the maverick Peters, derided the 'doctrinaire' approach in favour of the active encouragement of business, but agreed with the need to deregulate the labour market and move beyond the 'half-way house of corporatisation' to sell the Bank of New Zealand (BNZ) and other state-owned enterprises. Sceptical about the 'beneficent magic' of the market without any state intervention, the pragmatists assured Kerr of the NZBR of 'our mutual and common objectives' despite differences about the role of government.[1]

Negotiating a compromise between the 'evangelical fervour' of Richardson and the 'vociferous pragmatists', National, under Bolger's leadership, convinced the business community to abandon Labour and such unacceptable reforms as 'pay equity'. To the rest of us Bolger pledged to deliver the 'Decent Society'. A 'new era of new faces, new ideas, [and] new people' could rescue us from 'disordered and chaotic' policies.[2] The Labour incumbents, after an interminable journey in the wilderness of market reforms, lost in a landslide as National reoccupied the Treasury benches.

Almost as soon as the election was over, we discovered that the march to market freedom had not ended. We had replaced the demoted Douglas with a female Moses. The new Government's policies surprised many of its most devoted supporters. Another term − 'Ruthanesia' − entered our political lexicon as the new Minister of Finance became the most controversial member of the National Cabinet. As New Right true believers, Richardson and her ideological allies took swift action to save us from another 'crisis', this time stemming from budgetary deficits and the threatened collapse of the BNZ, through budget cuts directed at beneficiaries and the refusal to lift the super tax. It was a case, as New York Yankee Yogi Berra once said, of 'déjà vu all over again'. The 'apostles of the New Right' gained important portfolios but also faced a determined opposition who set about defeating the 'economic fundamentalists'. We marched forward under the leadership of an Irish Catholic dairy farmer, several accountants, two All Blacks, three policemen, the 'wet' Michael Laws, the ultra 'dry' Max Bradford, a former television host, the unpredictable Peters, the newly named 'Brat Pack', 'nine stroppy women', 'several fundamentalist Christians', a mushroom millionaire and assorted farmers.[3]

Joining Richardson, Shipley sought to inject 'small town values' into her Social Welfare portfolio, ably supported by the CIS and the NZBR, who called for welfare 'to go private'. Drawing in part on her

Presbyterian upbringing, Shipley believed that families should take 'the first brunt of responsibility' for their own welfare. Upton touted user pays in health and education. 'Market rents' and the sale of state housing became official policy, benefits became targeted, the universal family benefit disappeared and individual contracts replaced union contracts courtesy of the ECA as National delivered on its promises to business. The 'mother of all budgets' slashed benefits after an ebullient Richardson naively repeated a journalist's allusion to the Gulf War. Together Shipley and Richardson earned a reputation for relentlessly applying a 'doctrinaire approach bordering on inflexibility' and speaking the 'jargon of the new right' in a repetitive style overlaid by 'layers of rhetoric, cliché, bluster'. As though the British Conservatives' toppling of 'Iron Lady' Thatcher had left a space for a certain kind of public persona, Shipley and Richardson assumed the armour of steely determination as the media inserted them into a mythical framework about powerful and destructive women. The major characters in this 'Book of Ruth' appeared in cartoons as a frightening mixture of harpies, gorgons and Valkyries. Noticing signs of ideological disenchantment, Bolger edged away from Richardson as backbenchers and even a Cabinet minister called for 'common sense' to 'prevail over ideology'.[4]

Shell-shocked by the betrayal of electoral promises by the proponents of the 'Decent Society', we responded by punishing the National Government when the pollsters asked our opinion. Richardson and Shipley particularly attracted negative responses. Even the 'moderate' Burdon became known as 'First-Class Phil' after an outburst over the service on Air New Zealand. Asking why the Minister of Commerce had not shown the same 'outrage at the fiasco over user-pays for social services', an enraged journalist bestowed upon the Government a reputation for being 'right out of touch' and 'ideological ruthlessness'. Party membership declined from about 100,000 in 1990 to 40,000 within the first three years of office. Academics criticised the 'high priests' of the Chicago School, the CIS and the NZBR and the elevation of the market from an 'economic mechanism to a moral force'. Churches criticised benefit cuts when food banks began to serve rising numbers of beneficiaries. Pensioners complained about the surtax on superannuation. The sales of iconic New Zealand institutions such as the BNZ and NZ Railways caused anguish as firms like Fay and

Richwhite sometimes ingeniously bought and sold the same corporate assets. We fretted about bulk funding, health restructuring, the ECA and an article published by Richardson's speech-writer in the *Wall Street Journal* calling us poorly educated and lacking the work ethic.[5] Was this the 'good news', the Gospel of decency, promised by 'St Jim'?

Churches criticised the New Right reform agenda in the early 1990s as they pointed to the 'increasing evidence of poverty, social distress and financial hardship' following the benefit cuts. After the budget and the passage of the ECA, Catholic bishops expressed 'grave concern' about the application of 'monetarist theory', the 'return to liberal capitalism', and the assertion that the welfare state was obsolete. Insisting on the 'duty to act in solidarity' and the 'sinful' nature of the 'all consuming desire for profit', the bishops pleaded with the Government to modify the legislation. Human beings are 'always more important than capital', they insisted.[6]

Eleven denominations produced a *Social Justice Statement* in July 1993 and later published *Making Choices: Social Justice for Our Times*. Asking for 'moral accountability', the statement argued that a 'basic moral test of society' was how 'its most vulnerable members are faring'. The authors defined social justice as 'fairness in the distribution of incomes, wealth and power' and in the 'social, economic and political structures' that 'enable all citizens to be active and productive participants in the life of society', in language that reiterated the conclusions of the Royal Commission on Social Policy. Widely interpreted as a criticism of Government policies, this intervention challenged the moral claims made by the New Right.[7]

Acutely aware of flagging support for another bout of market liberalisation and moral reformation, the NZBR intensified its efforts to convince us to stay the course. Its publications alternated between technocratic analyses of economic issues and exhortatory literature on the need to accelerate the pace of reform. In the *Independent* Kerr defended 'free markets' as a 'moral training ground' in contrast to the 'coerced exchange' of the welfare state. The *NBR* warned against a retreat to 'Fortress New Zealand' and of the dangers of trying to 'mollycoddle' a 'mob of industrial cripples long overdue for weaning' as it reacted to the decision to slow down tariff reforms. *Dominion* editorials railed against 'poor pulpit politics'. Catholic conservative

Agnes-Mary Brooke denounced the 'muddled thinking' of the churches. Upton objected to their meddling with politics and John Terris portrayed them as wanting to 'turn back the clock'. Michael Irwin of the NZBR, himself a former theology student, warned against confusing the Gospel with 'ideologies' and prepared a paper about the *Social Justice Statement* that Kerr privately circulated. Irwin, a participant in Gospel and Cultures seminars in the early 1990s, helped to create the 'specialised mission society' DeepSight. It distributed writings by leading New Right moralists including Green, Epstein, Kerr, Novak, George Weigel, Peter and Brigitte Berger as the forerunner to a future 'Christian think tank' that could contest the 'social justice' theology favoured by mainstream church leaders.[8]

These visitors and their publications entered into an ongoing debate that was raging in Australia and New Zealand. A deep recession in the early 1990s created an opening for challengers to the New Right, often called 'economic rationalists' in Australia. Michael Pusey's *Economic Rationalism in Canberra* proved particularly influential after its publication in 1991. Pusey complained about the 'Darwinist' notion of domination over nature and civil society inherent in market liberalism. He lamented the 'professional separation' of law and economics from the humanities and social sciences as hindering lawyers and economists from developing a 'moral vocabulary capable of connecting social realities' to legal, political and economic institutions. An Australian version of the critiques written by Jesson, Kelsey, Easton and other critics of our New Right, Pusey's denunciation of economic rationalism evoked a powerful positive response but an equally determined counter-attack.[9]

A group associated with CIS and IPA published *A Defence of Economic Rationalism* in 1993, with a foreword by John Hyde accusing their critics of wanting prosperity without 'self-discipline'. In a New Right narrative ritually repeated on both sides of the Tasman with local variations, Hyde wrote about Australia as a 'nation in decline' which had been enjoying the 'third or fourth highest standard of living' in the 1950s but had precipitously slipped over the subsequent decades. Stone, Evans, Michael James, Michael Warby and Judith Sloan accused critics of promoting a 'moral panic' and advocating 'anti-rationalism'. The market, they insisted, was both morally and economically superior in its outcomes to those produced by state intervention. James attacked the 'moral myths of collectivism', drawing upon both Hayek and Popper. The market inculcated the virtues of 'honesty, fairness, truth-telling, responsibility, reliability and promptness', reduced 'transaction costs' and created efficiency, profits and 'trustworthiness' among the participants in market exchange. By contrast, 'non-market forces' allowed individuals to 'disregard the more remote consequences of their actions'. Citing New Zealand historian David Thomson, James claimed that the welfare state had generated 'suspicion, anxiety and selfishness' among New Zealanders while enabling 'looting' by Australian workers through 'wage-fixing'. James and the other contributors to *A Defence of Economic Rationalism* produced a moral critique of the vices allegedly caused by the immoral forces of socialism, trade unionism and state-provided welfare.[10]

In Australia and New Zealand similar arguments circulated, with a more strongly voiced moral conservatism in the Australian case. CIS publications and sympathetic journalists articulated a 'moral logic' as necessarily compatible with the 'market logic' they also vigorously advanced. Combining imported and internally generated moral commentary, the CIS emphasised the 'traditional role of the father' to rear a child instilled with 'respect for authority and a sense of obligation to comply with social rules' within the context of a 'moral community' that enforced 'standards'. Traditional male-headed families constituted 'moral microcosms of great power and importance in establishing rules and habits of duty and obligation' that should not be interfered with by courts, governments or feminist critics. This moral institution could be damaged irreparably by foolish 'claims to freedom, equality and rights', the 'entitlement' state, 'welfarism', public education and divorce. Inevitably in a welfare state enterprise suffered from 'dependence on the favours of the state', civic virtue declined and the 'moralising performance' of the family, school and other 'voluntary' institutions deteriorated. In fact, the government inflicted 'a moral wound' on citizens by taxation and welfare provision.[11] These Australian versions of the New Right's moral project influenced our own debates and policies as they found their way into the publications of the NZBR, the Treasury and Social Welfare and in our libraries and our media.

Despite these moral exhortations, a sizeable number of us continued to oppose New Right reforms, as opinion polls indicated.

Conflicts between Bolger and Peters, discontent over the health reforms and opposition to Richardson's financial policies increased the Government's unpopularity. Although Richardson was able to secure the reappointment of Brash as Governor of the Reserve Bank, she gradually became aware of her own political peril. Her ally, McTigue, lost his portfolios, as did Upton. This danger increased when the National Government decided to keep one promise in its 1990 manifesto – a referendum on electoral reform – during the 1993 election. Focused on a choice between Mixed Member Proportional Representation (MMP) and the traditional system – First Past the Post – we gained a vent for anger against both major political parties even if we did not choose to vote for alternatives such as Peters and his newly formed New Zealand First or the Christian Heritage Party. Seeking to curb the 'elected dictatorship' of a one-house Parliament, a slim majority voted for MMP despite the scare tactics used by Shirtcliffe, Brian Nicolle and other members of the NZBR and the business network. Campaigning on behalf of 'the spirit of recovery' in the same election, National's percentage of the vote fell to 35 per cent, McTigue lost his seat and Richardson's majority severely declined. National won back the Treasury benches with a margin of only one seat.[12] We had clearly decided to send a message about broken promises and our distaste for the endless repetition of 'there is no alternative' to the New Right agenda.

Assuring us that the relentless reform offensive was now being slowed to a sedate stroll, the new National Government promised a kinder, gentler version of the 'Decent Society'. Richardson and her New Right allies took the blame for its near defeat. She soon surrendered her portfolio to Bill Birch, the former champion of 'Think Big' and now a moderate proponent of New Right reforms. Shipley moved from Social Welfare to Health to replace Upton, a fading political 'star' who had failed to convince voters that user pays and Crown Health Enterprises had actually improved the health system. The demoted Richardson soon resigned from Parliament and McTigue departed for a position as High Commssioner to Canada, where he made friends with the local New Right fraternity, eventually securing a position at Mercatus in a rare reversal of the usual flow of expertise between the US and New Zealand. Those of us who hoped for an end to New Right reforms, however, endured additional rounds of asset sales, proposals for vouchers and bulk funding for the compulsory educational sector, green and white papers for tertiary education, an attack on the Employment Court as biased in favour of workers, the drive for the privatisation of the electrical system and still more proposals for market reforms in roading, water supply and almost every other aspect of public life where a quasi-market could be imposed.[13] The march resumed toward the still-distant Promised Land of market freedoms and prosperity despite obvious signs of reluctance and reform fatigue.

New parties contested the 1993 election or formed in response to the opportunities offered to them by MMP. The Greens negotiated an agreement with NewLabour, the Social Democrats and Mana Motuhake to form the Alliance in 1992. In addition to NZ First, formed after Peters parted company with the National Party, Douglas and other New Right activists founded the Association of Consumers and Taxpayers (ACT) Party. Lindsay Perigo and Deborah Coddington launched Libertarianz at an Auckland restaurant function complete with a whip-wielding 'nanny state' to symbolise the 'creeping welfarism' they hoped to destroy. Perigo called upon his followers to join him on the 'long march' towards freedom. Ross Meurant established the short-lived Right of Centre Party and Graeme Lee founded the Christian Democrats. Some Labour MPs, including Peter Dunne, and a few moderate National MPs coalesced into the centrist United Party. A series of retirements, including Lange's, made clear that New Zealand politics was undergoing a transition to an as yet unpredictable destination.[14] The surviving members of the major parties needed to adapt to a new, more fluid mixture of personality and fluctuating political allegiances.

Australian politics showed the same unexpected twists and turns. Despite conflicts between Hawke and Keating, Australian Labor clung to power into the mid-1990s benefiting from the internecine leadership conflicts among the Liberals. New Right activists from CIS circles, the IPA and special interest 'front' groups, such as the H. R. Nicholls Society for labour reform, fretted at the difficulties in gaining support for their agenda from the Keating Government. When the 'dry' John Hewson lost the 'unlosable' election in 1993, he eventually succumbed to Alexander Downer, who yielded in turn to Howard in 1995. Styling himself as the spokesman for the 'battlers', Howard adroitly combined a 'socially conservative vision with an economic rationalist reform program', deftly aided by Costello, a founding member of the H. R. Nicholls Society, and other Liberals who saw that approach as essential to create a winning political coalition.[15]

Acutely aware of the importance of moral issues to the success of the Christian Coalition in the 1994 US elections, New Right activists sought to apply that lesson to Australian and New Zealand politics. Undoubtedly nervous about the impact of MMP, the NZBR renewed its efforts to convince us of its policies as 'recovery-leading'. The CIS and the NZBR pointed to our reforms as a 'successful new model' which Australians should emulate rather than content themselves with a 'half-reformed economic order' under Labor. It brought Novak, the 'Christian apostle for capitalism', on a visit to Australia and New Zealand in 1995 to praise the 'moral-cultural system of democratic capitalism'. Australian economist Wolfgang Kasper praised our wisdom in abandoning the dream of a 'paradise' created by 'collective action'. Epstein argued against our Human Rights Act, anti-discrimination legislation more generally, teachers' unions, MMP and other 'moral hazards' as he visited in 1995 and 1996. Warnings about the dangers of 'moral neutrality' grew more heated during the electoral campaigns in 1996. Father Sirico admonished us that 'statism' caused 'cultural decline, family collapse and widespread secularisation'. To prevent those disasters, he believed that 'the majority needed careful tutelage in essential values'. These New Right circuit riders travelled through New Zealand and Australia to ensure political victory for their political allies.[16]

Importing yet more New Right evangelists in the election year of 1996, the NZBR brought Green from IEA to declaim 'with right-wing Christian-like zeal' that 'welfarism' had 'tended to impair human character' by preventing us from exercising 'personal responsibility'. Green told us that the market needed a 'moral order consistent with freedom' to operate properly. The NZBR brought Charles Baird, another repeat visitor, to call for the elimination of grievance procedures and the scrapping of the Employment Court. Under the auspices of the Employers' Federation, Evans, a sponsor of CIS and H. R. Nicholls, joined the attack, as did Sloan while praising other aspects of the ECA as a model for Australia to follow. The *NBR* headlined an article 'Welfarism's evil empire' in an obvious reference to Reagan's rhetorical attack on the Soviet Union and asserted the need to 'cleanse New Zealanders of their welfare mentality'. Sowell lectured against 'creating new injustices in the pursuit of social justice' as he quoted Friedman to prove that freedom must take priority over equality. The casual reader of our newspapers might have wondered why so many visitors thought we needed moral tutelage. A journalist gave us his answer, cynically asking whether these moral missionaries sold 'capitalism' or 'claptrap'.[17]

Enthusiastically preached, the mix of moral conservatism and market liberalism succeeded, if just barely, in the 1996 elections in New Zealand and won more convincingly in Australia, producing two coalition governments. The Liberal–National Party Coalition took power in Canberra, ratifying what one critic called 'hard liberalism' slightly softened by programmes carefully tailored to the needs of specific groups of electors to achieve political success. Anti-immigrant and nationalist rhetoric in combination with Maori disillusionment with Labour gained Peters and NZ First the kingmaker or 'queen maker' role in the aftermath of the election. Arduous negotiations extended for eight weeks after the elections, resulting in a coalition agreement with National.

Forced to make tactical concessions, Bolger engineered a series of coalition agreements with minor parties. An unwieldy partnership between old political adversaries put Peters in charge of finance in association with Birch, to the chagrin of his New Right critics but also to the disappointment of many supporters. Social conservatives in the NZ First caucus joined similar elements in the National caucus, while Howard and Costello presided over a similar combination in Australia. The elections in this part of the world suggested that the New Right in Zealand and Australia resembled their American counterpart in the advocacy of a moral agenda and the use of scapegoat tactics towards vulnerable minorities.[18]

The Coalition Government in Australia certainly developed a successful New Right reform strategy that contrasted markedly with Rogernomics and Ruthanesia in its speed. As 'gradual revolutionaries', Howard and Costello, like their Labor predecessors, incrementally introduced more stringent requirements for unemployment benefits, imposed user-pays social services, privatised government enterprises, reduced support for health and tertiary education and cut public programmes. Enthusiastic cooperation with Australia's leading corporations and multinationals, fund managers, ratings agencies and the US government ensured a good 'business climate' often favourably compared with our situation. The adroit use of 'fear tactics' and 'electoral trickery' further strengthened the Coalition's grip on power as it enabled its corporate allies to take advantage of the 'opportunities offered by globalization'. The CIS, the IPA and front groups enthusiastically contributed by mounting campaigns against aboriginal rights activists, environmentalists, trade unions, feminists, 'new class' academics, bureaucrats and the 'left radicalism' of Australian churches. They brought visitors like Novak and Sirico but also created their own forms of 'moral education' with an emphasis on the poisonous nature of 'vague Marxism', the welfare state and opposition to the 'fatal conceit' of an 'earthly utopia'.[19]

On this side of the Tasman, however, the National–NZ First Coalition Government found it more difficult to create the 'parliamentary foundations for an emerging conservative consensus'. The greater scope for single-issue organisations in a federal system provided a stronger basis for coalition-building in Australia than did New Zealand's unitary state. Australian Catholics, reared on fervent anti-Communism and conservative British and Irish Catholic traditions, mobilised more readily in support of 'right to life' and family values. When Bruce Logan began the Education Development Foundation in 1994 to turn conservative Christians into a 'useful strategic constituency for centre-right parties' in New Zealand, he found it difficult to make headway. After a disappointing result for the Christian Coalition composed of Christian Heritage and the Christian Democrats in 1996, Logan found the National Party reluctant to endorse his agenda. Only two MPs from the minority ACT Party – Muriel Newman and Stephen Franks – appeared willing to campaign against 'welfare dependency', adolescent sexuality and anti-gay issues. A strong core of socially liberal New Right advocates, notably including the ambitious Shipley, kept the Coalition from appealing to the 'hot button' moral issues and employing the scapegoat techniques used by Howard and the American New Right.[20] Howard's recipe for political success was difficult for our jerry-built Coalition to emulate because of the explosive Maori component in NZ First, recurrent scandals such as the Tuku Morgan 'undie-gate' saga, the replacement of Bolger with 'hard-line right winger' Shipley in November 1997 and the ructions that split NZ First between 'waka jumpers' and Peters loyalists during the acrimonious disintegration of the NZ First–National Coalition.[21]

In Australia, the CIS continued its own moral crusade, criticising 'rights-talk' as destabilising the 'moral habits' and 'free institutions' essential to maintaining a free society. Hyde published *Dry: In Defence of Economic Freedom* to argue that markets depended 'utterly on adherence to codes of behaviour that ought to be regarded as good'. He quoted Novak's *The Spirit of Democratic Capitalism* to support the argument that 'certain moral and cultural presumptions about the nature of individuals and their communities, about liberty and sin' were essential to make capitalism work. Former Treasurer Stone continued his own battle against 'wets', the 'soft left', and human rights activists. In close association with the Coalition Government in which Howard, Costello, Abbott and the Kemp brothers maintained frequent contact with CIS and IPA, the self-described Australian 'dries' reiterated their messages through the Murdoch- or Fairfax-dominated press with relative ease.[22]

The very fragility of our Coalition Government and the continuing signs of our unease with the reform agenda spurred our New Right tutors to redouble their efforts to educate us in correct virtues and market values. Perhaps sensing that the Coalition's days might be numbered, the NZBR and its allies trumpeted the success of our 'remarkable reforms', to use Brash's title to a speech he gave to IEA in London in 1996. A year later he boasted that the influence of our Reserve Bank 'runs around the globe'. Kasper, courtesy of the CIS, added his own praise for New Zealand's legal framework as a model emulated by twenty other countries. He applauded our Government for enshrining the theories of Buchanan's 'public choice' and Friedman's monetarism. We understood the need to chop 'off the dead hand of the state', according to the admiring reviewer of Kasper's book in the *NBR*. Rather than advancing us to new achievements, however, we appeared willing to rest on our laurels.[23]

Other visitors came to tell us that we had more reforms to undertake before we had perfected our society. Sister Connie Driscoll came in 1997 to speak about the 'tough love' regime at her Chicago institution that refused to help the 'undeserving' poor as a model that

Social Welfare should follow; Sirico, her associate at Acton, soon arrived on a similar mission. But even these clerical visitors faced an increasingly incredulous public. We appeared unwilling to listen to their advice. Our scepticism extended to Catholic challenges of Sister Connie's credentials as a nun and towards Sirico's claims that the welfare state lacked 'biblical roots' and that Catholicism 'promoted the free market'. Tom Frewen satirised Sirico's theology as 'God is the market and the market is God'. Raising the treaty issue with visits from Kenneth Minogue and Epstein gained relatively little traction for the NZBR. A journalist described the 'NZBR knights' as having to 'slog through rough country' as they dispatched their emissaries to prod us to 'keep up the momentum of governmental reform'. The sneering tone suggested that the New Right no longer inspired us but poked us from behind to keep us moving as the NZBR worried about our lack of 'fiscal discipline' and our 'imprudence'.[24]

In the 1980s and early 1990s Australia and New Zealand apparently offered a similar picture of the 'triumph of liberalism', but our political cultures had diverged as the next election neared. We had come to the end of what Helen Clark later described as 'fifteen years of neoliberalism'. Somewhere on the long march towards market freedom, many of us had decided to desert. Shipley's role as a 'stern rural chastiser' intent on rectifying our character provoked resentment rather than acquiescence. By the late 1990s, talk of 'a Third Way' and 'a coherent centre-left policy prescription' competed with shrill denunciations of the 'nanny state' for our rhetorical allegiance. Although we had been celebrated midwives to the transnational 're-birth of the liberal creed' and junior members in good standing of the New Right network, many of us now wanted to disconnect or attach ourselves to another global circulation system that brought us something more than earnest sermons about market verities and moral commandments.[25]

The short and sad history of the Code of Social Responsibility, discussed in a later chapter, indicated the national mood of truculence and our stubborn refusal to continue to march on command. As Chris Trotter summed up the situation, 1998 was the 'year the paradigm shifted and left the government behind'. Introduced in 1997 by Bolger and Roger Sowry, the code became associated with Shipley after the split with NZ First, as talk of the 'nanny state' began to be used against her. The Prime Minister, who had supported the reduction of the welfare state, found herself cast as 'big sister' or an 'old-fashioned J2 teacher' scolding us for our lack of discipline. Even subjected to criticism by the visiting Sirico because the 'state has no business laying down a moral code', the code met a derisory reception from both expected and unexpected quarters. Defended as a 'catechism' by Shipley and as a 'new mantra' by Sowry, the minority Coalition Government entered an ideological tangle from which it found it hard to extricate itself. Simultaneously accused of moral authoritarianism and of denigrating the individual by treating people as 'economic units', the code failed to connect moral conservatism and New Right economics in a politically appealing blend.[26]

The 'D-Day' for the code passed without a declaration of victory as the two-million-dollar exercise produced a return rate of 7 per cent for its survey of our attitudes. This rejection, according to the *Nelson Mail*, reflected our belief that the Government was 'fiddling' in the 'private' lives of citizens. A *Dominion* reporter wrote about the difficulty of getting Cabinet ministers to talk about their own 'family values' that lent itself to their being accused of double standards or 'rank hypocrisy' by their opponents. The year ended with reports about declining support for the Government in the polls, business abandoning a 'sinking Shipley' and other stories that corroborated Trotter's analysis. Neither the New Right nor Jenny's code appeared to have sufficient popularity to retain our continued support.[27]

The irony that Shipley, selected as National's leader to demote Peters from his position of power, governed only because of the 'motley' support of Dunne, the 'tight five' waka-jumpers, two other NZ First defectors and Alliance defector, Alamein Kopu, was a cause for ridicule. Agnes-Mary Brooke asked her readers, 'Did we vote to bring on the clowns?' A columnist in the *Independent* described Labour as being nourished on the 'humus of National's decay' as Clark, the leader of the Labour opposition, benefited from the negotiation of *détente* with Anderton and the Alliance. Sniffing the political breeze, a journalist described the Shipley Government as having a 'gangrenous whiff about it' at the end of 1998. As New Right evangelists admonished us against backsliding in 1999, Kerr and his comrades prowled the countryside seeking to lure back the lapsed members of their faith. The note of desperation did not go undetected despite the brave words and new reforms being relentlessly promoted.[28]

The high drama of the disintegration of the Labour Government in the fallout between Douglas as Moses and the Hamlet-like Lange had now reached a farcical re-enactment in the dissolution of the Coalition Government. The audience rejected the cast and the script as 'boringly repetitive'. Scandals about 'dinnergate' and 'glitzy' Work and Income New Zealand (WINZ) conferences added to the Government's troubles. Brash came in for criticism in the business press for having 'kept the brakes' on the economy 'too hard and for too long'. Pronouncing the public verdict, a letter to the editor of the *Dominion* described the NZBR in words that also applied to the Government. Both suffered from the 'same terminal disease – non-performance leading to public ridicule'. Kerr's claim that the 'rot' had started in 1993 was an admission that he also saw signs of irreversible decay.[29] The New Right leading players yielded the parliamentary stage in November as the election produced a Labour–Alliance Coalition Government.

In the next chapters, detailing the debates over New Right policies in education, welfare and sexual issues, we explain these deviations from the path of market rectitude and the New Right triumph in the US and Australia. This is a complex story that could easily have encompassed the prison system, health, broadcasting, foreign policy and many other areas of New Zealand life in the 1980s and 1990s where similar conflicts ensued. We focus on our chosen areas to illustrate the reasons why many of us refused to heed the moral missionaries described in this chapter. Rather than reflecting a distinct lack of national virtue, many of us thought in moral categories like 'social justice' and 'social responsibility' that did not easily fit with market efficiency. In place of personal sin and moral failings, we sometimes thought about market failures. Some of the heretics among us even considered that dependency might be a necessary part of the human condition at certain times and situations in our lives rather than always constituting a 'moral hazard'. In the next chapters we show the existence of competing moral frameworks and related notions of citizenship while discussing our conflicts over sexual politics, education and welfare reform and the debates between New Right and 'new rights' advocates.

CHAPTER EIGHT

Sexuality for Sale?

> *Moreover thou shalt not lie carnally with thy neighbour's wife, to defile thyself with her. And thou shalt not let any of thy seed pass through the fire to Molech, neither shalt thou profane the name of thy God: I am the LORD. Thou shalt not lie with mankind, as with womankind: it is abomination.* LEVITICUS 18:20–22

Just as we were beginning our march towards market freedom, we debated the decriminalisation of homosexuality, broke away from the nuclear alliance with the US and extended the powers of the Waitangi Tribunal. These simultaneous occurrences create interpretative problems. Were we marching left or veering right? The results of our vociferous debates about sexuality suggest that we marched in an intricate chain step interweaving leftist and rightward steps that defy rigid ideological classification. In contrast to the onward march of America's Christian soldiers, we did not appear willing to obey strict moral marching orders. Our New Right found sexual liberalism compatible with market liberalism, making an alliance with moral conservatives, at least in the 1980s and early 1990s, difficult to consummate.

Ancient myths about contamination and moral impurity conflict with the New Right's professed devotion to the 'free market'. Debate over what can and should be sold, like what kinds of sexual practices can be legal, forces us to negotiate between notions of freedom and moral laws. What is sacred? What is secular? What can be sold? Who should be free to express his or her sexuality? Can we rent our sexual partners or sell sexual services? These questions created controversies in the 1980s and the 1990s with significant consequences for the fortunes of the New Right. In the religious culture of the US, market liberals found it prudent and essential to political success to forge a complex coalition including Christian conservatives, neoconservatives and aggressive nationalists. Indeed, controversies over 'hot button' issues of sexual morality may have enhanced the political appeal of the US New Right, a strategy clearly understood by the current president and his advisors. Here, our political system did not require the same complicated negotiations.

Our much simpler New Right coalition, composed primarily of market liberals, more single-mindedly focused on market freedoms. In contrast to their American cousins, our moral conservatives never negotiated a satisfactory partnership with the pro-market New Right. As a consequence, two parallel circuits carried different kinds of New Right language, policies and personnel between the US, Australia, Britain and New Zealand. Our New Right experience shows the impacts of these separate networks and the consequences of the failure to connect them into a political coalition. More closely resembling our British counterparts, we thus diverged from the US New Right and also from Australia, where ties between the Liberals and moral conservatives developed in the past decade as Howard and Costello energetically courted the growing ranks of Pentecostals and evangelicals.

Sexual controversies, one of the major consequences of Adam and Eve's expulsion from the Garden of Eden, contributed to the 'rise' of the US New Right and may be strengthening the Coalition's grip on power in Australia. As a logical corollary, the loss of influence on the part of our New Right can, in part, be attributed to its failure to use sexual morality to gain support from moral conservatives. Critics of the welfare state may decide to invigorate their cause by launching a 'moral panic' and targeting a scapegoat or two. Howard's and Bush's success may inspire erstwhile political leaders to play the 'moral' card. The recent emergence of Maxim and Destiny, the repeated attacks on 'political correctness', 'pink think' and 'social engineering' by Dunne and other politicians in the debates over prostitution and civil unions suggest that the still existing forces of the New Right may be drawing a lesson from the history that we will now sketch.

This history of our sexual controversies throws up a curious feature. We usually think of ourselves as living in a predominantly secular society, despite the evidence of our Christian heritage. This may be another indication of our fondness for simple myths that obscure the complicated aspects of our culture. When public debates broach sexual issues, however, the Bible is always a reference for at least some of us. At least one famous verse surfaced from the Book of Leviticus, despite our general ignorance of the Old Testament. The law at issue in the mid-1980s obviously reflected that biblical focus because it criminalised male homosexuality but not same-sex female sexuality. A man should not lie with another man as he would lie with a woman is the biblical paraphrase that echoed through submissions to select committees and letters to the editor in the 1980s and surfaced again in the condemnation of the civil union legislation. In grappling with homosexual law reform, we diverged from the US New Right and have continued to diverge, as well as moving away from our Australian neighbours, who passed a 'defence' of marriage law like American states. There are some New Zealanders, however, who want to return to traditional values as they chant 'enough is enough', repeat the familiar biblical passages and warn about the power of the 'sisterhood'.

That battles that raged in the mid-1980s and the early 1990s form part of a series of moral confrontations that continue to agitate the moral conservatives amongst us. Beginning in 1970, moral conservatives mobilised here to protect us from the baleful effects of the sexual revolution convulsing Britain and the US Copying British moral conservatives, the Society for the Protection of the Unborn Child (SPUC) and the Society for the Promotion of Community Standards (SPCS) emerged to campaign against sex education, abortion, pornography, feminism and gay rights. Responding to these moral pressure groups, Parliament tightened the abortion law, removed a provision for sex education and refused to include 'sexual orientation' in the Human Rights Act in 1977. The Council of Organisations for Moral Education continued to patrol these moral barricades in parallel to the establishment of the Moral Majority and the TVC in the US whose leaders, the Reverends Falwell and Sheldon, came to play a role in our own debates about moral issues.

In the US this Christian Right allied itself with the Republican Party. In Britain it voted for the Conservatives. Our New Right, even in the National Party, boasted a younger leadership, often young adults who came of age in the 1970s, rather than the 1940s and 1950s generations that dominated American and British politics. Like the

US we also produced a gay rights movement, heavily influenced by its American counterpart, which claimed sexual freedom as a human right, a form of sexual citizenship and a matter of 'gay pride'. In contrast to the American and Australian cases, however, where such battles occurred at the state and local levels, ours took place in Parliament, where these activists found political allies, particularly among the feminists in the Labour Party who came to power in 1984.[1]

This new development alarmed conservative Christians. Concerns about sex education and abortion gave way to worries about the possible ratification of the UN Convention against Discrimination against Women and the looming threat that homosexuality might be legalised. A Labour caucus that included Maori activists, feminists, trade unionists and peace campaigners might advance all kinds of changes opposed by moral conservatives. The Labour Manifesto advocating sex education, reproductive rights, a Working Women's Charter and ratification of the UN Convention threatened a moral apocalypse in the view of religious conservatives, who organised a resistance movement led by Women for Life, the Concerned Parents' Association, the SPCS and the evangelical newspaper, the *Challenge Weekly*.[2]

The first skirmish in this moral battle occurred in an attempt to prevent the ratification of the UN Convention. In defence of the housewife and the traditional family, hundreds of conservative Christian women poured into the Women's Forums intended to formulate the agenda for our newly created Ministry of Women's Affairs. The *Challenge Weekly* sympathetically covered the campaign that featured a visit from an Australian representative of Women Who Want to Be Women, an anti-feminist group connected to the NZ and Australian League of Rights and the US anti-feminist Eagle Forum. These groups combined Cold War fears about Communism and the UN, anti-leftist worries and antagonism to feminist challenges to the male-headed family that dated back to the origins of feminism and sexual reform.

Our moral crusaders, like anti-feminist Americans, predicted that lesbian marriages would be recognised and housewives forced into the workplace if the UN Convention were ratified. A moral catastrophe threatened New Zealand if the 'liberal humanist world-and-life-view' expressed in the UN Convention ushered in the 'one-world, anti-Christ government' described in the Book of Revelation. They defended the 'traditional-conservative world-and-life view', bursting into Christian hymns at some of the meetings.[3] Unable to prevent Lange and the Labour Cabinet from ratifying the Convention late in December 1984, our moral guardians remained in a state of high alert anticipating yet another threat from sexual liberationists.

When Labour MP Fran Wilde introduced a member's bill seeking to include 'sexual orientation' in the Human Rights Act and decriminalise homosexuality, both sides geared up for a moral Armageddon. Keith Hay and Sir Peter Tait with four MPs organised a petition drive against the bill. Rowdy public meetings, advertisements, pamphlets, submissions to the select committee, letters to the editor and emotional reports in the *Challenge Weekly* argued the conservative moral case. That famous verse from the Book of Leviticus, claims of the unnaturalness of anal intercourse, warnings about the seduction of the young and predictions of our decline into depravity poured out to persuade the rest of us to join the crusade. Similar claims flowed into Parliament to be repeated in testimony, impassioned debate and letters to MPs.

Moral missionaries from the US and Australia exhorted us to prevent the passage of this pernicious legislation. Sheldon of TVC and Jack Swann, a veteran of anti-gay campaigns in New York and a member of the anti-Communist Committee for the Free World, visited us in August 1985. The NZ League of Rights brought over Jackie Butler, president of Women Who Want to Be Women, to oppose homosexual law reform and feminism threatening our traditions. That same year we received the spiritual guidance offered by anti-abortion activist Francis Schaeffer. In 1986, Rousas Rushdoony, the Christian Reconstructionist from the Chalcedon Institute, told us about the need to incorporate the Bible into all our laws, including capital punishment for homosexuality. His supporters in Reformed churches in New Zealand preached the same need for a theocratic state and biblically correct legislation. Simultaneously some of us received pamphlets citing the controversial research of psychologist Paul Cameron providing 'scientific' evidence for the dangers of homosexuality. We found ourselves enlisted in a moral battle in which the military leaders for one side sometimes spoke with American accents and at least one spoke Australian.[4]

Inspired by Sheldon's TVC and Falwell's Moral Majority, the Coalition of Concerned Citizens (CCC) organised to carry on the moral campaign after their American visitors departed our shores. Seeking to challenge the 'gay rights' framework, the CCC sternly expressed 'great suspicion' about our 'talk of rights, deeming it to be humanistic, egotistical and overly optimistic about human nature'. Rather than sexual citizens free to exercise our sexual choices, we must think of ourselves as 'sinners' having 'no rights before God'. Like the earlier opponents of the UN Convention, CCC leaders claimed that appeals to human rights justified 'licentious lifestyles' and incited 'human rebellion against the law of God'.[5]

Arguing for what some of us perceived as a theocratic state, the CCC alarmed those who did not want New Zealand to become a literal 'Godzone'. A petition, ostensibly bearing 800,000 signatures, arrived at Parliament in late September 1985 under the banner 'For God, For Family, For Country'. It was a remarkable display of religious fervour, flag waving and hymn singing that bore the hallmarks of the flamboyant US Christian Right. Uplifting to the organisers, frightening to the secularly inclined, this spectacle marked the emotional centrepiece of a campaign that continued until July 1986.

Aware that many of us thought in the language of universal human rights, the supporters of homosexual law reform appealed to these beliefs. Their submissions to the select committee made claims about social justice, equal rights, the freedom to express our innate sexuality and against unjust discrimination and described homosexuals as an oppressed minority. This language could be traced to back to the US Civil Rights movement, feminism, trade unions, social democracy, the *Universal Declaration of Human Rights* and our own battles about apartheid during the 1981 tour.[6]

The religiously inclined among the supporters of the bill drew upon other parts of the Bible. They pointed out Christ's silence about homosexuality and the Gospels' injunctions to judge not others lest we be judged. Contrasting the 'loving' Christ of the Gospels to the stern patriarchal God of the Old Testament, these arguments for 'social justice' deployed a liberal biblical interpretation against the morally conservative interpretation. The Gay Christian Group claimed to speak on behalf of our Christian majority as expressed by the official positions of the Presbyterian, Anglican and Methodist faiths. This support, expressed in newspaper ads, aided these efforts to counter the fundamentalist, evangelical and reformed versions of the Bible with their focus on sexual sin and damnation.

Although gay rights activists and supporters imported arguments, organisational structure and language from the US, they found a way to deflect the allegations that their cause was a part of an 'international homosexual network' made by their opponents. Lange's debate with Falwell in 1985 immeasurably aided this strategy by appearing to place the Christian fundamentalist leader on the wrong side of the nuclear issue for the majority of New Zealanders. At a time when the *Washington Post* and *New York Times* wrote about our 'nationalistic' pride and cautioned the White House against becoming the heavy-handed Goliath to our anti-nuclear David, the timing could not have been worse for our religious right to have Falwell stage the debate with Lange. Lange's victory was a national triumph. Our pleasure at being at the centre of 'geopolitics' was enhanced by the feeling that we held the 'moral high ground' and that Falwell, despite his position as self-proclaimed leader of the Moral Majority, did not. Playing to these sentiments, the supporters of homosexual law reform turned our Christian Right into collaborators with an alien power, the nuclear-armed US.[7]

The CCC became 'our equivalent of America's Moral Majority' in the rhetoric of supporters of the decriminalisation of homosexuality. The Reverend Michael Blair, an Anglican, argued that public and media attention had been captivated by the 'roar of fury from a small group of fundamentalists' whose fervour he compared to the 'same mania that fired the Ku Klux Klan'. Critics charged that Sheldon represented an effort by 'outside powers to undermine our national sovereignty', shown by his nefarious connections to Falwell and his support for Reagan's election. The nationalist myth that many of us wanted to believe in 1985 put gay rights activists onto the side defending our national autonomy as we exited from the Cold War four years before the fall of the Berlin Wall. The overlap between aggressive anti-Communism and the Christian Right reinforced the 'left' and the sexual liberationists simultaneously.[8]

Continuing this rhetorical strategy, Selwyn Dawson, a retired Methodist minister, published 'God's Bullies' in *Metro* magazine. Dawson described the opponents of homosexual law reform as the 'counterpart of the American Moral Majority or New Right' supported by moral conservatives among us. He recited the 'dubious achievements' of the US Christian Right, pointing to Reagan's election, the defeat of the Equal Rights Amendment, the censorship of textbooks, the persecution of homosexuals and the restoration of the death penalty. We, of course, did not want to follow their benighted example. Our moral crusaders had been bewitched by a 'vision of the traditional family', their fears of women's equality and their belief that sexuality could only be 'exclusively heterosexual and confined within marriage'. Dawson separated himself and his enlightened readers from these frightened souls. Flattering to those who shared his views, Dawson appealed to nationalist sentiments to justify support for decriminalising homosexuality and to prove that we were capable of moral and political 'self-sufficiency'.[9] As a minister, he also undercut the notion that there was only one kind of biblically sanctioned morality.

Through such arguments that implicitly labelled the opponents of reform as backward looking, the campaign to decriminalise homosexuality gained a narrow majority in Parliament, drawn primarily from Labour but including a few National MPs, in July 1986. The opponents prevented the inclusion of sexual orientation in the Human Rights Act through their passion, the widespread appeal of their arguments and their credible threats of political retaliation. Newspaper headlines like 'Gay Rights: MPs Say Yes' demonstrated, however, that the sexual reformers won the rhetorical battle in the mainstream media by moving the emphasis from sex to human rights. Endorsing this framework, editors and journalists, most of whom were also cheering on the New Right market reforms, described the decriminalisation of homosexuality as a victory for 'moderation, tolerance and compassion'. Editorials described the debate as marked by the 'extremes of zealotry and bigotry' and lamented that Parliament had not provided protection for homosexuals against being 'hounded from their homes and jobs by those who choose to discriminate'. They predicted, however, that the opposition would 'wane over time'.[10] Gay activists and their allies had won the discursive battle through appeals to social justice, our self-image as urbane and enlightened and nationalist sentiments that set us distinctly apart from American 'nuclear cowboys' and religious 'bullies'.

Anxious to demonstrate its political clout, the CCC promised to punish Labour in the 1987 election. The *Coalition Courier* appeared as an insert in the *Challenge Weekly* to continue the battle against sexual liberalism. The *Courier* placed its crusade in the context of a larger war against secular humanism, Communism, socialism and feminism. Their arguments revealed their strong Cold War allegiances to American- and Australian-style anti-Communist groups. The *Courier* exhorted its readers to beware of Communist subversion, sexual education and the other dangers of sexual liberalisation as it urged them to vote. Several veteran moral campaigners secured nominations from the National Party but only in Labour strongholds such as Mt Albert, firmly held by Labour progressive Helen Clark. The CCC also circulated material from the John Birch Society and other anti-Communist groups under the auspices of their parliamentary ally, National MP Graeme Lee. These tactics failed to punish their opponents in the 1987 election. Their extremely conservative views, especially their opposition to the 'new economic order', made it highly unlikely that the National Party, then coming under New Right dominance, could consider even a tactical alliance at the next election. The moral campaigners had lost yet another battle in their war against sexual liberalism.

The election of a National Government in 1990 committed to the 'Decent Society' did not halt the trend towards either sexual and market liberalism. Carefully studying anti-gay tactics in the United States, supporters of gay and lesbian rights developed a strategy to amend the Human Rights Act to include sexual orientation. They sought to avoid the controversy that had erupted in the mid-1980s and used public relations professionals to orchestrate the campaign carefully. Rather than using a sexual citizenship framework, the advocates of the new legislation framed the issue as a matter of public health in keeping with the portfolio held by its sponsor, Katherine O'Regan, the Associate Minister of Health. Spokesmen from the AIDS Foundation acted as the public face of the campaign to keep it within a health framework. The authors of the bill included heterosexuality and bisexuality as a part of the definition of 'sexual orientation' to guard against the 'special rights' accusations that had been effective in the US. There was to be no repeat of the 1985–86 political firestorm.

The electoral weakness of the CCC in the 1987 campaign encouraged members of the National Cabinet to endorse the legislation this time, but the Prime Minister, Jim Bolger, had not changed his mind. In deference to such internal conflicts, the Government supporters of the legislation proposed it as a 'special supplementary paper' rather than as part of the Human Rights Act Amendment bill. It was thus treated as a 'conscience' issue. Steered carefully through the parliamentary agenda, the legislation's ministerial sponsors arranged to have Bolger make out-of-town appointments that took him away from Parliament during crucial votes.[11] Everything was done to keep the debates from heating up within Parliament, to avoid embarrassment for the Government and to stifle the potential for frenzied moral debate like those that had occurred in the mid-1980s.

Although during the debate a few MPs stridently attacked homosexuality as a perversion, immoral and as causing disease, the supporters' tactics leached most of the passion from the issue. The number of submissions tapered off in comparison to the response to the Homosexual Law Reform bill of 1985. The 1993 addition to the Human Rights Act completed the legislative victory for gay rights by prohibiting discrimination on the basis of sexual orientation. A majority in the Cabinet and both major party caucuses decided that sexuality should be a matter of individual 'conscience' rather than a criminal activity or a valid reason for discrimination. The very fervour of the opposition in the mid-1980s, its connections to Cold War fervour and its reliance upon American tactics had apparently backfired on the CCC and other moral crusaders.

The political misfortune of Christian Heritage and other Christian parties offered further evidence that moral conservatives lacked sufficient electoral appeal to persuade a major party to follow the example of the Republican Party in the US. With the exception of New Zealand First and a member or two of the ACT caucus, our 'moral majority' appeared to be a politically impotent moral minority in the 1990s. In the US, by contrast, continued controversy about homosexual rights, including a reluctance to decriminalise homosexual acts, built political support for a New Right coalition that advocated market freedoms and moral restraints.[12]

By the end of the 1990s, the contrast between New Zealand and the US appeared even more marked. In the US a president was impeached for lying about an extra-marital affair while in New Zealand we paid almost no attention to the sexual lives of our politicians. There a network of religious right organisations relentlessly fought against the 'gay rights agenda' and engaged in the prolonged scandal hunt that eventually won the White House for a 'born again' Christian in 2000. Our scandals on this side of the Pacific usually involve money, speeding limousines, high-priced underpants, 'he said, she said' news reports, tennis balls in the mouths of talkative students or genetically modified corn, not sexual escapades. These differences partially account for the greater longevity of the New Right and its version of 'moral politics' in the US than in our own 'Godzone'.

Our New Right concentrated on the pursuit of market freedoms, leaving sexual choice to those who could afford the consequences. One advocate of homosexual law reform even used market language to argue his case. David Bisman wrote 'Homosexuality and the "Free Market"' asking, 'How can it be a matter of principle that a business man should be permitted to charge any interest rate that he wishes on a loan', but not 'be allowed to sleep with another male who wishes to sleep with him'? The New Right among us could embrace Bisman's argument by defining ourselves as sexual consumers rather than sexual citizens, free to make choices.[13] This argument, however, was rarely made by the supporters of homosexual law reform or civil unions, where the focus usually is on the equal rights of citizens. Living in a society where the radical student generation of the 1970s came to power in the 1980s and 1990s, we participated in a revolution against the older generation, our imperial masters and the Cold War itself in the mid-1980s. We came out in sexual terms at the same time that we came out from under the nuclear umbrella, four years before the Germans walked through the Brandenburg Gate.[14] The coincidence of libertarian rebellions against a 'repressive' past meant that our New Right was also our New Left, a hybrid political form that the term 'Third Way' somewhat clumsily describes.

At the same time, the comparison with the United States suggests that a New Right that only focuses on market freedoms is more fragile and fleeting than one that includes moral conservatism at its ideological core, a conclusion that may now be reshaping the strategies of opposition parties, moral conservatives and their journalistic allies such as Ian Wishart's *Investigate*. The US New Right delves deeper in people's psychic interiors with its focus on emotionally volatile issues and its ability to generate fear and hostility towards sexual deviants or other 'outlaw' groups. Under such tutelage, Americans are encouraged to think of themselves as members of a God-fearing 'moral majority' and to focus on individual, particularly sexual, sins as requiring punishment. Both domestically and internationally, they fight against 'evil-doers' who must be destroyed. They define themselves against an 'immoral' minority who are portrayed as threatening 'family values'.[15] Thousands of articles about Monica Lewinsky, stem cell research, abortion and gay marriage clog the American press and the electoral debates while comparatively little attention is paid to corporate malfeasance, the spending of billions on warfare and weapons or the numbers of Americans imprisoned in what may be the most costly 'welfare' system in the world.

We thought differently about moral questions from Americans in the 1980s, as the puzzled commentary and grudging admiration in their press coverage suggested. We debated the morality of nuclear weapons, the rights of the tangata whenua, gay rights and the 'social justice' of New Right reforms at the same time. This coincidence may have reinforced an understanding of morality as involving social and cultural dimensions rather than focusing on individual sin and virtue. At a time when our leaders spoke widely about freedom, we may have taken that concept much further than it was intended. If so, we began to practise the freedom to make choices and take responsibility for those choices in our sexual lives and even to change our political system. Rather than looking back to the past and genuflecting before the sacred texts, as American conservatives are wont to do, we moved forward towards sexual liberalism even as we heard calls to return to Victorian liberalism in our economic practices. This, of course, was what we did in the 1980s and 1990s. Will we continue on this path towards sexual liberation or heed the calls from those, like Maxim and Destiny, who want us to emulate the US and Australia?

PART FOUR

Numbers: Learning the Law

He hath said, which heard the words of God and knew the knowledge of the most High, which saw the vision of the Almighty, falling into a trance, but having his eyes open. NUMBERS 24:16

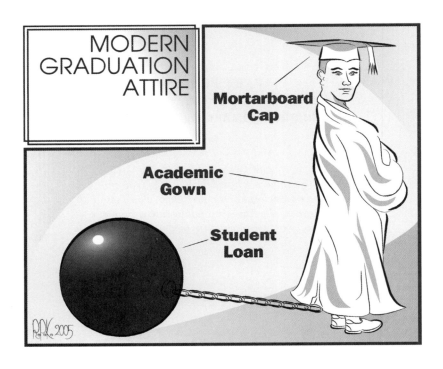

CHAPTER NINE

Education for Enterprise

*And they have turned unto me the back and not
the face: though I taught them, rising up early
and teaching them, yet they have not hearkened
to receive instruction.* JEREMIAH 32:33

*Receive my instruction and not silver: and
knowledge rather than choice gold.* PROVERBS
8:10

This chapter will examine the impact of New Right reforms on
education. As we have already demonstrated, the New Right intended to restructure both the private and public sectors to create
an 'enterprise society'. In relation to the public sector, New Right
reformers sought to reduce the government's direct costs and
involvement in the provision of services, by turning government
enterprises into businesses that could be more profitably managed
by private entrepreneurs. They sold off these 'businesses' where they
could and contracted for services, reducing government's role to that
of purchaser of educational 'outputs'. The model chosen, which we
call the 'competitive privatising of risk' (CPR), creates quasi-markets
while maintaining a high degree of centralised control through
contractual and statutory compliance requirements and, of course,
the purchase of the products and services. The CPR model insists
upon the separation of purchasing from provision, at least formally,
and draws a clear distinction between ownership and purchase,
in keeping with the assumptions of the school of 'public choice'
economics. The New Right thus introduced market processes into the
educational system while distancing government from responsibility
for the actual delivery of education, in order to shrink the 'state',
enlarge the 'private' sector and teach us to think like consumers for
whom 'choice' was our primary value.

Publicly funded education became a crucial battleground between the New Right and state interventionists on both the social democratic left and the paternalistic right because it was both a major consumer of public resources and an important crucible of character formation that moulded civic-minded future citizens or, in the New Right vision, produced self-interested consumers and entrepreneurs. Free-marketeers viewed the sort of public schooling that had developed under egalitarian principles as the cause of economic inefficiency, a pervasive lack of entrepreneurship and a non-competitive ethic antithetical to the free play of market forces. New Right publications, workshops, seminars and campaigns advocate the CPR kinds of reforms. Their authors tout the wonders of education vouchers, competitive markets, user pays, consumer 'choice' and 'personal responsibility' and write about the value of education exclusively in terms of its contribution to economic growth and private advancement to create an 'enterprise culture'.

The reform of education became a test case for the efficacy and 'truth' of market approaches in which success was measured by increased outputs and a decline in unit cost per student and qualifications produced, leaving quality to be determined by the individual consumers and their future employers. The CPR reform of education therefore, was essential to the creation of a market-driven society and the implementation of the New Right programme, redefining formerly considered public goods, such as education, and limiting government intervention, now increasingly derided as 'social engineering'.

From 1984 until 1999, we witnessed just such an attempt to transform education – from pre-school to universities – closely paralleling New Right reforms in the US, UK, Australia and Canada. The impact of educational reforms in our public schools was especially high because of our proportionately greater state-funded education (including the integrated schools) than that of those countries, the government's near monopoly on the funding and the extent of direct management of schools by the Department of Education. As there have been analytical studies of the pre-school and primary and secondary school changes, we give more attention to the tertiary sector, where the so-called 'private benefits' of education became the most strongly entrenched and the CPR model was most fully imposed. The underlying New Right ideology of creating market mechanisms in the previously 'public' sectors drove the changes in the 'education industry'.

Parliamentary act after act, working party after working party and compliance report after compliance report proposed massive changes of the CPR sort. As a consequence, the twelve years from 1987 until 1999 were a time of ideological and institutional turmoil in our educational system. Schools and universities found themselves constantly shaken in the persistent throes of restructuring and facing enormous compliance costs, experiencing uncertainties in terms of funding and responding to rapid changes in work practices and conditions, often beyond that required by legislation. Teachers mastered new qualifications and scrambled to adjust to changes in management and governance. Likewise, school students faced new assessment procedures and qualifications and tertiary students acquired large debts in the 1990s as user pays surged into the tertiary sector.

The range of reforms was broad but the general CPR dictates were clear, paralleling changes in other parts of the 'public sector'. Kindergartens, schools, colleges of education, wananga, polytechnics and universities gained a degree of independence and autonomy in exchange for being managed like businesses that deployed resources, including 'human capital', to produce the largest numbers of 'products' at the most efficient and competitive unit price. Educational institutions shouldered almost the entire burden of business risk as they sought to attract increasing numbers of education consumers, while government ministries created incentives, enhanced competition and acted as advisors, auditors and assessors. The funding mechanisms created a new system of competitive bidding and new models of governance developed to enhance managerial and financial controls over these educational 'enterprises'. This commodification of education directly linked schools and universities to the market, subjected them to the vagaries of consumer choice and forced them to pursue a 'bums on seats' approach to increase their revenue stream. The architects of the new education intended these institutions to 'grow' future enterprising New Zealanders – flexible, creative, computer literate, technologically adept and eager to participate in a growing national economy fully integrated into the global economy.

Reflecting a similar Conservative call for 'back to basics' in Britain, Merv Wellington, the Minister of Education, released *A Review of the Core Curriculum for Schools* in March 1984, detailing the core subjects and the minimum time to be spent on them. Labelled restrictive and dictatorial by the Labour Opposition, the policy document ensured that the 'crisis' in education became one of the campaign issues in the 1984 election. Concerns about class sizes and adequate funding featured in political debates, along with the issue of university student bursaries, the quality of education and the need to increase the numbers of those gaining qualifications. Educational reform thus appeared prominently on the political agenda when Labour captured the Treasury benches in 1984.

During Labour's first three years in government, however, Marshall, of the Labour left, presided over the Education portfolio, keeping New Right reformers at bay. A review committee on schools consulted widely and received more than 20,000 public submissions containing recommendations that ranged from the teaching of peace studies and Te Reo to all New Zealand students to the reforms desired by the New Right's increasingly vocal education lobby, including the Employers' Federation. The business lobby demanded job training and qualifications specifically designed for the marketplace.[1] The Department of Labour concurred with this lobby, agreeing that students were inadequately prepared for employment and endorsing vocational education and training.

When interviewed by us, Douglas and Prebble claimed to be unaware of the campaigns for free-market schooling, including vouchers and student loans, endorsed by New Right think tanks such as the IEA and by luminaries like Friedman.[2] Despite these denials, some government departments, notably the Treasury and the Department of Labour, advocated radical educational reforms, even in the earliest days of the Fourth Labour Government. In response to rising unemployment and pressure from employers, an informal cabinet committee, chaired by Prebble, looked at education and training. A discussion paper prepared by Prebble proposed the US model of students paying fully for their tertiary education, along with the notion of publicly funded education ending at fifteen. From that point, qualified students might receive vouchers to be cashed in for three to five more years of education or training from providers of their own choosing. Occupied with financial and other economic reforms, Douglas and Prebble allowed Marshall and the Labour left to continue to implement a social democratic conception of education during the first term.

This redefinition of education as a commodity subject to market forces that could be bought and sold in the domestic and international marketplace gained fuller expression in *Government Management: Brief to the Incoming Government*, received by the Labour Cabinet after Labour's re-election in 1987.[3] This document extended the neo-liberal model to education, social welfare and social services to construct educational markets from pre-school- to tertiary-level education. The Treasury report focused on the relationship between education and the economy, the lack of consumer choice in education and the neglect of efficient management practices. It began by declaring that the first Labour Government's commitment to suitable 'free education' for all New Zealanders might have been appropriate forty years earlier to achieve 'the social ideal of equality', but contended that this was no longer the correct vision needed for our educational system in the future. Instead, we needed to recognise that the current system had failed, as shown by the numbers of truants and early school leavers and the lack of skills of many young workers entering the labour market. Furthermore, public education had failed to satisfy Maori educational aspirations and those of many other New Zealanders. What was needed was an educational system designed for a small country forced to make its way in the competitive 'international economy'.

The authors of *Government Management* employed an explicitly Hayekian perspective highlighting the imperfect knowledge that prevented government bureaucrats or other centralised planners from making effective policies. Following Hayekian principles, they stressed the need to 'free up demand and supply' to (re)create a free market in educational products to be purchased by individual consumers better aware of their individual preferences, tastes and interests than government officials. Only such a market could guarantee that the supply of educated labour could meet employers' demands. This new, efficient delivery system did not require additional funding – a claim based on a single American study that unlinked financial 'inputs' from 'quality' educational outputs – but needed to be freed from direct government intervention to unleash the 'power' of consumer choice. Echoing Thatcher's 'there is no such thing as society' claim, the authors of *Government Management* insisted that that so-called 'public goods' like education were mostly reducible to private benefits accrued to individuals, with only residual benefits spilling over to other New Zealanders.

According to these Treasury officials, 'education shares the main characteristics of other commodities traded in the marketplace'. It could be operated according to market principles with a clear focus on the issues of who pays, who chooses, who consumes, who benefits and who is accountable for the efficient provision of educational products. Although the payer had previously been the government, mistakenly understood as funding the production of free or 'virtually free' products, this false assumption needed to be corrected to recognise the actual balance between public good and private benefit. Weighing the relative allocation of benefits for the recipients of tertiary qualifications, the Treasury economists argued that the greatest benefits accrued to the individual students, who enhanced their 'human capital', and to their future employers. Ultimately the 'worth' of the knowledge and skills attained would be recognised through the market for these educational products.[4] Mechanisms to determine 'realistic comparative assessments of public and private benefit' and new modes of governance would ensure that there was transparency and accountability regarding the use of public funds. The report advocated less central control and greater parental involvement – 'a partnership with parents' – to enhance market operations by bringing suppliers of educational products and consumers into closer contact. Many of the equity issues such as limited access to pre-school and tertiary education for Maori and Pacific Island communities gained acknowledgement in this document. The remedies differed from earlier proposals: the 'hidden hand' of the market would magically produce the required services at the right price to these new groups of consumers. The Treasury officials also recommended the recruitment of overseas students by secondary and tertiary institutions to further reduce the direct costs to government and encourage entrepreneurial behaviour among these business competitors.

According to this document, government intervention had distorted the educational system by reducing 'freedom and responsibility', preventing supplier competition, denying consumer choice and failing to provide economic incentives for teachers and schools. Once these barriers had been removed, improvements in education would automatically result from the free operations of the market.[5] Within this new market, student–teacher relations would become contractual, freeing individuals from the bureaucratic constraints of a state-sanctioned and -funded network of providers to pursue their own self-interest.

Delivered shortly after the 1987 election, Gerald Grace's inaugural lecture as Professor of Education at Victoria University of Wellington exposed the unexamined assumptions in the Treasury blueprint for education. Entitled 'Education: Commodity or Public Good?', Grace's lecture focused on the ideological transition from the 'right' to free education as a public good intended to produce intelligent citizens to education as a personal investment designed to produce market competitors.[6] Grace declared that the Treasury claim that a beneficial outcome can be considered a 'public good' only if it is 'non-exclusive' was incorrect.[7] Rather than describing education as a 'scarce' commodity, Grace described it as a collective taonga that did provide non-exclusive benefits, such as the promotion of democracy, equality and social justice. Paying lip service to this, subsequent government documents admitted that there was a public benefit to education but usually limited that benefit to an ill-defined 'social cohesion'. Still committed to the market, these officials could only accept a sort of 'trickle-down' or 'spill-over' conception of residual benefits to other participants in the market through the enhancement of productivity. Ideas about citizenship and social justice continued to be rejected for the same reasons that Hayek had advanced.

The Labour election victory in 1987, the result in large part of the perceived successes of the New Right economic reforms and an independent foreign policy, was the signal for Douglas and his allies to extend reforms to education, labour, health and social welfare. Brian Picot, a businessman, chaired the Task Force to Review Education Administration. The wide-ranging Picot Report, *Administering for Excellence*, appeared in April 1988.[8] Guided by its principles, two working parties, established under the auspices of Deputy Prime Minister Palmer's Cabinet Social Equity Committee, examined early-childhood and post-compulsory education and training. Each committee produced detailed recommendations for reforms along CPR lines that eventually appeared in legislative form in the 1989 Education Act.[9]

The clash between Lange and Douglas over Labour's future direction and the speed and scope of New Right reforms came to a rancorous public dispute in 1988. Lange removed Douglas as Minister of Finance, slowing the pace of reforms and relieving the pressures on a public sector reeling from extensive structural change, and he assumed the role of Minister of Education. Despite his rejection of Douglas's reform agenda, he endorsed almost all the Picot recommendations. A Ministry of Education replaced the Department of Education and the raft of recommended reforms sailed on in its legislative form and ministerial policy to reshape our educational system.

The proponents of the Picot reforms intended to shift responsibility for educational decision-making from government bureaucracies to the educational customers or their agents. In schools, parents and others from the local community became boards of trustees to govern these new educational enterprises. These boards contractually employed the principals, ensured effective management of the schools and assumed responsibility for meeting the needs of the local community. They became responsible for compliance with educational policy and developed a direct contractual relationship with the Ministry rather than with district education boards. In exchange, the school boards could freely purchase services. The Picot Report argued that bulk funding provided the freedom for boards to pay the salaries of teachers and make other decisions about school expenditures.[10] A school charter, or contract, set out the purposes and outcomes of the school as a collaborative undertaking by the board, principal, staff and community. This document, subject to approval by the Minister of Education, included relationships with employers. The report also advocated a new national body of trustees, appointed by the Minister, to offer guidance to local school boards.[11]

As the new system developed, changes to some of the original proposals, generally towards greater Ministry control, began to occur. For example, *Tomorrow's Schools* granted additional powers in charter negotiations to the Ministry who set the terms of both Ministry–school and school–community contracts and, by the time of the 1990 charter framework, the 'community' had largely been excluded from the process. In the following years policy amendments to the Education Act concerning the charter coupled with the Ministry's directive and curriculum-setting authority meant that power had formally returned to the centre for primary and secondary schools. The Lough Report in 1990 reported that boards of trustees experienced information gaps, lack of clear direction from the Ministry and confusion over their legal responsibilities.[12]

The Educational Review Office, an external review agency formally independent of the department, assumed the role of assessing the progress made by individual schools. The New Zealand Qualifications Authority was designed to create a unified national system that recognised both academic and vocational training. A single system and authority greatly facilitated movement between different institutions and increased flexibility. Originally intended to include the universities within this system, this part of the plan met fierce resistance and was only partly achieved.

The Picot Report recommended that Maori students should have an alternative to existing education that included the opportunity of learning in a secure 'Maori environment', conducive to the development of positive Maori identity. Its authors recommended the use of Te Reo and whanau-supported learning as the levers for raising Maori educational attainment.[13] *Tomorrow's Schools* stressed the importance of Maori participation on boards of trustees and the links between school and community.[14] At the pre-school level, support for the kohanga reo movement led to a large increase in language immersion kindergartens. At the school level, the successful involvement of communities and parents effectively promoted programmes in primary and secondary schools. Finally, the establishment of wananga brought the teaching of Te Reo and other relevant Maori courses to the tertiary level, creating a new diversity in our educational system.

The election of National to government in 1990 brought new market-oriented reforms in education. The title of Lockwood Smith's 1991 *Education Policy:Investing in People: Our Greatest Asset* made clear its pro-market agenda. Smith announced that by 're-ordering priorities in education funding, the Government will achieve its goal of maximising New Zealand's economic performance with a more highly skilled, better educated and more adaptable workforce'.[15] National's policy did not promise extra funding but simply declared the goal of redistributing funds to special education and bulk-funded schools, thus further reducing the ministry's risks. It also proposed, in keeping with the ECA, the replacement of national employment agreements with separate pay scales to allow for incentives to reward 'better' teachers. This last possibility provoked strong resistance from unions and most teachers, effectively restricting bulk funding to a minority of schools. The 1993 Curriculum Framework added new priorities in computers and technology education in keeping with the goal of expanding training and teaching marketable skills.[16]

The NZBR established the Education Forum in 1992 to publicise and promote the privatisation of education and other New Right educational policies as it cheered on the efforts of the National Government to bring market disciplines to the educational system. Clearly these New Right lobby groups believed that they had begun to achieve their educational goals. They championed a system of incentives for successful schools and teachers to reward quality outcomes. Reports advocated maximising parental choice to enhance competition between schools and create an environment conducive to the expansion of private schools. At the tertiary level, the NZBR claimed that the current system restricted individual economic capacities, set limits to the pursuit of individual self-interest and thus limited our 'democracy'.[17] The NZBR recommended the complete privatisation of tertiary education by removing all state funding in the development of a nationally and internationally competitive 'client-driven' system, modelled on the US system.[18] Its aim was for tertiary institutions to 'compete both for finance . . . and for clients in relatively free markets' so that these institutions 'face true incentive to meet their clients' . . . needs in the most efficient manner'. The NZBR insisted on the importance of 'facilitating private sector competition in the provision of tertiary education' as part of 'any reform process'.[19] Consumer choice and market competition were to transform New Zealand education at all levels.

In the policies directed towards the tertiary sector, we can trace the emergence of an official discourse, initially fostered by *Economic Management*, that lumped together all post-compulsory institutions and ignored differences between education and training. The specificities of each of its component parts became difficult to address under this conception of a single tertiary market. The New Zealand Vice-Chancellors' Committee (NZVCC) commissioned a report, *New Zealand's Universities: Partners in National Development*, published in 1987.[20] Understanding education as a 'right', it conceded that university education clearly did have a degree of private benefit to the students concerned but cautioned that developing criteria to calculate the proportions of private versus public benefit would be difficult. The NZVCC called for substantial additional funding to ensure international parity but accepted the reality of funding constraints. It conceded that user pays was inevitable and that fees should be limited to 20 per cent of the cost. This concession from the university sector itself contributed to an environment in which the significant issue to be debated was not whether students should pay fees at all but whether 20 per cent was the right amount.[21] A second issue highlighted here, that would become a central feature of the debates over the next decade, was the need to improve access to tertiary education.

The Hawke Report and the government follow-ups, *Learning for Life* and *Learning for Life Two*, returned to the principles outlined in *Government Management* and the broad guidelines of the Picot Report.[22] The main institutional change was the recommendation that the University Grants Committee (UGC) be disbanded and that universities be funded directly from the Ministry. The report advocated this to avoid the distribution politics of the UGC and to give greater autonomy to individual universities. As funding was still largely centrally controlled, this amounted to the application of the CPR model to universities. According to the Hawke Report, universities should be encouraged to raise some non-government funds and other income by setting their own fees, exercising greater budgetary control and selling their services where they could do so. Students would pay fees and be able to obtain loans along the lines of an existing Australian model. A Chief Executive Officer, appointed on a fixed-term contract by a reduced-size university council, would run each university. Each tertiary institution would be held to the terms of its charter and performance agreements would be made with the Ministry. Finally, the Hawke Report recommended that research and teaching be decoupled in the interests of cost-effective resource allocation.[23]

Market competition among universities, between universities and other tertiary institutions and among private providers would guarantee that desired services would be offered cost-effectively. The Hawke Report advocated the need for lifelong learning in a rapidly changing world and stressed the need for greater access to tertiary education, to increase participation rates necessary for economic growth and on the grounds of equity. The recognition of the need for institutional diversity reflecting the diversity of the market was part of the argument for greater devolution and decentralisation.[24] The two *Learning for Life* reports further blurred the differences among tertiary institutions – universities, colleges of education, polytechnics and wananga – recommending competition between them and supporting that idea that degree-granting status should no longer be restricted to universities.

Of particular importance to tertiary institutions was the new funding system. A new system based directly on the past year's equivalent number of full-time students (EFTS) would replace the previous system of five-year block grants. Although EFTS had been used in the past, this measure now assumed a new importance. A university's government revenue was calculated as the total of EFTS in different subject cost categories as set by the Ministry. The EFTS formula operated across the tertiary sector to foster competition between universities and other providers.

The 1989 Education Act incorporated these proposals into legislation and along with the State-Owned Enterprises Act (1986), the State Sector Act (1988) and, the Public Finance Act (1989), provided the legal framework for CPR in New Zealand education. The schools, universities, colleges of education, polytechnics and wananga effectively paralleled the former state-owned enterprises except that they still had the government as their largest customer. The government's assets (owned by the Crown) were protected by the provision for taking direct business control when these were threatened. CPR entailed the privatisation of both risk and management, forcing schools, universities and other tertiary providers to develop quasi-commercial administrative procedures and processes. Governance broadly followed Picot Report recommendations. In the case of universities and other tertiary institutions, this entailed a redefinition of the structure and powers of councils, now to be made up of representatives of staff, students, the Ministry and other stakeholders. The Education Act (1989) made provision for the councils to appoint a CEO as their sole employee, who in turn became the employer of all other staff. The tertiary institutions thus became restructured along prevailing corporate lines. The issue of who owned the assets of these public institutions is still contested and ownership details unresolved. The Education Amendment Act (1990) redefined charters to give schools less independence but increased autonomy for universities. Legislation in 1990 also introduced tertiary student fees along with the right for different tertiary institutions to award qualifications and degrees.

The new National Government continued the education reforms. In 1991 student fees were effectively doubled and the new EFTS funding formula introduced. Smith launched the Study Right Scheme (SRS) to encourage students into tertiary education and training. Students under 22, during their first three years of tertiary study, received 95 per cent of tuition costs. Other students received only a 75 per cent subsidy of course costs. Opposition to this scheme prevented it from being fully implemented. Tertiary student numbers increased steadily during the 1990s and at a much faster rate than government funding, so that funding per student markedly decreased. The student loans scheme finally began in January 1992. Throughout the 1990s Treasury, the Ministry of Education and the NZVCC debated the funding of the growth in tertiary education.

In response to this debate a Ministerial Consultative Group (MCG) chaired by Jeff Todd began to explore the funding options for the sector in 1994. The Todd Report concluded that tertiary education and training generated both public and private benefits and therefore should continue to be funded by individuals and the state.[25] It assessed the public benefits in terms of the government's 'economic vision' of a growing 'competitive enterprise' economy and 'reducing unemployment'. In determining the public:private benefit balance, it argued that public benefits include economic growth, cultural development and social tolerance. The report concluded that a 25 per cent private and 75 per cent public funding split was appropriate and recommended that any future change to this ratio would require a full analysis of the risks involved. Members of the MCG voiced equity concerns, such as the differing abilities of families to support student members.[26] Their views divided between the need to address these inequities directly or not.[27] The Todd Report noted that Smith's SRS threatened the government's stated goal of encouraging lifelong learning by discriminating against older students and recommended its disestablishment.[28]

The Treasury's briefing paper to the incoming Coalition Government in 1996 advocated further refinements to the CPR approach.[29] It advised policy changes to ensure that private tertiary institutions competed with the existing public ones. Government funding should be levelled across the sector, giving increased competition and student choice. Treasury also proposed enhanced monitoring and closer management of government funding to ensure 'value for money'. Many of these proposals appeared in the tertiary memorandum leaked into the public domain in July 1997. The same document proposed the introduction of that old favourite of the New Right think tanks, the transferable education voucher, and argued that 'increased competition would improve the level of innovation and responsiveness to student needs and place a downward pressure on prices'.[30] Closely paralleling the NZBR's emphasis on market competition, the Ministry of Education and the Treasury endorsed market-oriented reforms and yet also insisted upon closer scrutiny by the government as 'owner' of educational assets and purchaser of educational products.

The Coalition Government released its Green Paper, *A Future Tertiary Education Policy for New Zealand: Tertiary Education Review*, in September 1997.[31] It dealt with funding and tuition costs for students, the funding and assessment of research, regulation and quality assurance, ownership and organisational form and issues relating to governance and accountability. It fostered a competitive market by supporting the end of the autonomy of the universities in awarding degrees by recommending that all degrees be recognised by the NZQA. Beyond faith in the market and the belief that competition must generate benefits in price and quality there were no guidelines for what would constitute effective competition between public and private tertiary providers.

In November 1998, the Tertiary White Paper, *Tertiary Education in New Zealand: Policy Directions for the 21st Century*, was released.[32] It proposed a new Universal Tertiary Tuition Allowance

(UTTA) to subsidise costs for students enrolled in approved courses and provided for Private Training Establishments (PTEs) to receive identical funding subsidies as public tertiary institutions, beginning in 2000. Consistent with New Right dogma, this was an attempt to create a competitive tertiary market and effectively subsidised PTEs at the expense of public tertiary institutions. This led to government support of profit-making opportunities for entrepreneurs.

The lack of consistent principles is evident in relation to governance. The draft legislation mandated that the CEOs be members of the governing bodies of tertiary institutions, overturning the Green Paper's earlier recommendation that CEOs be removed from councils. The same White Paper recommended the reduction of university councils from 12–20 to 7–12 members, appointed on the basis of 'expertise' in order to increase 'efficiency' and 'effectiveness'. It also recommended that the number of 'internal stakeholders', that is, students and staff, be reduced and that a majority of councillors be 'external' to the tertiary institution. Betraying a suspicion of academics and students, these proposals promoted a shift in power from the members of the institution to the business community and ministerial appointees.

The proposed legislation re-designated universities and other public tertiary institutions as 'Crown companies'. In return for taking on an even greater degree of business risk by assuming greater responsibility for 'their' assets, tertiary institutions would be required to pay a capital charge for the use of 'their' public resources. The White Paper, repeating the Green Paper, insisted that public tertiary institutions must achieve particular levels of returns on their assets, as if the monies had been invested in the marketplace. In addition, financial reporting requirements and quasi-external financial monitoring were to be intensified. Tertiary institutions were to be reassigned from the fifth to the sixth schedule of the Public Finance Act 1989 and thus required to submit for Ministry approval not only a charter but a detailed Statement of Intent with performance targets. Each institution would be required to meet the financial performance levels determined by the Tertiary Ownership Monitoring Unit. The Minister acquired new powers of intervention, including the assumption of direct control when an institution was held by the Ministry to be at risk.

Following the Hawke Report's recommendation for the de-coupling of teaching and research, the White Paper opened the way for teaching-only institutions and full research universities. The White Paper provided a rationale for this change. It would lower the barriers to entry and thus increase access to tertiary education while at the same time significantly reducing costs by removing the costs of research at most tertiary institutions. Research funding, which had previously been a proportion of all EFTS income, was to be withdrawn and set aside as a contestable pool. Institutions would bid for funding, on the basis of targeted research, which it defined as 'advanced, high quality research with a strong strategic focus'.[33] This fund was to start at 20 per cent of research income, rising over a number of years to 80 per cent.

The breaking of the research–teaching nexus galvanised opposition from the NZVCC and academic university staff. These critics argued that the international standing of New Zealand universities would be compromised and that the proposal would create an unprecedented degree of government, or other agency, control over research undertaken in New Zealand. The NZVCC reiterated university opposition to the divorce of research and teaching.[34] These Coalition educational policies allowed the proliferation of new courses of study, particularly by new providers in the areas of high demand. This led to the duplication of programmes and a lowering of entry standards for many courses. The capping of EFTS created internal competition between and within public tertiary institutions. When the EFTS cap was removed in 1998, this encouraged an even more dramatic increase in courses seeking government EFTS funding, while the problem of quality was largely left to the consumer and the provider to determine.

Commenting on educational reform in New Zealand in 2003, Gary Hawke claimed that few of those involved in education desired a return to the pre-1984 situation. This is undoubtedly true but hardly a useful test of the efficacy of the reforms or a validation of them.[35] Looking back on those feverish fifteen years it is clear that many of the same issues are still being addressed and that few lasting solutions were found. There are ongoing concerns about school leavers and their preparedness for the workforce, Maori and Pacific attainment levels and increasing participation in the tertiary sector. The reforms also created a series of new concerns over the quality of courses, particularly private courses at the tertiary level. The high and increasing levels of student debt are also a growing concern. A few theoretical principles drove the educational reforms: that competition lowers costs; that costs should be split between the funder and the provider; and that the market will deliver quality education at the lowest possible cost. Access to tertiary education did increase although with compromises in quality. In the terms set by the reformers, the promised results have just not materialised. The Ministry has also grown in size and budget as have the other government-funded educational agencies.

The levels and costs of compliance have greatly increased and the Coalition Government in 1999 was as interventionist and controlling as pre-reform governments. The nature of this control, however, is different. First, there is what Nicholas Rose calls 'governmentality', that is, the introduction of new forms of total governance across the educational sectors. These new modes of accountability have dramatically changed the management of every educational institution and their internal structures to ensure heightened levels of central control. This has taken place despite a rhetoric of greater institutional autonomy and consumer choice. Secondly, these New Right new accountabilities, measured in dollars and outputs, under CPR have shifted the entrepreneurial and enterprising risks and responsibilities to the providers. The New Right reform of education in New Zealand has yet to demonstrate all of the promised benefits. It certainly has not produced the enhancements of quality that were predicted nor the dramatic lowering of costs. In terms of new rights, the involvement of parents and communities has succeeded in creating a more participatory and democratic educational system, particularly at the school level. The provision of pre-school education has reached new groups of children. Education is certainly less monocultural than it was in the early 1980s for all New Zealand students. Access to tertiary education has improved. These are genuine achievements, although they could have occurred outside of the CPR framework. In fact, these successes appear to have occurred, not because of the market, but in spite of the imposition of market mechanisms.

We now have an educational system where market imperatives, managerial systems and moral conflicts persist often without recognition of the underlying source of the tensions. Well-intentioned teachers and entrepreneurial institutions develop curricula that explicitly or implicitly endorse the logic of commodification. Students learn to think of themselves as consumers and future executives; universities seek to market their educational products and the public alternately bemoans and applauds the results. Debates about whether consumers should dictate the price and quality of education emerge alongside laments about falling standards and inadequate controls by bureaucrats and the government. Parents and politicians celebrate 'consumer choice' as a supreme virtue while also insisting that the government intervene where the market fails to deliver. Simultaneously condemning the lack of competition and warning about the loss of educational rigour, the New Right and its political allies continue to advocate market forces in education while denouncing their inevitable consequences.

PART FIVE

Deuteronomy: Saving Us from Corruption

*They have corrupted themselves, their spot is not
the spot of his children: they are a perverse and
crooked generation. Do ye thus requite the LORD,
O foolish people and unwise? is not he thy father
that hath bought thee? hath he not made thee and
established thee?* DEUTERONOMY 32:5–6

CHAPTER TEN

The Restoration of Virtue

And the Levite, (because he hath no part nor inheritance with thee,) and the stranger and the fatherless and the widow, which are within thy gates, shall come and shall eat and be satisfied; that the LORD thy God may bless thee in all the work of thine hand which thou doest. DEUTERONOMY 14:29

In the 1970s our welfare state expanded through the introduction of the DPB and, in 1975, a generous superannuation system. Almost as soon as that legislation was passed, however, an attack was under way against DPB beneficiaries. Bert Walker, the Minister of Social Welfare, described DPB recipients as 'bludgers living off the state', while Prime Minister Muldoon speculated that they preferred the overly generous DPB to honourable marriage or honest work. At exactly the same time, the US New Right and its British counterpart began a welfare reform offensive, blaming poverty on individual behaviour and personal morality. In all three societies, a moral rectification project was under way.[1] As this chapter will show, these attacks were more than simple coincidence. The evolving New Right network transmitted moral arguments through the circuits linking us to Australia, Britain and the United States.

In the view of our New Right disciplinarians, we needed moral rectification. Many of us had been corrupted by prolonged exposure to a 'welfarist' mentality. In contrast to the 'dual' US welfare state of 'good' benefits earned by wage-earners or veterans and 'bad' benefits bestowed on the non-working poor, we had been overly cosseted in a welfare system that provided far more generous universal benefits than the minimalist US system. Our welfare state system had extended its tentacles to almost every citizen while failing to stigmatise the recipients as thoroughly as the US had done. All of us received the benefits of 'socialised medicine', a system that the US New Right had successfully defeated whenever it had been proposed. An overwhelming majority of us attended public school, thus 'capturing' welfare benefits for the middle and upper class. We attended public universities, often supported by the government and thus committed the sin of 'churning' by receiving benefits for which we then paid taxes to finance them. Mothers received a family benefit. Many of us had drunk subsidised milk and had our teeth drilled in government-run 'houses of pain'. We often worked in government enterprises. Arbitration fixed our wages. In contrast to the Americans we could receive the dole even if we had never worked and keep on receiving it long past the six months' time limit imposed in the American system. Subsidies supported 'private' businesses and licences controlled imports. In short, we had experienced the moral degradation of 'cradle-to-grave security'. Only by breaking the apron strings that tied us to the 'nanny state' could we become 'moral, thinking beings'. Would we accept the necessary discipline and embrace self-reliance?[2]

Our New Right, like its counterparts in the US, Britain and Australia, set about this task determined to free us from 'modern collectivism', which its spokesmen rightly saw as their 'biggest challenge'. Those dedicated to scraping away the 'corrosive effects of welfare' focused on the problems of 'dependency', illegitimacy and solo-parent families that inevitably came from a welfare state that interfered 'with the natural order of things'. Words and phrases like decency, personal responsibility, the 'work ethic' and the 'moral hazards' of benefits featured in government policies, public debates and media commentary. As the *New York Times* claimed in an article discussing our 'embrace of market discipline', we acted like 'an antipodean echo of a worldwide phenomenon'. This new enthusiasm for 'market discipline' meant that all of us must give priority to efficiency, productivity and profit, the cardinal virtues of the market. Seeing the welfare state as a major obstacle to the development of 'bourgeois' values and virtues, our New Right went to work to 'roll back' that impediment to our moral reform.[3]

Our erstwhile moral tutors, often ensconced in Treasury in the early 1980s, took cues from the British New Right's celebration of self-reliance, thrift, prudence, industriousness and other Victorian 'virtues' predating the welfare state, the values essential to the restoration of the 'enterprise society'. Linked think tanks, the IEA in Britain, the CIS in Australia and the NZBR, circulated blueprints for our remoralisation. The essential arguments, drawn from an eclectic mix of 'Protestant ethic', public choice, monetarist and neoclassical economics, can be found in *Economic Management*. A fuller version appeared in *Government Management* as Treasury economists and ex-officials in the private sector pressed for reforming the welfare system as the next important stage of our New Right transformation.[4]

The New Right intended to reverse the expansion of rights and welfare programmes that had occurred in the British welfare state, in the US 'war on poverty' and welfare rights movement of the 1960s and, in our case, as a result of the reports of the Royal Commission in 1972 that advanced the right to full participation in a mass consumer society. These policies and our increasing immersion in so-called 'rights discourse' alarmed New Right moralists concerned that this insidious language of 'entitlement' might hinder their efforts to restore the 'primacy of the market'. Sharing Hayek's disdain for the 'mirage of social justice', they embarked on a moral restoration project to teach us to think as consumers, taxpayers and entrepreneurs.[5]

These New Right efforts were aided by the results of the reforms already implemented. The old 'informal welfare state' based on the regulation of wages and the labour market together with protection for local manufacturing had disappeared in the flurry of economic reforms. From the floating of the dollar and replacement of protected employment with 'pure market forms' to the removal of tariffs, the elimination of subsidies and the introduction of 'enterprise' models, New Right reforms had eliminated the props that sustained a system that sceptical economists called 'disguised unemployment'. The disappearance of publicly financed 'full employment' and regulatory weapons meant increased pressure on our benefit system that it had never been designed to confront. Lange's establishment of the Royal Commission on Social Policy in 1986 clearly intended to produce a 'social justice' answer to this problem, signalling to our New Right reformers that they must deliver a 'full market' solution instead.[6]

Already integrated into a transnational network, our New Right could import experts and 'off the shelf' solutions from the US, Australia and Britain. Neoconservative journals with their ongoing critique of the welfare state could be found in our university libraries. The scholarly outputs of US and British New Right think tanks and conservative foundations circulated through the New Right network and could be cited by sympathetic journalists and reform-minded politicians. Economic journals supplied arguments to Treasury economists interested in eliminating expensive programmes and replacing public service time-wasters with an efficient contractual regime.

Books by New Right intellectuals were an important resource to our reformers. In 1984, Charles Murray's *Losing Ground: American Social Policy 1950–1980* attacked anti-poverty programmes in the US and disputed the principle of 'social' citizenship. According to Murray, welfare programmes had perversely increased poverty and demoralised the poor. He accused the welfare system of rewarding the irresponsibility of the 'individual' recipients of benefits and encouraging unmarried motherhood, crime and other forms of deviant behaviour. Shifting the public debate from poverty to welfare dependency, the New Right network secured maximum publicity for this attack on the concept of public responsibility for welfare provision. Two years later Lawrence Mead's *Beyond Entitlement* argued for the imposition of obligations upon welfare recipients in an explicit form of 'paternalism' that required the poor to work as a way to reform their characters. The influential Heritage, linked to IEA, CIS and our NZBR, gave Stuart Butler major responsibility for developing its welfare reform package. Transmitted by books, media reports and visits from ideological entrepreneurs, these New Right critiques of welfare appeared in Treasury briefing papers, NZBR reports, CIS publications and, frequently, in our daily newspapers.[7]

Britain, undergoing its own version of New Right reform, exported a version of this moral restoration project. Thatcher claimed that the welfare state had 'demoralised communities and families' by substituting 'dependency' for independence and by rejecting 'traditional values'. Acknowledging her own debt to Murray, she also defended 'Victorian virtues' and stressed the need to restore the 'self-discipline' of the 'undeserving' poor. Income-tested benefits displaced universal benefits, with an emphasis on 'targeting' that appealed to Treasury economists interested in cutting expenditure while avoiding 'poverty traps'. The IEA, the CPS and the ASI sought to devolve responsibility for their own welfare upon individuals and families. Still maintaining a more generous welfare state than the US, these British reform initiatives encouraged our New Right to use the same arguments and implement the same policies.[8]

Government Management agreed with this imported critique of the welfare state. Treasury wanted to limit the government to defining 'a clear set of rights' that encouraged 'individuals to voluntarily transact between one another in order to pursue their own well-being'. Smith's 'invisible hand' allocated rewards and punished the lazy or incompetent. Bureaucrats should neither interfere with the market nor rescue people from the consequences of their own failures.[9] Intent on rebuilding our characters using this moral blueprint, the NZBR led by ex-Treasury economist Kerr watched as Lange and Douglas came to blows over the future of our welfare state. As the Lange–Douglas partnership dissolved, our New Right advocates began to look elsewhere for political allies to undertake our moral reformation.

Eager to take advantage of the government disarray, Richardson quickly demonstrated that she agreed with the need for moral reform. The Shadow Minister of Social Welfare pointed to the sad consequences of welfare dependency. Interviewed in the *NBR*, she explained her position. According to Richardson, an equitable society was based upon giving us the opportunity to 'exercise choice' rather than through a generous welfare state. Her goal was to 'match the market economy with market culture', an 'enterprise culture' which includes 'standing on one's feet'. Faithfully reciting the arguments made by American and British critics of dependency, Richardson offered herself as an eager New Right disciple anxious to teach us market discipline.

Objecting to teenage mothers' receipt of the DPB, Richardson explained, 'My view is that there should be no automatic payment'. If the 'child parent can't make family arrangements to look after the infant', she recommended adoption as a 'viable option'. Perhaps recognising that she might be labelled as cold-hearted, she declared herself as 'an advocate for the vulnerable', which she insisted was the child, rather than the mother. 'I will not salve my conscience by simply paying money', she told the *NBR*.[10] Richardson continued to build her connections to the New Right network as she waited expectantly for the Labour Government to collapse.

A month after Richardson's interview appeared in print, Murray arrived under the auspices of the CIS to share his insights into 'The American Experience with the Welfare State' in both New Zealand and Australia. He spoke at a Wellington conference attended by prominent politicians, businessmen and government officials exploring 'the intellectual foundations of the welfare state'. The participants discussed ways to combat 'dependency' and prevent the 'political capture' of welfare policies by self-serving bureaucrats. According to Murray and other speakers, state-provided welfare deprived 'individuals of the personal challenges that give meaning to their lives'.[11] Murray's ability to repeat existing beliefs satisfied his hosts. Certain that the next election offered the opportunity to put these plans into action, the New Right endorsed aspiring leaders like Richardson.

The claims that the welfare state rested 'on morally flawed foundations' justified cuts to welfare programmes as beneficial to the recipients and soothed any scruples the public might feel. The requirement to seek a low-wage job completed the moral instruction. Soft-hearted members of the public must realise that the welfare system impaired everyone's moral constitution by discouraging private charity and direct personal assistance to help the 'deserving' poor. Later encapsulated by the term 'compassionate conservatism', these reassuring messages countered critics who wailed about overly harsh benefit cuts or accused the New Right of 'beneficiary bashing'. Mingling pro-market liberalism and moral conservatism, this blend of reassurance and stern discipline bore the hallmarks of the hybrid version of New Right ideology brought to us by neoconservatives like Murray, Mead, Novak, Sirico and Epstein.[12]

Among the keywords in this moralising interpretation of the welfare system was the concept of 'dependency' that established wage earning and market participation as the only valid definition of adult status. Often ignoring the work involved in motherhood, this discourse insisted that families must be supported through participation in the market by at least one parent. Traced back to an earlier period where political rights could be exercised only by property-owners who thus possessed the requisite 'independence', this pejorative notion of 'dependence' had once been applied to all persons kept in a state of permanent non-adulthood – wives, servants, the poor, children, slaves and apprentices. Updating this usage, New Right spokesmen described 'dependency' as an 'incomplete state of life'. Conversely, 'completed men and women stand on their own feet'. Now adapting their rhetoric to a 'post-feminist era', they insisted that women must display the same 'independence' that had once been reserved for male property owners. This attack on dependency, however, paid no attention to the actual consequences of motherhood, the costs of childcare and low wages on women's ability to 'stand on their own feet'. Since this usage evolved at the same time as widespread discussions of the dangers of drug addition, 'dependency' acquired another negative connotation. Passing through the New Right circuit, this keyword appeared in news reports, speeches and research, especially in the *NBR* and NZBR publications.[13]

Murray's visit occurred at precisely the strategic moment when the Labour Government, re-elected earlier in the year, had begun to address the social issues neglected during its first term. Anxious to deliver on the social dividend promised his supporters after the 'pain' of the reforms, Lange now confronted New Right proposals for cutbacks that envisaged the creation of the 'minimalist' American model.[14] Although the Royal Commission on Social Policy was still inquiring into the 'goals, values and principles' of social policy in a reconstructed welfare state, the New Right wanted to deconstruct that state rather than allow it to be reformed.[15] Murray's visit was thus an effort to short-circuit the Royal Commission's report from influencing our attitudes about the 'welfare burden'.

Speaking on behalf of the CIS, Alan Gibbs, who attended an MPS conference that same year with Upton and Jenny Gibbs, plunged into the debate, repeating Murray's arguments. According to Gibbs, 'the welfare system is flawed' because it operated on the basis of 'entitlement' and not 'incentive'. Gibbs claimed that the 'state system' had destroyed a vibrant civic 'support system'. Remote, 'impersonal' bureaucrats deprived people of a 'sense of personal responsibility for others'. The 'Rogernomes' in Labour and National's New Right faction eagerly endorsed Gibbs's arguments. They opposed a 'rights-based' welfare policy that treated the poor as citizens entitled to support. Instead, the poor must work their way out of poverty with only a minimalist 'safety net' for those unable to support themselves.[16]

Words and phrases like opportunity, 'enterprise culture', the 'morally bankrupt' welfare state, warnings of 'moral hazards' and concerns about 'middle class capture' conveyed these views to the readers of our newspapers. The press published reports about welfare 'bludgers' and fraudsters in our version of Reagan's exaggerated account of a Chicago 'welfare queen'. Sympathetic editors and journalists asked, in the case of the *New Zealand Herald*, if 'discrimination' against beneficiaries was 'necessarily such a bad thing'. Citing abuse of the benefit system, the *Herald* concluded that anti-beneficiary prejudice was preferable to the 'acceptance of dependence'. The *Press* wanted the 'work ethic' restored. One reporter moaned that he wanted to enjoy the 'luxury' of being 'underprivileged', while another described state support for abortions as rewarding 'irresponsible' sexual activity. A *Dominion* cartoon depicted an overburdened man labelled 'work force' being ridden by ACC, DPB, solo parents, sickness and unemployed beneficiaries to illustrate the accusation that beneficiaries exploited the hard-working taxpayer.[17]

The multi-volume report of the Royal Commission on Social Policy lay unread on library and office shelves as the Labour Government collapsed in the aftermath of the 1987 crash and internal strife. Richardson and her New Right colleagues eagerly anticipated their election to the Treasury benches as they heated up their rhetoric against the legacy of 'economic and social paternalism', which had deprived us of a 'sense of responsibility for our own destiny'. The welfare state had trapped us in a 'self-reinforcing cycle of dependence'. The New Right gained ascendancy in the National caucus as Richardson became the Shadow Minister of Finance and passed the Social Welfare portfolio to friend and confidante, Jenny Shipley. National's policy on welfare proposed to 'improve incentives' and usher in the 'Decent Society', drawing upon research from New Right think tanks. Journalists described the policy as 'getting tough on young solo parents' and encouraging beneficiaries out of the 'poverty trap'. Speaking about the need to restore 'moral capital', the National Party declared that a dose of 'self-discipline' could lift the 'underclass' out of its lethargy.[18] The New Right reform juggernaut was about ready to 'roll back' what remained of our welfare state.

Newly elected, Bolger announced the policy of 'stiff medicine', eliminating the universal family benefit and cutting other benefits, tightening eligibility and increasing health costs through user pays. These policies, he claimed, expressed the principles of 'fairness, self reliance, efficiency and greater personal choice'. Richardson advised the Wellington Chamber of Commerce of her intention to 'transform a dependency culture into an enterprise culture'. The severe slashing of benefit levels, retention of the surcharge on superannuation and the passage of the ECA ushered in a new 'contract' regime. Richardson told us of her intentions to produce moral reform and a change in our attitudes. 'Things will change because the Government will change the rules to change the attitudes.' She intended to instil a 'strong work ethic' by making it more difficult to survive on benefits and by reducing the ability of unions to raise wages. Richardson and 'soul-mate' Shipley proclaimed the need for a 'social revolution' from which the family might be 'reborn as the central economic unit'. Richardson assumed the image of the 'tough mother' by warning beneficiaries not to 'expect the state to nanny everyone'.[19]

Not all of us were willing to accept these reforms. The National Government and their New Right allies endured a torrent of criticism, particularly from the churches opposing the benefit cuts. Methodists and Anglicans denounced the 'creed of greed'. In early 1992 eleven churches prepared their *Social Justice Statement* asking the Government to give priority to the needs of the poor. They spoke about 'our responsibilities' to create a 'just social order'. Although this did not dissuade the Richardson and Shipley from pursuing welfare reform, the *Statement* urged us to think about the so-called 'structures of sin' that caused poverty and social exclusion according to the 'social justice' advocates.[20]

Disturbed about this challenge to the morality of their welfare reforms, the CIS sponsored Sirico's first visit in 1993 to provide a theological justification for free markets and the 'entrepreneurial vocation'. He characterised the *Social Justice Statement* as 'confused' and 'ill considered'. Instead of criticising New Right policies, churches should instruct the poor in thrift, industriousness and personal responsibility. The rich should offer charity to the poor but not be coerced by the state to redistribute their wealth through taxes to dispense morally hazardous state welfare. The CIS published Sirico's views to make sure that we had an opportunity to understand the market-compatible way to address the needs of the poor.[21]

As earlier discussed, this visit did not persuade all of us to accept New Right policies. Pension cuts and the retention of the surtax outraged superannuitants. Many of us expressed anger over user pays in health and education and the impact of the benefit cuts. We objected to language such as 'spill over' describing the 'residual' public benefit of education. This public anger, manifested by the passage of MMP, a drastic decline in National Party membership and its one-seat victory in 1993, did not stop the efforts to eliminate 'welfarism' despite Richardson's demotion. More visitors arrived, sponsored by the NZBR and CIS, to criticise 'welfare dependency' and urge us to support these reforms.[22]

In 1995 the CIS brought Novak from AEI and the NZBR brought Epstein. Novak defended capitalism as morally just. He praised welfare reform in the US and urged us to follow the New Right reform agenda. Epstein warned about the 'moral hazards' of welfare, unions and the 'socialisation' of education, suggesting that we should revert to the 'state of nature' in which families and charitable organisations supplied children's needs for education and income. He described the problems for orphans attendant on the death of parents as like those that came from the 'non-diversification of your portfolio'. Offering no suggestions as to how children could acquire additional parents to diversify their welfare investment, Epstein spoke about 'incentive', and the purchase of 'inputs' in a 'relatively efficient fashion' to describe how education and other services should be supplied through the market. Novak and Epstein's application of market logic to welfare, familial relationships, education and the legal system met with the approval of their New Right hosts but puzzled some of their listeners.[23]

Green in 1996 declared that 'the benefit system sends the wrong signals'. Kerr concurred with his British guest, pointing to the 'underclass' developing here and claiming that the welfare state had worn away our 'moral underpinnings'. Green lectured throughout New Zealand arguing for a 'welfare that works'. Green's book, *From Welfare to Civil Society*, summarised by the NZBR, circulated widely. Green reminded his readers of Murray's *Losing Ground* and Mead's *Beyond Entitlement* while bringing to our attention Marvin Olasky, another Acton associate and the moral tutor of Governor George W. Bush. According to Green, the welfare state had harmed 'those who need help but also the people capable of providing the assistance'. We must return to an 'older tradition' from before the welfare state, when charity was a 'personal duty' rather than a matter of 'politics'.[24]

Determined to eliminate the state from the provision of any social services, Green advocated the privatisation of hospitals, education and universities. He also wanted to lift the age for superannuation to seventy, thus requiring us to work for longer periods of our lives without any public assistance. Sceptics asked where we would find the time and energy to practise the 'moral virtue' of charity while engaged in the 'competitive market economy' he prescribed for us. One reviewer claimed that we might lack the time to donate to voluntary involvement and accused Green of being unable to tell the difference between his romantic fantasy of a 'perfect world' and the 'one that we actually live in'. Another critic objected to Green's 'rosy-hued' view of the pre-welfare-state Britain described in *Hard Times*, pointing out that New Zealand had been populated by refugees from Victorian England who obviously had not been as pleased as Green with the quality of life there.[25]

Although an Anglican bishop approved Green's preaching of 'old-fashioned virtues' and *NBR* praised his emphasis on the 'moral imperative of self-help, personal responsibility and independence', this applause was not universal. Critics wrote about 'dark Satanic mills', 'capitalism without a human face' and nineteenth century workhouses as 'symbols of an uncaring and punitive ruling class'. A sceptical Cardinal Thomas Williams concluded, 'The man's crazy!' He asked whether Green knew how much the 'churches and voluntary organisations are doing' and how his 'new moral order' could actually acquire the necessary resources. Suggesting that Green really wanted to restore an obsolete 'moral order', Rosemary McLeod mocked him as a 'good Victorian patriarch' worried about rescuing 'fallen women'. One critic pointed to the 1950s, when 'dependency was all but universal', to disprove Green's claims about the corrosive effects of the welfare state on the 'work ethic' since employment was high during that period and crime was low. Another described him as a 'neo-rightist' trying to turn the 'clock back' instead of recognising that state welfare has 'improved the lot of the disadvantaged'.[26] Clearly Green had struck a nerve by straying beyond 'beneficiary bashing' to try to reform us all.

Despite this flurry of criticism, Green's visit heralded a renewal of the universal moral rectification project. Our unwillingness to work harder, retire later, pay for our own health, fund our children's education, nurse the sick, tend the dying and care for the downtrodden suggested that we needed a stronger dose of moral exhortation. After the 1996 MMP election, the Coalition Government received a briefing from Bazley's Department of Social Welfare (DSW) advising the new Cabinet on how to create a 'virtuous' society.[27] In the next few years many more visitors arrived to lecture about moral values, market efficiency and personal responsibility.

We were not alone in this emphasis on moral restoration. In the US the New Right, including its strong Christian membership, emphasised the role of religion in accordance with Olasky's *Tragedy of American Compassion* and Sirico's insistence on 'faith-based' charity instead of state-funded social welfare. According to Olasky, government programmes turned compassion into a destructive force. The US New Right blamed welfare and 'political correctness' for illegitimacy, crime and family breakdown. Only faith-based charity could convert the poor to the moral behaviour that freed people from poverty through marriage, hard work and self-discipline. Here, however, the New Right faced difficulties in applying a 'faith-based' solution because of the conflicts between the New Right and the churches. Journalistic allies of the New Right complained about the 'shrill polemic' emanating from church welfare agencies and accused them of espousing 'dripping wet liberalism'. Columnist Agnes-Mary Brooke described the churches as joining the 'infantilised queues demanding that the Government solve problems'. Such comments put our New Right into an ideological quandary as to how charity could be dispensed once that 'voracious monster' called the welfare state had been killed.[28]

Trying to sustain their reform agenda, our New Right looked to the US for inspiration. In 1996, President Clinton signed into law the Personal Responsibility and Work Opportunity Reconciliation Act, ending welfare 'as we know it'. The new legislation set lifetime limits for welfare benefits, financed incentives for marriage, provided for faith-based delivery and transferred funding to the states. The Coalition Government wanted us to follow this example by moving 'away from a welfare mentality to a greater acceptance of social obligations'. Wisconsin was its new inspiration, a reformist utopia where 'welfare dependency' was trending down through a workfare programme. Doing its part, the *NBR* published an essay from the *Wall Street Journal*, blaming the welfare state for having created a 'spiritual crisis', destroyed the family and spread 'social pathologies'.[29]

A month later DSW sponsored a conference with support from Electronic Data Systems, an economic beneficiary of welfare reform in the US. The 'Beyond Dependency' conference featured Mead as one of the major speakers with Jean Rogers, the head of the Wisconsin welfare programme. Rogers spoke about the requirements to work for unemployment benefits and for mothers to find work when their children had reached twelve weeks of age. Describing the Wisconsin reforms, she told her audience that 'adults in many ways are grown-up children. They like a little direction and to know what the boundaries are as well.' There should be no sense of 'entitlement' to welfare benefits, she told us. To remove incentives, the Wisconsin programme refused to increase benefits for larger families. Wisconsin state officials had turned the welfare state into a 'stern parent' rather than a benevolent 'nanny', to Rogers's evident satisfaction.[30]

Presenting himself as one of the key intellectual architects of the 'new paternalism', Mead spoke about 'working-age adults' as the 'core of the social problem' without mentioning that most of them were mothers with dependent children. The 'culture of poverty' could be overcome by enforcing the duty to work on all adults. Poor people must be required to 'function in improving ways'. He referred to Murray's *Losing Ground* and claimed success for welfare reform in the US in achieving the goal of abolishing 'dependency'. Mead applauded the focus on morality, marriage and 'personal responsibility'.[31]

The NZBR contributed to the concerted drive for welfare reform. NZBR brought Kris Mauren from Acton and Sister Connie Driscoll. A year later, Sirico returned to discuss not only the Code of Social Responsibility but welfare reform. Depicted in the media as a welfare-knowledgeable nun and priest, Driscoll and Sirico countered the criticisms from our churches. Driscoll labelled welfare a form of social insanity. At her programme in Chicago she provided support only to poor women who lived up to her rigorous moral standards. Having testified before Congress about the need for 'faith-based' organisations, Sirico argued that our welfare system should be abolished to enable churches, charities and individuals to take care of the poor. Complaining about the hostile response from churches and university students, Driscoll and Sirico appeared unable to convince the churches or many of the public of the desirability of relying upon faith, hope and charity to alleviate poverty.[32]

ACT joined in the praise for the Wisconsin reforms. Newman, the ACT spokeswoman on welfare, told the readers of *NBR* and *North & South* about the successes of the Wisconsin workfare policies, based on her brief visit to that state. Later Tommy Thompson, the governor credited with the Wisconsin reforms, chatted to Kim Hill about the 'success story' that ultimately secured him a place in the Bush Cabinet during its first term. Taking credit for the reforms, Thompson did not mention the support received from the Hudson Institute who designed the legislation, the funding from the Bradley Foundation or the contributions of the local New Right think tank in lobbying for his programme. He also did not mention the influence of outside influences upon state elections. Like Driscoll's association with Acton, parts of the story of Wisconsin's welfare reform 'success' did not appear in commentary by ACT or our American visitors.[33]

Advocates of 'new rights' attempted to be heard in the midst of the moralistic clamour about dependency. New Right opponents organised a 'Beyond Poverty' conference, timed to coincide with the 'Beyond Dependency' conference. This group argued that poverty, exacerbated by benefit cuts and harsh DSW policies, rather than dependency, was the issue that needed to be addressed. One participant warned us to beware the 'powerful system of mutually reinforcing myths' being circulated through New Zealand by the speakers at the 'Beyond Dependency' conference and our other New Right visitors. The so-called 'independent individual' was a New Right myth. Anne Else pointed to the benefits of welfare provisions in alleviating poverty, while Mike O'Brien traced the origins of the focus on 'dependency' back to false distinctions between the deserving and undeserving poor.[34]

Not discouraged by these critics, Bazley welcomed the New Right visitors. She saw her mission as encouraging people to become self-sufficient in a policy shift called 'from welfare to well being'. She wanted to 'contribute to the goals of economic growth and social cohesion', visiting Wisconsin and Washington to study US policies.[35] Riding on a wave of media enthusiasm for these initiatives, the Coalition Government introduced a bill to cut benefits to people who turned down job interviews. Editors agreed on the need to 'free people from dependency'. Using verbs like 'cure' to transform 'welfare dependency' into the verbal equivalent of an addiction, editors like Long of the *Dominion* praised Bazley for organising the conference and Sister Connie for her message of 'tough love' to wean women away from welfare.[36] Aided by the favourable publicity, the DSW reorganised into a workfare-oriented 'Work and Incomes New Zealand' or 'WINZ'.

When introduced, the Government moderated the Wisconsin model to the extent that DPB beneficiaries were not forced to take on part-time work until their child reached the age of five or find fulltime work until the child reached fourteen. Counter-attacking, the Labour Opposition complained about the 'Victorian approach to social security, with its echoes of the poorhouse', criticised policies that emphasised 'punishment' and described the Wisconsin scheme as 'cruel'. Accusations of 'turning back the clock' and 'blaming victims for their own demoralisation' countered the moralising discourse of the New Right. Critics asked, 'Is it moral to force people to work?' Impressed by this vigorous response, New Right arch-critic Kelsey described us as having emerged 'from the paralysis induced by the blitzkrieg of the past 12 years' and becoming aware that New Right doctrines were neither 'economic truth' nor 'immutable'.[37]

Some of these criticisms of the welfare reforms may have stemmed from our reaction to another Coalition Government initiative, the ill-fated Code of Social Responsibility. Intending to drive home the New Right lessons of 'personal responsibility', the authors of the code had tried to speak the language of 'social obligations'. Peters, the Deputy Prime Minister, announced the intention to reform the 'dysfunctional' welfare family, but his National Party colleague Sowry emphasised that the code addressed all of us. As interpreted by Jane Clifton in the *Listener*, the Coalition Government's proposal to cut benefits for 'bad' parents meant that it was alternating between two versions of the state: the 'avenging nanny' and a softer version that encouraged good behaviour, the 'interfering auntie'. Shipley's ascension as Prime Minister reinforced the harsher image of the Government as a moralistic scold trying to make us conform to her moral precepts. Less than 10 per cent of us responded to the discussion document for the proposed code. Surprisingly, the Government headed by a New Right politician acquired the almost unshakeable negative stereotype of the 'nanny state' in its efforts to pursue welfare reform while appealing to 'middle New Zealand'.[38]

Aware of this threat to their goals, the reformers tried to narrow the focus. Newman assailed the DPB as 'anti-family, anti-marriage and anti-work'. A CIS researcher complained about the inflation of 'rights' as undermining personal responsibility. Australian James Cox, writing a report for the NZBR, suggested that we adopt the US model of workfare to move our beneficiaries towards 'personal independence' and prosperity. At the ACT conference Sirico declared that the poor needed a 'good kick' to restore their self-respect. Sirico and ACT denounced the concept of 'social responsibility' as contrary to their goal of restoring 'personal' responsibility. The media endorsed the work-focused WINZ programme, but no one appeared able to rescue the Coalition Government from the 'strategic muddle' of the code and its own internal conflicts as the Coalition came unhinged.[39]

Continuing its challenge to the New Right, the churches spoke out again in the name of social justice. The Anglican Church sponsored the Hikoi of Hope, chanting 'enough is enough' in a phrase destined to be used against another target a few years later. The Hikoi travelled through New Zealand from September to December 1998.[40] Juxtaposing one moral vision against another, this spectacle effectively spelled the end of the New Right campaign for welfare reform and the Government's misbegotten code. It was also the beginning of the end for our position as an official laboratory for New Right experiments. Unable to claim exclusive possession of the concept of 'moral' and forced to use the term 'social' rather than 'personal', the Government had already conceded the difficulties of persuading us to follow the American example in welfare reform.

This episode clearly shows the activities of the New Right network operating to achieve welfare reform. A New Right coalition – politicians, government officials, editors, think tanks, organisations, ideological missionaries – engaged in a twelve-year moral rectification project. Enjoying success in the early 1990s, this coalition never dominated our political system without challenge, particularly from 'social justice' advocates. These New Right 'moral reformers' preached a form of market morality designed to turn us into self-reliant competitors and, in our leisure hours, charitably inclined compassionate conservatives. Ignoring the conflict between these two moral models of self-interest and altruism, these moral entrepreneurs also faced a determined opposition. Partly based in the churches, but also including other New Zealanders who thought in terms of 'social responsibility' and 'social justice', this opposition ultimately exposed the contradiction between New Right 'freedom' and its moralistic 'underpinnings'. This group of 'new rights' advocates intervened to stop the march to the New Right Promised Land.

PART SIX

Beyond Myths and Market Morality

*And the LORD said unto him, This is the land
which I sware unto Abraham, unto Isaac and
unto Jacob, saying, I will give it unto thy seed: I
have caused thee to see it with thine eyes, but thou
shalt not go over thither.* DEUTERONOMY 34:4

CHAPTER ELEVEN

New Rights New Zealand:
Myths, Moralities and Markets

*And all that handle the oar, the mariners and all the
pilots of the sea, shall come down from their ships,
they shall stand upon the land.* EZEKIEL 27:29

No man is an island, intire of it selfe. JOHN DONNE,
DEVOTIONS

Lest we create our own myths about our virtues, it is time to pause
and reflect. We stayed on the march towards the Promised Land for
fifteen years, a tribute either to our slavish deference to our leaders
or the clever exercise of power by small overlapping elites. Perhaps
these leaders understood our hopes and our fears. They spoke in
a familiar language that resonated with some of our values. As
experienced seafarers, we may agree with those leaders who loudly
insist that everyone should 'man' the oars and that no one deserves a
free ride. This may be why we sometimes jumped at the opportunity
to point accusing fingers at beneficiaries or other 'bludgers'. We
sometimes appeared willing to toss some people overboard to lighten
our own load. Our prison system boasted the second-highest rate
of imprisonment in the world, lagging only behind the US. Despite
adverse Maori statistics, the claims of 'special privilege' for Maori
often evoke a positive response from the non-Maori population.
Many of the victories for 'new rights' have been achieved through
incredibly narrow margins after considerable drama and ferocious
debate. Are we really more compassionate than our American,
Australian or British counterparts?

And yet, we are different in an important way, even if the claim
of our moral superiority is questionable. Currently we are diverging
away from the New Right direction being taken by our trans-

Tasman and trans-Pacific neighbours. Equality, however deformed by pettiness or envy, is one of our principles as a small society. We cannot aim for world domination or even for the privilege of being Uncle Sam's nephew, so our goals may be more modest as befits the pessimism of a small nation. Our history avoids grand adventures or heroic battle scenes. We talk of our wars through tragic massacres and strategic miscalculations in which we have acted as imperial pawns. Maybe in some ways this sort of anti-heroic mythic past makes us less prone to utopian fantasies, nationalist hubris or abstract visions. Our alternatives are most often our famed pragmatism, a kind of improvised making-do. Douglas and the Treasury officials operated only on the basis of the very broadest New Right principles. Much of the implementation of New Right policies was *ad hoc* and opportunistic. Even our ideologues were pragmatists. This proved to be the principal strength and weakness of our New Right.

We may also lack the same intense insecurity that is the other side of ambition for power. The very target of New Right reforms, the welfare state, underpinned this security and gave us 'cradle-to-grave' protection. Why would we trade that away for some promised freedom in the 'never-never', many of us may have asked. Without that insecurity, we may not need to rely upon an authoritative book, the abstract purity of dogma, the insistence on infallible authority, rigid doctrines and the certainty that comes from having it all written down in a sacred text. Even our truncated welfare state offers us a degree of security and certainty that appears to make us less susceptible to prophets armed with such texts. In fact, we may refuse to listen to them. Perhaps this helps to explain why we took a 'left turn' in 1999.

Our experience of New Right reform over a decade and a half has thus provided the foundation for our current experiment with 'Third Way' pragmatic politics. New Zealand's evident need for structural reform in the 1980s has been widely accepted but the methods for achieving those changes continue to be questioned. Parallel developments in Australia suggest that a more graduated approach might well have achieved the same ends without the social turmoil and disruption. During the 1980s and 1990s the recognition of the fragility of New Zealand in the global economy became almost inescapable. Our dependence on exports and the fluctuating international value of our currency has highlighted the need for us to remain globally competitive, but this competitiveness depends on government policies and direction. At the same time, we learned that we do not respond very positively to moral exhortation, moral disciplining or the politics of exclusion as the means to increase our individual and collective productivity. This has renewed our support for New Zealand's traditions of the provision of statutory welfare, health and education as the most effective way of ensuring our survival in the global economy.

This study of our New Right as a moral enterprise ends, as our title suggests, with the recognition that we experienced several New Rights because of different ways of conceiving of the relationship between morality and markets. Moral conservatives and pro-market activists found it difficult to create a political coalition like the American 'New Right'. Many politically powerful 'New Right' activists in New Zealand espoused a liberal or libertarian approach to both markets and sexual freedom, in strong contrast to the US where there was and is a coincidence of support for market freedoms and sexual constraints. The Labour Party, with its feminist and gay activists, could not consummate such an alliance here. Just as importantly, our New Zealand moral conservatives resembled the 'extreme' American right wing in their objections to the 'new world order' and big business. This alienated them from both the National Party and its corporate supporters such as the NZBR. So, unlike the New Right coalitions of moral conservatives and market liberals in the US, Britain and now taking shape in Australia, New Zealand's religious right remained separate from the pro-market New Right.

By failing to provide convincing proof of their electoral power, our moral conservatives offered little reason for the National Party to risk alienating its own individualist feminist contingent, led by Richardson, Shipley and O'Regan, who were committed to individual freedoms for men and women. This prevented the possibility of a workable coalition over issues of sexual morality and 'family values'. The current National Party leadership no longer displays this same commitment to individualist feminism, thus opening up the possibility of an American-style moral–market coalition. This parallels the strategy adopted by United Future, New Zealand First and ACT. The Maxim Institute, founded in 2001, is actively promoting this sort of strategic alliance of moral conservatives and market liberals.

To return to our title, alongside our history of the New Right in the upper case our analysis has focused on the challenge of 'new rights' in the lower case. The New Right of Douglas, Richardson, Gibbs and Kerr has been resisted by the advocates of 'new rights' for women, for workers, for gays and for Maori. The proponents of these 'new rights' tempered the full impact of market policies. Environmentalists and peace activists added further complications. These proponents of 'social justice' opposed the notion that atomised individuals pursuing their own narrowly defined self-interests could promote the general welfare. Where the New Right championed political, civil and property rights, 'new rights' activists defended social, cultural and economic rights. These battles, as everyone who reads the press or watches television news can testify, continue in sneering references to political correctness and open debate about the 'nanny state', powerful women and the place of the Treaty.

Perhaps with the intention of placating these 'new rights' advocates in the Labour Party, the Labour New Right justified the free-market agenda as removing 'privilege' and promoting equality. New Right Labourites tactically supported 'new rights' activists, facilitating victories on homosexual law reform, women's issues, the Treaty of Waitangi and the anti-nuclear cause. When the New Right moved on to the social welfare terrain, which had been ceded to the Labour left in the first term, their egalitarian rationale no longer convinced their 'new rights' colleagues. The Fourth Labour Government collapsed as a result of conflict between its pro-market 'New Right' and the proponents of 'new rights'. The National Government eventually faced a version of the same dilemma in its recurrent battle with 'social justice' advocates, who included the poor among those with rights, and those in its own ranks who favoured the 'new rights' of Maori, gays, women and beneficiaries. Although imported New Right evangelists argued against the morality of 'entitlements' and 'rights discourse', these other claimants refused to be silenced. Simultaneously upper and lower cased, 'new rights' and 'New Right' remained resolutely plural and contested as current political battles make indisputably clear.

New Zealand itself was just as important a *causa belli* in this rancorous history of the 1980s and 1990s as the multiple meanings of 'new rights' and 'New Rights'. New Right evangelists arrived at a crucial moment in our process of nation building. Having been forced to redefine our colonial relationship with Britain by having our economic ties cut, some of us may have looked for another imperial big brother or uncle. Many of us, however, saw this as a time to grow into nationhood. When New Right prophets began to preach, some of us asked whether this substituted one form of colonial conformity for another, replacing one imperial system based in London with a virtual empire headquartered in Washington and New York. Nationalism, as the proponents of homosexual law reform understood, was one of the forces reshaping our identities in ways not always compatible with New Right goals.

The loud and harsh Australian and American tones delivering New Right advice were both a positive and a negative in regards to our willingness to listen. Our right-wing Christian denominations can most often be traced to the US, but their cultural rituals and the emotional displays disturbed those of us with more reticent British-derived religious preferences. The market jargon of some New Right pro-market visitors sounded strange to us, particularly when delivered by enthusiastic salesmen. Negative stereotypes of Americans prone to fanaticism contributed to a certain wariness about New Right ideas associated with a particular form of zealotry by 'God's Bullies'.

The dangers of the application of ideological models of the perfect market to any given reality are that the specificities of that reality are neglected and overlooked. For example, while it is the case that competition can lower unit price, the creation of privatised monopolies is unlikely to yield this optimum result. Another example is the end of political commitment to full employment. As policies fostering employment are jettisoned and unemployment rises, there necessarily will be additional demand for social welfare. If this implementation of the market model leads to the reduction of government spending in the welfare sector, then we have a failure of theory in relation to reality. The market in practice continually failed to deliver the promised benefits. This, in turn, undermines, perhaps fatally, the moral claims for allowing the market to operate freely.

The curious coincidence of New Right reforms with our decision to end the nuclear alliance with the US points to both contingency and nationalism as crucial factors. The links between the market and military ties might not be immediately apparent, but recent controversies over free trade and the Iraq War make those connections more visible. Our own nationalist upsurge in the mid-1980s over the nuclear issue reinforced resistance to military power as one of the major instruments for the realisation of the New Right's global project. By charting our own independent course to an early end to our part in the Cold War nuclear alliance, we also may have set limits to our ideological incorporation into the New Right as a global enterprise.

The ideological missionaries who visited us did not always speak our language. Their certainties, their absolutes and their denial of alternatives contradict our pragmatism and our pluralism, fostered by our own colonial, cultural and class realities. The American language of 'possessive individualism' and 'personal responsibility' required translation into an appropriate Kiwi idiom by those New Right catechists seeking to teach us to think of ourselves as 'autonomous individuals'. Our small population enhances our interconnectedness and interdependence. Our ancestral memories trace journeys to Aotearoa by sea or, more recently, by air, that have entailed dependency upon the other people in the same vessel. As island-dwellers, subject to the movements of the earth, the ebb and flow of tides and wind currents from all directions, we are difficult to convert to a project that stresses total self-reliance, the absolute pursuit of self-interest and the strict calculation of costs and benefits. Market myths derived from societies with endless frontiers and overseas and overland journeys that leave others behind do not fit easily with our traditions.

A careful reading of the Bible, as we hope our use of exemplary verses has made clear, has a prophylactic effect against New Right utopias. Those of us who know the Bible know that there can be no return to the Garden of Eden, nor did Moses and the original marchers reach the Promised Land. The biblical Moses, descending from Mount Sinai after receiving the first set of the Ten Commandments, discovered his countrymen feasting and worshipping the Golden Calf that they had pressured his brother Aaron to build. In spite of Moses' second ascent of Mount Sinai to receive another set of tablets and the people's acceptance of them, Moses and the Jews who left Egypt wandered for forty years in the wilderness until all of the original generation had died. The Promised Land is always a promise for the next generation. The biblical Moses, like our Moses, was allowed to see the Promised Land, but denied entry, as were we all. Beneath the siren call of obfuscating myths lie complex historical realities whose interpretation promises guidance for our future.

The New Right myth of the 'undeserving poor' to be targeted, excluded and morally reformed clashed with our own egalitarian myth of New Zealand's basically 'classless society'. The moral reformers with their calls for 'social responsibility' risked being seen as 'wowsers', prudes and hypocrites. The New Right paternalistic plan to pressure the poor into better behaviour resulted in accusations of endorsing the 'nanny state'. The reliance upon the coercive power of the government to rectify the immorality of beneficiaries while simultaneously advocating the reduction of the state and its powers was a difficult contradiction to escape. When, as in the case of the Code of Social Responsibility, the Government, facing this contradiction, was forced to invoke our egalitarian myth by directing its strictures at all of us, we resented this moral high-handedness. Since the New Right project demanded the moral reform of almost all of us, it ran up against this cultural resistance. Only the most adroit use of language could avoid the dangers of either flouting our commitment to equality or of being considered puritanical and overbearing. Successive governments failed to escape this dilemma.

If myths of a never-ending desert journey no longer resonate with us, what then should we learn from this recent period in our history? What emerged was a hybrid of New Rights and 'new rights'. We marched in a spiral, moving alternately to the left and to the right, mingling identity politics and moral politics, in a complicated pattern. This pattern is unique even as it partly parallels developments elsewhere. We seemed to have decided in 1999 to stop our travelling toward the New Right utopia and instead to stand on our own land, flowing with more milk and honey per capita than any mythical Promised Land. Before we declare these myths dead it is important to note that the New Right 'true believers' have survived and continue to have influence among us. Their call to arms is often class-biased, divisive and sometimes carries racial undertones as they seek a revival of their former influence. Our egalitarian beliefs continue to be used to mount attacks on 'racial privilege' against Maori claims in the name of 'one law for all'. These veteran New Right spokesmen often speak of 'family values' while demanding that DPB recipients be required to work, as though only two-parent, heterosexual families are entitled to respect. Just as vehemently, they demand tax cuts without specifying how the costs of education, healthcare and other social services are to be paid, no doubt relying upon the unpaid and low-waged to carry on that work for which they do not want to pay.

Called again to march by a new Moses, we might well respond. When we discuss beneficiaries who depend upon the state for support, moralism still seems to evoke a positive response in condemning their 'dependency' and moral failings. Echoes of this discourse still inform the contemporary debate over the funding and extent of welfare as DPB recipients get the blame for failed marriages and poorly brought-up children. Certainly we demonise criminals and lobby for more stringent punishments while also displaying a tendency towards vigilante activities against suspected criminals. The recent controversies over prostitution reform and civil unions have mobilised the moral marchers and produced new institutions such as Maxim seeking to unify the New Right moral- and market-conservative constituencies. As long as myths justifying the marginalisation of minorities continue to exert appeal, there is a possibility of success for New Right prophets calling upon us to resume the march toward the Promised Land.

For the likely outcome should we heed such appeals, we need only look back to the history that we have just recounted or to our neighbours in the United States, where the New Right coalition of market liberals, moral conservatives and aggressive nationalists have come to dominate the White House and Congress. Currently, this coalition seeks control of the judiciary to pursue its moral and market agenda. We can observe the price of such victories in the rates of imprisonment, the poverty, the third-world health statistics for the disadvantaged and the instability of family life. Ironically the divorce rates are highest in the very states that most enthusiastically endorse the 'family values' crusade. Education costs continue to soar for American students seeking a university education while the ownership of the nation's wealth becomes more concentrated. The much-trumpeted tax cuts have largely benefited those already advantaged while draining the support for social services. Billions are spent on the military and large sums on the police and prisons. Is this the 'free market' and 'moral' model that we should emulate?

If, on the other hand, we reject mythologised versions of our recent past, we may recognise that we were neither prisoners trapped in a test tube of global capitalism nor victorious champions playing on the field of dreams of New Right visionaries. If we can keep our feet planted on this land while maintaining essential connections to the wider world beyond its shores to which the poet John Donne eloquently referred, we may be able to reclaim equality from the realm of myth and to work towards it in our economic and political decision-making. For this to occur, we must realise that we can neither assume that everyone is equal nor deny that some of us possess unearned advantages. This stricture applies to Maori and non-Maori alike since claims of unalloyed benefit flowing from the private and exclusive possession of property and the unconstrained market can be heard from many quarters. By understanding that markets are simply mechanisms of often unequal exchange rather than moral instruments justly rewarding each participant, we can free ourselves from New Right mythology. As the members of a small nation, we also need to recognise that the state is often the only guarantor of the rights of citizens that can ensure a measure of equality unattainable in the cut and thrust of the marketplace where resources are unequal. Just as profoundly, we must abandon the nostalgia for a lost golden age, whether it lies in pre-European culture, the zenith of the welfare state, the glories of the conformist and morally upright 1950s or a state of pristine isolation from the evils of the global economy. Having confronted our past and our present stripped of comforting illusions, ideological disguise and enticing myths, we will be better equipped to engage in the continuing debates about economic, cultural and social policies in which the New Right and advocates of 'new rights' continue to clash.

Notes

INTRODUCTION

1 For a clear and insightful definition, see Jonathan Boston, 'New Zealand's Welfare State in Transition' and 'Social Justice and the Welfare State', Jonathan Boston, Paul Dalziel and Susan St John (eds), *Redesigning the Welfare State in New Zealand: Problems, Policies, Prospects*. Auckland, 1998.

ONE: GARDEN OF EDEN OR PHARAOH'S EGYPT? NEW ZEALAND BEFORE 1984

1 Arthur Koestler, *The God That Failed: Six Studies in Communism*. London, 1950, 25–82.

2 Douglas Myers, *What I've Learned in Business*. Auckland, 1999, 55; James Belich, *Paradise Reforged: A History of the New Zealanders from the 1880s to the Year 2000*. Auckland, 2001, 413.

3 Roger Douglas, *There's Got to Be a Better Way!* Wellington, 1980, 9, 12.

4 Ibid., 57.

5 Douglas, 'Economic Policy Package', NZ Labour Party, 1983; Douglas, *Towards Prosperity*. Auckland, 1987, 35; Economic Summit Conference, 'A Briefing on the New Zealand Economy'. Wellington, 1984; Treasury, *Economic Management: A Briefing Paper to the Incoming Government*. Wellington, 1984.

6 Harvey Franklin, *Cul de Sac: The Question of New Zealand's Future*. Wellington, 1985, 2, 3, 5.

7 Wolfgang Rosenberg, *The Magic Square: What Every New Zealander Should Know about Rogernomics and the Alternatives*. Christchurch, 1986, 121, 11, 10–14, 25–8.

8 Simon Collins, *Rogernomics: Is There a Better Way?* Auckland, 1987, 1–17, 16, 38, 49, 172.

9 Brian Easton, 'The Commercialisation of the New Zealand Economy: From Think Big to Privatisation', 'The Unmaking of Roger Douglas?', Brian Easton (ed), *The Making of Rogernomics*. Auckland, 1989, 114–21, 127, 171–87; Easton, 'From Reaganomics to Rogernomics', Alan Bollard (ed), *The Influence of United States Economics on New Zealand: the Fulbright Anniversary Seminars*. Wellington, 1989, 69–95, 69–70, 76, 79.

10 Bruce Jesson, *Fragments of Labour: The Story behind the Labour Government*. Auckland, 1989, 20, 22, 25, 31, 33, 43, 82; Jesson, *Behind the Mirror Glass: The Growth of Wealth and Power in New Zealand in the Eighties*. Auckland, 1987, 9, 10.

11 Chris Trotter, 'Shut out of the Quarter Acre Paradise: Toll Gates Blocking the Promised Land', *NBR* 23 March 1990; Trotter, 'Greedy Steal from the Needy: Paradise Lost and There's No Way Home', *NBR* 30 March 1990; David Novitz, 'Rational Discussion in Times of Crisis', David Novitz and Bill Willmott (eds), *New Zealand in Crisis: A Debate about Today's Critical Issues*. Wellington, 1992, 3–16.

12 Ruth Richardson, *Making a Difference*. Auckland, 1995, 11, 13.

13 Ibid., 56, 72, 115, 230.

14 Douglas Myers, 'Fatal Delusions', Sir Ron Trotter, 'The Myth of the Middle Way', Alan Gibbs, 'New Zealand Economy: Future Challenges', Roger Kerr, 'Labour Market Reform: The Role of Public Opinion', NZBR, *Sustaining Economic Reform*. Wellington, 1990; Kerr, 'Achieving a Positive Economic Direction', 'The Next Five Years: What Now?', 'A Battle of Teacups', NZBR, *From Recession to Recovery*. Wellington, 1992.

15 Colin James, *New Territory: The Transformation of New Zealand 1984–92*. Wellington, 1992, 5, 8, 36, 37, 276, 245, 293; see also James, *The Quiet Revolution: Turbulence and Transition in Contemporary New Zealand*. Wellington, 1986.

16   Myers, 'Two Scenarios for New Zealand', Bob Matthew, 'The Old New Zealand and the New', NZBR, *The Old New Zealand and the New*. Wellington, 1994; Kerr, 'Kiwis Can Fly', NZBR, *The Next Decade*. Wellington, 1994.

17   St John, 'The State and Welfare', Andrew Sharp (ed), *Leap Into the Dark: The Changing Role of the State in New Zealand since 1984*. Auckland, 1994, 89–106, 94; Jane Kelsey, *Rolling Back the State: Privatisation of Power in Aotearoa/New Zealand*. Wellington, 1993; Kelsey, *The New Zealand Experiment: A World Model for Structural Adjustment?* Auckland, 1995; Kelsey, 'Aotearoa/New Zealand: The Anatomy of a State in Crisis', *Leap into the Dark*, 178–205, 178, 179.

18   Sharp, 'Pride, Resentment and Change in the State and the Economy', *Leap Into the Dark*, 225, 245, 246, 247, 245.

19   Kelsey, *The New Zealand Experiment*, 353, 46–68, 75–6; Belich, *Paradise Reforged*, 395–460; Nigel Haworth, 'Neo-liberalism, Economic Internationalisation and the Contemporary State in New Zealand', *Leap into the Dark*, 19–40, 22, 21; Kelsey, *Rolling Back the State*, 15, 16, 18–20, 21, 133–44; Kelsey, 'Aotearoa/New Zealand', 178–205, 182, 185, 186; Kelsey, *The New Zealand Experiment*, 20, 22; Kelsey, *Rolling Back the State*, 23, 304.

20   Easton, *The Commercialisation of New Zealand*. Auckland, 1997, 73, 9; Easton, *The Whimpering of the State: Policy After MMP*. Auckland, 1999, v, 3, 6, 7, 104, 241.

21   David G. Green, *From Welfare State to Civil Society: Towards Welfare that Works in New Zealand*. Wellington, 1996, 5–30; Green, 'A Personal Duty to Help Others', *Dominion (Dom)* 27 March 1996; Michael James (ed), *Exploring Civil Society: Essays on David Green's* From Welfare State to Civil Society. Wellington, 1998; see also 'About Civitas: Staff, Director Dr. David G. Green', Civitas website, www.civitas.org.uk; Green, *The New Right: The Counter Revolution in Political, Economic and Social Thought*. London, 1987; Green, *Reinventing Civil Society: the Rediscovery of Welfare without Politics*. London, 1993; Green, *Community without Politics: A Market Approach to Welfare Reform*. London, 1996.

22   Ibid., 29–30; Norman Barry, 'Economism, Civil Society and Welfare', Roger Dale, 'Civil Society: Organisational Alternatives or Victorian Values?', *Exploring Civil Society*, 17–30, 129–42; Myers, 'Identity, Culture and Society', NZBR, Wellington, 28 November 2000, NZBR website, www.nzbr.org.nz.

23   Donald Brash, 'New Zealand's Remarkable Reforms', Hayek Lecture Institute of Economic Affairs, London, 4 June 1996, Reserve Bank of New Zealand, Speeches, website www.rbnz.govt.nz/speeches/0031201.html#P83_4786; 'Brash Out of Line in Broaching Politics', *Waikato Times* 8 June 1996; Alan Williams, 'Why Free Markets are Preferable', *Press* 1 July 1996; Linda Sanders, 'Banking Expert Defends Brash's Right to Speak', *Evening Post (Post)* 6 June 1996; 'Brash Releases Book on NZ Reforms', *Post* 13 January 1997; Karl Du Fresne, 'Provocative Attack on Welfare Spending', *Post* 2 April 1996; Michael Belgrave, 'Dark Satanic Mills No Jerusalem', *Post* 12 April 1996; Ruth Smithies, 'Soup Kitchens and Social Policies', *Dom* 10 April 1996.

24   *Someone Else's Country*, directed, written and produced by Alister Barry, 1996; *Revolution*, directed by John Carlaw, written by Marcia Russell and Carlaw, produced by Russell, 1996; Russell, *Revolution: New Zealand from Fortress to Free Market*. Auckland, 1996; Russell Campbell, 'The New Right and Documentary Film in New Zealand: *Someone Else's Country* & *Revolution*', *Illusions* 29, Winter 1999, 2–7, 3.

25   Campbell, 'The New Right and Documentary Film in New Zealand', 5, 4, 7.

26   Myers, 'Wake Up New Zealand', Kerr, 'Is New Zealand on the Right Track or the Wrong Track?', Kerr, 'Why is New Zealand Not Doing Better?', NZBR, *Wake Up New Zealand*. Wellington, 1999.

27   Jesson, *Only Their Purpose is Mad: The Money Men Take Over NZ*. Palmerston North, 1999, 7, 14, 15, 37, 52, 54, 55, 57, 67, 69, 70, 78.

28   Koestler, *The God That Failed*, 25.

TWO: EXEGESIS: INTERPRETATIONS AND COMMENTARY

1   Ranginui Walker, *Nga Tau Tohetohe/Years of Anger.* Auckland, 1987, 29.
2   Ibid.
3   Ibid., 179, 193, 213, 241, 69, 54, 22; Ranginui Walker, *Nga Pepa a Ranguinui/The Walker Papers.* Auckland, 1996.
4   Donna Awatere, *Maori Sovereignty.* Auckland, 1984; Donna Awatere Huata, 'Choice in Education', ACT New Zealand, *Common Sense for a Change.* Wellington, 1996.
5   Jesson, *Fragments of Labour*, 54; Kelsey, *Rolling Back the State*, 9, 15–21.
6   Jesson, *Fragments of Labour* 34, 36–8, 22.
7   David Steele, 'The NZBR II'. Wellington, 1989; Paul Harris and Linda Twiname, *First Knights: an Investigation of the NZBR.* Auckland, 1997; Kelsey, *Rolling Back the State*, 15–21, 110, 129–31, 133–40; Jesson, *Fragments of Labour*, 34, 36–8, 41–3, 49, 53, 60, 63–4; Barry, *Someone Else's Country.*
8   Jesson, *Fragments of Labour*, 29, 32, 47–8.
9   Kelsey, *The New Zealand Experiment*, 11, 69–81, 335.
10 Easton, *The Commercialisation of New Zealand*, 73, 85, 112–21; Bryan Philpott, 'A Debate with the NZBR', *Research Papers in Economic Policy Internal Paper 217.* Wellington, May 1990.
11 Simon Sheppard, *Broken Circle: The Decline and Fall of the Fourth Labour Government.* Wellington, 1999, 16, 17, 18–27, 111–70.
12 James, *The Quiet Revolution*, 1–2, 7, 54–72, 73, 79, 165; James and Alan McRobie, *Turning Point: The 1993 Election and Beyond.* Wellington, 1993, 7–9. 32–63; James, *New Territory*, 5, 9, 47, 71, 86, 93, 99, 112, 141, 197, 234, 293.
13 Jonathan Boston and Martin Holland, 'The Fourth Labour Government: Transforming the Political Agenda', Boston and Holland, *The Fourth Labour Government: Radical Politics in New Zealand.* Auckland, 1987, l–14, 5, 10; Boston and Paul Dalziel, *The Decent Society? Essays in Response to National's Economic and Social Policies.* Auckland, 1992; Boston, John Martin, June Pallot and Pat Walsh (eds), *Reshaping the State.* Auckland, 1991; Boston (ed), *State under Contract.* Wellington, 1995; Boston, Stephen Church, Stephen Levine, Elizabeth McLeay and Nigel S. Roberts, *Left Turn: The New Zealand General Election of 1999.* Wellington, 2000.
14 Belich, *Paradise Reforged.*

THREE: PILGRIMS, PRAGMATISTS AND PROFITEERS

1   Stuart Sim, *Fundamentalist World: The New Dark Age of Dogma.* Duxford, 2004, 129, 105, 133, 134.
2   Serge Halimi, 'New Zealand, From Welfare State to Market Society: Test Tube Miracle of Total Capitalism', *Le Monde Diplomatique* April 1997; Donald Brash, 'New Zealand's Remarkable Reforms'; Brash, *American Investment in Australian Industry.* Canberra, 1966, vii.
3   Greg Whitwell, *The Treasury Line.* Sydney, 1986, 179, 271–2, 17, 26, 30–5, 37; Michael Pusey, *Economic Rationalism in Canberra: A Nation-building State Changes Its Mind.* Cambridge, 1991, 6–7; 'The Men who Run Australia': Part l, 'Our Leading Public Servant', Part 2, 'Fraser's Brawls with the Treasury', *National Times* 2–28 October 1978, 29 October–4 November 1978.
4   Whitwell, *The Treasury Line*, 3–4, 176, 85–188, 199–207; Lee Eckermann, 'The Lucky Country Joins the Club: Recession, Price Control and Incomes Policy in Australia', Sudha Shency, *Wage–Price Control: Myth & Reality.* Turramura, 1978; Peter Samuel, 'Capitalism Becoming Respectable', *Bulletin* 18 April 1978.
5   Deborah Coddington, 'Face to Face: Douglas Myers', *North & South* November 2000, 74–8, 81; Douglas Myers, 'A Tiger on Your Tail', H. R. Nicholls Society Keynote Address, ww.hrnichols.com.au/Nicholls/nichvol12/vol12key.htm.
6   'State's Bazley Top Businesswoman', *Dom* 8 September 1987; Jenni McManus, 'The Changing Face of New Zealand's Power Elite', *Independent* 16 August 1996; 'Transport's Staff-slashing Bazley Shifts to Social Welfare', *Independent* 4 June 1993;

Leslie Watkins, 'Bazley Betrays Kids to Save Face', *Truth* 17 October 1997; Ray Lilley, 'Bazley Wields The Big Stick Over Reform', *NBR* 28 May 1999; Graeme Hunt, 'Social Welfare Head Far from Politically Correct', *NBR* 7 February 1997; David McLoughlin, 'Face to Face: Margaret Bazley', *North & South* April 1999, 116–9; 'Damehood a Relief after Mrs Battle', *Dom* 7 June 1999; Hunt, 'Tireless Public Servant Steps Down', *NBR* 17 November 2000; 'Govt's "Hatchwoman" to Retire', *Post* 13 November 2000; 'Tough Love', *Press* 20 March 1997; 'New Broom at the Fire Service', *NBR* 28 March 1999; 'Boss of the Beneficiaries', *Post* 10 August 1996; 'How to Manage Tough Changes', *Dom* 5 June 1993; 'Bouquets and Bullets', *Post* 29 September 2001.

7   Monica Allard, 'Ehud Barak and Hugh Morgan', Australian Broadcasting Corporation, *Sunday Profile*, 10 March 2002, www.abc.net.au/sundayprofile/stories/s556366htm.

8   Georgina Murray and Douglas Pacheco, 'Think Tanks in the 1990s', www.anu.au/polsci/marx/interventions/thintanks.htm; Greg Lindsay, 'Greg Lindsay Speaks Out about the Early CIS', *Policy* Winter 1996, www.cis.org.au/glint.htm; 'Contributors', H. R. Nicholls Society, www.hrnicholls.com.au; 'Volume 11: Appendix l: Contributors', Samuel Griffith Society, www.samuellgriffith.org.au/papers/html/volume11/v11app1.htm; Paul Chamberlain, 'Mining Chief Lashes Mabo', *Sydney Morning Herald* 1 July 1993; 'Senior Management', WMC, 2004, www.wmc.com/about/management.htm; Proceedings of the Inaugural Conference of the Samuel Griffith Society, Melbourne 24–26 July 1992; 'The Lavoisier Group: Australian Greenhouse Corporate Front-Group', www.geocities.com/jimgreen3/lavoisier.html; Chairman's Address, 2004 Annual General Meeting, WMC, www.wmc.com/pubpres/agm04/address.htm; Hugh Lorton-Carnegie, 'The Business Council Turns 21', www.crikey.com.au/business/2004/03/22-0003.html; Fran O'Sullivan, 'Aussie Stallion Heads Right', *NZH* 6 October 2003; Hugh Morgan, 'Free Trade: We've Only Just Begun', *Australian* 11 August 2004; 'Morgan Departs with 9.5m', *Courier Mail* 23 March 2003; Ray Evans, 'A Retrospective', H. R. Nicholls Society, www.hrnicholls.com.au/nicholls/nichvo17/volxv014.htm; Evans, 'Surveying the Thirdwayers' Ambitions: What Sort of Australia Do they Want?', H. R. Nicholls Society, www.hrnicholls.com.au/nicholls/nichvo20/Evans99.html.

9   Murray and Pacheco, 'Think Tanks in the 1990s'; John Hyde, *Dry: In Defence of Economic Freedom: The Saga of How the Dries Changed the Australian Economy for the Better*. Melbourne, 2002, vii, 2, 4, 9, 59, 67-70.

10 Shaun Carney, *Peter Costello: The New Liberal*. Crows Nest, 2001; Philip Mendes, 'From Keynes to Hayek: The Social Welfare Philosophy of the Liberal Party of Australia, 1983–1997', *Policy, Organisation & Society* 15, Summer 1998, 65–87; David Potts, 'The Think Tanks', *Australian Financial Review* 19–21 May 1981; Lindsay, 'Rekindling the Flame: The Revival of Liberalism', *Institute of Public Affairs Review* April/June 1979; *Bulletin* 26 May 1981, as quoted in Dean Jaesnsch, *The Liberals*. Sydney, 1994, 159; 'Volume 7: Contributors', H. R. Nicholls Society, www.hrnicholls.com.au/nicholls/nichvo17/volxv002.htm.

11 Paul Kelly, *The End of Certainty: Power, Politics & Business in Australia*. St Leonards, 1994, 35, 109–10, 121; David Marr, *The High Price of Heaven*. Sydney, 1999, 28, 31; Jaesnsch, *The Liberals*, 143–75.

12 'Volume 2: Contributors', H. R. Nicholls Society, www.hrnicholls.com.au/nicholls/nichvo12/vol2cont.htm; Richard Glyuas, 'Two Decades on, Tough Calls Still Rattle Big Biz Castle of Cards', *Australian* 1 October 2003; 'Volume 1: Profile of Contributors', H. R. Nicholls Society, www.hrnicholls.com.au/nicholls/nichvo11/vo11prof.htm; David Kemp, 'The Occasional Address', www.hrnicholls.com.au/nicholls/nichvo17/voxv011.htm.

13 Carney, *Peter Costello*, 71–3; Michael Duffy, *Latham and Abbott: The Lives and Rivalry of the Two Finest Politicians of Their Generation*. Sydney, 2004.

14 Coddington, 'Family Ties: Hearts and Minds', *North & South* September 2000, 28–9; McManus, 'The Changing Face of New Zealand's Power Elite'; Andrea Fox, 'A (quiet

wee) chat with the godfather', *Weekend Herald* 11 June 2005; General Workers Union in Denmark, *The Experiment in New Zealand: The Consequences and Experiences of the Reforms in New Zealand*. Copenhagen, 2001, http://www.psa.org.nz/; see also Stephen Harris, 'Mandarins Make Moves', *NBR* 17 December 1993; Anthony Hubbard, 'Crusader of the NZBR', *Listener* 4 May 1992.

15   McManus, 'The Changing Face of New Zealand's Power Elite'; 'Country loses key director and investor: Colin John Fernyhough, 1938–2003', *NBR* 14 February 2003; 'Fernyhough Loses Battle with Cancer', *Dominion Post (Dom Post)* 14 February 2003; McLoughlin, 'Nights of the NZBR: The Gang of 45', *North & South* September 1992; Hubbard, 'Crusader of the NZBR', *Listener* 4 May 1992; David Henderson, 'Labour Market Reform in the 1990s: The OECD Record and Its Lessons', H. R. Nicholls Society, www.hrnicholls.com.au/nicholls/nichvo20/Henderson99.html.

16   Vernon Wright, *David Lange: Prime Minister*. Wellington, 1984, 47, 56, 131, 135; Simon Sheppard, *Broken Circle*, 10–11, 30, 32; Harvey McQueen, *The Ninth Floor: Inside the Prime Minister's Office – A Political Experience*. Auckland, 1991, 196.

17   Roger Douglas, *There's Got to be a Better Way!*; Douglas, *Toward Prosperity*. Auckland, 1987; Simon Collins, *Rogernomics*. Wellington, 1987; Brian Easton, *The Making of Rogernomics*; Sheppard, *Broken Circle*, 11–12; McManus, 'The Changing Face of New Zealand's Power Elite'.

18   Geoffrey Palmer, *Unbridled Power? An Interpretation of New Zealand's Constitution and Government*. Auckland, 1987 revision of 1979 edition; Geoffrey Palmer and Matthew Palmer, *Bridled Power: New Zealand Government Under MMP*. Auckland, 1997; 'Populist Salvation: Review of *Unbridled Power? An Interpretation of New Zealand's Constitution and Government*', *Comment: A New Zealand Quarterly Review* 9, December 1979, 34–5; 'Geoffrey Palmer – a Late Flowering Strong Man', *North & South* December 1986; 'Master Plan', *Listener* 19 December 1987; Gordon Campbell, 'Smooth Operator', *Listener*, 28 May 1988; Linda Clark, 'Big 3 Loyal to Lange: Coup Fears Laid to Rest by Palmer', *NBR* 24 November 1988; Jesson, 'The Disintegration of the 4th Labour Government', *Metro* 8:89, November 1988, 138–54; James, 'Palmer and Clark: Can They Manage?', *Management* 8:36, September 1989, 34–7; Simon Collins, 'Palmer: Standing Firm on Centre Ground', *NZH* 9 August 1989; 'Sovereignty for Sale: The Law to be Privatised in Printing Office Move', *NBR* 8 December 1988.

19   Iain Morrison, Grant Cubis and Frank Haden, *Michael Fay on a Reach for the Ultimate: The Unauthorised Biography*. Wellington, 1990, 138, 139, 240, 241, 242; McManus, 'The Changing Face of New Zealand's Power Elite'.

20   Mike Moore, *Hard Labour*. Auckland, 1987, 86–7; Michael Bassett, *The Third Labour Government: A Personal History*. Palmerston North, 1976, 294–300.

21   Donna Awatere Huata, *My Journey*. Auckland, 1996, 61, 62, 63, 79.

22   Jim Bolger, *Bolger: A View from the Top – My Seven Years as Prime Minister*. Auckland, 1998, 38, 114, 116, 119, 260–1.

23   Rosemary McLeod, 'Jenny and Ruth: The Story of an Enduring and Powerful Friendship', *North & South* August 1991, 46–58; Warwick Roger, 'To the Manse Born', *North & South* November 1992, 10–11; 'Radical Ruth Speaks Out', *Dom,* 30 September 1995; 'Helping Us to Help Ourselves', *NBR* 9 August 1992; 'Ruth's Rules', *Listener* 28 January 1989; 'Benefits of Work', *Listener* 10 December 1988; Mike Jaspers, 'Ruth's Vision of a Leaner, Meaner State', *NBR* 30 March 1990.

24   Richard Cockett, *Thinking the Unthinkable: Think-Tanks and the Economic Counter-Revolution, 1931–1983*. Hammersmith, 1995, 122–242, 243, 279–83, 306–8; Marian Sawer, 'Political Manifestations of Libertarianism in Australia', Sawer (ed), *Australia and the New Right*. Sydney, 1982, 1–19, 1–2; Roger Douglas, Interview by Paul Morris, Wellington 27 August 2002; IEA spokesman, Interview by Paul Morris; Andrew Scott, *Running on Empty: 'Modernising' the British and Australian Labour Parties*. Annandale, 2000, 78–80, 81–5; Sawer, 'Political Manifestations', 3–9; Pusey, *Economic Rationalism in Canberra*, 227–9; 'Volume 1: Profile of Contributors', H.

R. Nicholls Society, www.hrnicholls.com.au/nicholls/nichvol1/vol1prof.htm; Sawer, 'Political Manifestations', 3–9; Herman Kahn and Thomas Pepper, *Will She Be Right? The Future of Australia.* St Lucia, 1980, xi, xv–xvi, 22–4.

25 Cockett, *Thinking the Unthinkable,* 122–242, 243, 279–83, 306–8; Sawer, 'Political Manifestations', 1–19, 1–2; The Tasman Institute website claims that CPS was founded in 1982, but this seems to be incorrect in terms of its actual presence and activities, as is its statement that it was founded in 1990.

26 Pusey, *Economic Rationalism in Canberra,* 227; Lord Ralph Harris, 'Taxation and Public Spending in a Modern Democracy', J. Wilkes (ed), *The Politics of Taxation.* Sydney, 1980; Wolfgang Kasper, 'Ignorance, Discovery and Choice – A Requiem for Economic Rationalism?', Joint Conference of the Australian Society of Legal Philosophy and the Centre for the Legal and Economic Study of Institutions, University of Queensland, St Lucia, Brisbane, 19 September 1997; Kasper et al., *Australia at the Crossroads: Our Choices to the Year 2000.* Sydney, 1980, 208; Kasper, *Australian Political Economy.* Crows Nest, 1982; Greg Crough and Ted Wheelwright, *Australia: A Client State.* Ringwood, 1982; Peter Coleman, 'James McAuley's 20 *Quadrant*s', http://www.the-rathouse.com/McAuley_20 quadrats-ns4.html; Frances Stonor Saunders, *Who Paid the Piper? The CIA and the Cultural Cold War.* London, 1999, 215, 395.

27 Richard Long, 'Fortress Japan: Are the Bulwarks Crumbling?', *Dom* 22 July 1995; Hubbard, 'Calling in the Newsman to Save the English Patient', *Sunday Star-Times* 4 May 2003; Long, 'Why Maori Plurals Take S in English Text', *Dom* 17 February 1998; 'If Only He'd Been First Past the Post', *Sunday Star-Times* 10 November 1996; Long, 'Ultimate War Weapon that Led to Peace', *Dom* 9 August 1995.

28 Kelly, *The End of Certainty,* 48; P. Swan, 'The Libertarian Challenge to Big Government', *Quadrant* September 1979, 5–11; John J. Ray, 'Is Equality Morally Obnoxious?', *Quadrant* November 1979, 68–9; *Australian* 10 Feb 1981; Sawer, 'Philosophical Underpinnings of Libertarianism in Australia', *Australia and the New Right,* 20–37; Mendes, 'From Keynes to Hayek'; Hugh Morgan, as quoted in Paul Collins, *God's Earth: Religion as If Matter Really Mattered.* New York, 1995, 33–4; Paul Christopher, 'The Chattering Class and Australian Social Cohesion', *The Observer* Autumn 2004; Sharon Beder, *Global Spin: The Corporate Assault on Environmentalism.* Melbourne, 2000, 17–8, 19–20, 81–3, 85, 89, 93, 96, 102, 103, 201, 210, 221–2, 278.

FOUR: LEAVING EGYPT: THE RIGHT MARCH ON WASHINGTON AND WESTMINSTER

1 'Frank H. Knight', 'The Chicago School', www.cepa.newschool.edu; Richard M. Ebeling, 'Aaron Director on the Market for Goods and Ideas', 17 September 2004, Foundation for Economic Education, www.fee.org; 'Aaron Director, Founder of the field of Law and Economics', University of Chicago News Office, 13 September 2004, www-news.uchicago.edu; 'Aaron Director, 1901–2004', 'Marginal Revolution: Small Steps Toward a Much Better World', www.marginalrevolution.com; 'Milton Friedman – Autobiography', Nobelprize.org, www.nobelprize.org; 'About Rose Director Friedman', 'About Milton Friedman', Milton Friedman and Rose Director Friedman Foundation, www.friedmanfoundation.org; 'Lord Ralph Harris', Interview, 17 July 2000; 'The Chicago School', 'Milton Friedman', 'George Schultz', *Commanding Heights,* www.pbs.org/wgbh/commandingheights/; 'Milton Friedman' www.disinfopedia.org; 'Milton Friedman', Nova Civitas, 60gp.ovh.net; George W. Bush, 'President Honors Milton Friedman for Lifetime Achievements', The White House, www.whitehouse.gov.

2 Mark Thornton, 'Biography of Fritz Machlup', Ludwig von Mises Institute, www.mises.org; 'An Interview with Fritz Machlup', *Austrian Economics Newsletter* 3:1, Summer 1980; 'Who is Ludwig von Mises?', Ludwig von Mises Institute, www.mises.org; Israel M. Krizner, 'Fifty Years of FEE – Fifty Years of Progress in Austrian Economics', www.libertyhaven.com; Nevenka Cuckovic and David L. Pryor,

'Mises, Hayek and the Market Process: An Introduction', www.libertyhaven.com; 'Profile of Friedrich von Hayek', *Commanding Heights*, www.pubs.org/wgbh/commandingheights/; 'The Austrian School', 'Neoliberalism', en.wikipedia.org; 'The Austrian School', www.cepa.newschool.edu; John Moser, 'The Origins of the Austrian School of Economics', *Humane Studies Review* 11:1, Spring 1997, www.gmu.edu/departments/his/hsr/s97hsr.html.

3   Mark Thornton, 'Biography of Fritz Machlup'; Henry Hazlitt, 'An Economist's View of "Planning": Regimentation on the Fascist Model, Says Dr. Hayek, Can Evolve From It, *The Road to Serfdom* by Dr. Friedrich A. Hayek', *New York Times* 24 September 1944; Richard M. Ebeling, 'Aaron Director on the Market for Goods and Ideas', 17 September 2004, www.fee.org; Christian Parenti, 'Winning the War of Ideas', *In These Times* 17 October 2003; Louis W. Liebovich, 'American Dreamers: The Wallaces and Reader's Digest: An Insider's Story', *Journal of American History* 84:2, September 1997, 705–6; Frederick Allen, 'Wally's Word – Theirs was the Kingdom: Lila and Dewitt Wallace and the Story of the *Reader's Digest* by John Heidenry', *Columbia Journalism Review* 32:6, March 1994, 53–4.

4   'James W. Fifield', 'Spiritual Mobilization', 'Leonard Read', 'Foundation for Economic Education', 'William Volker Fund', 'F. A. Harper', www.disinfopedia.org; Leonard Liggio, Institute of Humane Studies, Interview by Dolores Janiewski, Fairfax, Virginia, 8 April 2003; Mary Sennholz, 'Leonard Read, the Founder and Builder', *The Freeman* May 1996; Edmund A. Opitz, 'Leonard E. Read: A Portrait', *The Freeman* September 1998, www.libertyhaven.com.df.

5   'Foundation for Economic Education', 'F. A. Harper', 'William Volker Fund', www.disinfopedia.org; Paul L. Poirot, 'The Writings of F.A. Harper – A Review', *The Freeman*, www.libertyhaven.com; Llewellyn H. Rockwell, Jr, 'The Biography of Henry Hazlitt (1894–1993)', Ludwig von Mises Institute, www.mises.org; Gary North, 'The Moral Dimension of FEE', *The Freeman* May 1996, www.liberty-haven.com.

6   Midge Decter, *An Old Wife's Tale: My Seven Decades in Love and War*. New York, 2001; Irving Kristol, *Neoconservatism: The Autobiography of an Idea*. New York, 1995; Norman Podhoretz, *Making It*. New York, 1969, 73–6, 83–102, 109–14, 203–25; Carney, *Peter Costello: The New Liberal*, 72–73.

7   'Bretton Woods System', 'Washington Consensus', en.wikipedia.org; 'Conference at Bretton Woods', 22 July 1944, www.ibiblio.org/pha/policy/1944/440722a.html; William Finnegan, 'The Economics of Empire', *Harper's Magazine* May 2003, www.mindfully.org.

8   'About Hoover', 'About Hoover – Mission Statement', Hoover Institution, www-hoover.standford.edu.

9   Hazlitt, 'The Early History of FEE', *The Freeman* March 1984, originally presented at the Leonard Read Memorial Conference on Freedom, 18 November 1983, www.libertyhaven.com; Milton Friedman, 'Foreword', Fritz Machlup (ed), *Essays on Hayek*. New York, 1976, xxi–xvi, xxi; George C. Roche III, 'The Relevance of Friedrich A. Hayek, *Essays on Hayek*, 1–11, 6; as quoted in George H. Nash, *The Conservative Intellectual Movement in America Since 1945*. New York, 1976, 18, 19, 20, 21; Foundation for Economic Education, www.fee.org; Gerald Frost, *Antony Fisher: Champion of Liberty*. London, 2002, 39–40, 42–3; William F. Buckley, Jr., 'The Road to Serfdom: The Intellectuals and Socialism', *Essays on Hayek*, 95–106, 96, 106; Shirley Robin Letwin, 'The Achievement of Friedrich A. Hayek', *Essays on Hayek*, 147–67, 163; Friedrich von Hayek, *The Road to Serfdom*, 3–4; Reinhold Niebuhr, *The Children of Light and the Children of Darkness*. New York, 1944, 178, 189, 183, 185–7, 161–2; John Ehrman, *The Rise of Neoconservatism: Intellectuals and Foreign Affairs, 1945–1994*. New Haven, 1995, viii, 7–8, 12; Irving Kristol, Interview by John Ehrman, 21 July 1991; 'The General Meeting Files of the Mont Pelerin Society, 1947–1998', Liberaal Archief, www.liberaalarchief.be.

10   Richard Cockett, *Thinking the Unthinkable*; Atlas Economic Research Foundation, www.atlasusa.org; 'Lord Ralph Harris', *Commanding Heights*, www.phbs.org/

wgbh/commandingheights/; National Education Association, 'The Real Story Behind "Paycheck Protection": The Hidden Link between Anti-Workers and Anti-Public Education Initiatives: An Anatomy of the Far Right', 1998, www.nea.org/publiced/paycheckp 187; Atlas Economic Research Foundation, www.atlasusa.org; 'Atlas Economic Research Foundation' www.disinfopedia.org.

11   'Mission Statement', 'Herman Kahn, Founder', Hudson History', Hudson Institute, www.hudson.org; Herman Kahn, *On Thermonuclear War*. Princeton, 1960; Kahn, *Thinking about the Unthinkable*, New York, 1962; Kahn, *The Alternative World Futures Approach*. Croton-on-Hudson, 1966; S. M. Amadae, *Rationalizing Capitalist Democracy: The Cold War Origins of Rational Choice Liberalism*. Chicago, 2003, 32–47, 77, 134.

12   'AEI's Diamond Jubilee, 1943–2003'.

13   Leonard Liggio, Interview by Dolores Janiewski; James L. Doti, 'Henry Salvatori – A Man of Integrity', *The Freeman* October 1995, www.libertyhaven.com; Cockett, *Thinking the Unthinkable*, 4, 68–72, 74, 77, 92, 122–58; 'The Sharon Statement', *New Guard* March 1969, as quoted in Lisa McGirr, *Suburban Warriors: The Origins of the New American Right*. Princeton, 2001, 63; William F. Buckley, Jr, 'Morality and American Society', *Religion & Liberty: A Publication of the Acton Institute for the Study of Religion and Liberty* 2:3 May–June 1992; Patrick Allitt, *Catholic Intellectuals and Conservative Politics in America, 1950–1985*. Ithaca, 1993; Mary Brennan, *Turning Right in the Sixties: The Conservative Capture of the G.O.P.* Chapel Hill, 1995; John A. Andrew, *The Other Side of the Sixties: Young Americans for Freedom and the Rise of Conservative Politics*. New Brunswick, N.J., 1997; Clayborne Carson, *In Struggle: SNCC and the Black Awakening of the 1960s*. Cambridge, 1981; William Rusher, *The Rise of the Right*. New York, 1984; Gregory L. Schneider, *Cadres for Conservatism: Young Americans for Freedom and the Rise of the Contemporary Right*. New York, 1999; Nash, *The Conservative Intellectual Movement in America Since 1945*.

14   McGirr, *Suburban Warriors*, 34, 54–5, 60–3, 75–6; Nash, *The Conservative Intellectual Movement in America Since 1945*, 24; Steve Bruce, *The Rise and Fall of the New Christian Right: Conservative Protestant Politics in America, 1978–1988*. Oxford, 1988; J. Allen Broyles, *The John Birch Society: Anatomy of a Protest*. Boston, 1964; Dallas A. Blanchard, *The Anti-Abortion Movement and the Rise of the Religious Right: From Polite to Fiery Protest*. New York, 1994; Sara Diamond, *Roads to Dominion: Right-Wing Movements and Political Power in the United States*. New York, 1995; Diamond, *Not by Politics Alone: The Enduring Influence of the Christian Right*. New York, 1994; Robert C. Liebman and Robert Wuthnow (eds), *The New Christian Right: Mobilization and Legitimation*. Hawthorne, 1983; William C. Martin, *With God on Our Side: The Rise of the Religious Right in America*. New York, 1996; Clyde Wilcox, *God's Warriors: The Christian Right in Twentieth-Century America*. Baltimore, 1992; Gary North, 'It All Began with Fred Schwarz', www.lewrockwell.com.

15   Antonio Gramsci, *Selections from Prison Notebooks*. London, 1971, 57, 161, 181, republished as Antonio Gramsci, 'Hegemony, Intellectuals and the State', John Storey (ed), *Cultural Theory and Popular Culture*. Athens, 2000, 210–16; Nash, *The Conservative Intellectual Movement in America Since 1945*, 12, 258, 242.

16   Phyllis Schlafly, *A Choice, Not an Echo: 'The Inside Story on How American Presidents Are Chosen'*. Alton, 1964.

17   Doti, 'Henry Salvatori'.

18   Peter Coleman, *The Liberal Conspiracy: The Congress for Cultural Freedom and the Struggle for the Mind of Postwar Europe*. New York, 1989; Paul E. Montgomery, 'Magazine to Give Social Analyses', *New York Times* 23 October 1965; Peter Steinfels, *The Neoconservatives: The Men Who are Changing America*. New York, 1979, 83–90; Gary J. Dorrien, *The Neoconservative Mind: Politics, Culture and the War of Ideology*. Philadelphia, 1993, 68–132; Geoffrey Norman, 'The Godfather of Neoconservatism (and His Family)', *Esquire* 91:3, 13 February 1979; Irving Kristol, 'About Equality',

Commentary November 1972, reprinted in Irving Kristol, *Two Cheers for Capitalism*. New York, 1978, 153–87, 165, 174, 177, 184, 186, 177; Norman Podhoretz, 'Making the World Safe for Communism', *Commentary* 61:4, April 1976; Midge Decter, *The New Chastity and Other Arguments Against Women's Liberation*. New York, 1972, 180–1; Decter, *An Old Wife's Tale*; Decter, 'Neocon Memoir', *American Jewish History* June–September 1999, 183.

19 Diamond, *Roads to Dominion*, 178–202; Don Reynolds, 'A Push in the right direction: Financial Powerhouses Pollinate Campuses with big bucks and conservative ideas', www.influx.uoregon.edu/1997/cons/; see also Nash, 'From Unity to Fragmentation', *The Intercollegiate Review* April 1996, 55–8; Doti, 'Henry Salvatori'.

20 'Heritage Foundation', Right Web, www.rightweb.irc-online.org; Diamond, *Roads to Dominion*, 171; John D'Emilio and Estelle B. Freedman, *Intimate Matters*. Chicago, 1997, 347; Martin, *With God on Our Side*, 163–7; 197–8; Jerry Falwell, *Listen, America!* Garden City, 1980, 181–6; Ioannis Mookas, 'Faultlines: Homophobic Innovation in Gay Rights/Special Rights', Linda Kintz and Julia Lesage, *Media, Culture and the Religious Right*. Minneapolis, 1998, 345–61, 347; Margaret Cruickshank, *The Gay and Lesbian Liberation Movement*. New York, 1992, 15; Richard R. Cornwall, 'Queer Political Economy: The Social Articulation of Desire', Amy Gluckman and Betsy Reed (eds), *Homo Economics: Capitalism, Community and Lesbian and Gay Life*. New York, 1997, 89–122, 109; Godfrey Hodgson, *The World Turned Right Side Up: A History of the Conservative Ascendancy in America*. Boston, 1996, 174–9; Michele McKeegan, *Abortion Politics: Mutiny in the Ranks of the Right*. New York, 1992, viii–ix; Brennan, *Turning Right in the Sixties*; Diamond, *Roads to Dominion*, 161–77; Richard A. Viguerie, *The New Right: We're Ready to Lead*. Falls Church, 1981; Kevin P. Phillips, *The Emerging Republican Majority*. New Rochelle, 1969; Patrick Buchanan, *Conservative Votes, Liberal Victories: Why the Right has Failed*. New York, 1975; William A. Rusher, *The Making of the New Majority Party*. Ottawa, 1975; Clyde Wilcox, 'PACS of the Christian Right: A Longitudinal Analysis', *Journal for the Scientific Study of Religion* March 1988; 'Sex and God in American Politics: What Conservatives Really Think', *Policy Review* Summer 1984; Alan Crawford, *Thunder on the Right: The 'New Right' and the Politics of Resentment*. New York, 1980; Bruce, *The Rise and Fall of the New Christian Right*; National Education Association, 'The Real Story'; Anna Williams, 'Conservative Media Activism: The Free Congress foundation and National Empowerment Television', Kintz and Lesage, *Media, Culture and the Religious Right*, 275–94.

21 'Stuart Butler', www.disinfopedia.org; 'About the Heritage Foundation', 'About the Heritage Foundation – Our Staff: Stuart Butler', 'Publications by Stuart Butler', www.heritage.org; 'Heritage Foundation', www.mediatransparency.org; 'Heritage Foundation', People for the American Way, www.pfaw.org; Norman Solomon, 'The Media's Favorite Think Tank: How the Heritage Foundation Turns Money into Media', *Extra!* July/August 1996, www.fair.org/extra/; 'Heritage Foundation', Rightweb, www.rightweb.irc-online.org.

22 'Cato', www.disinfopedia.org.

23 Maurice Isserman and Michael Kazin, *America Divided: The Civil War of the 1960s*. New York, 2000; Rebecca E. Klatch, *A Generation Divided: The New Left, the New Right and the 1960s*. Berkeley, 1999; Bruce J. Schulman, *From Cotton Belt to Sunbelt: Federal Policy, Economic Development and the Transformation of the South, 1938–1980*. New York, 1991, 206–21; Peter Appleborne, *Dixie Rising: How the South Is Shaping American Values, Politics and Culture*. New York, 1996; Linda Kintz, *Between Jesus and the Market: The Emotions that Matter in Right-Wing America*. Durham, 1997, 52–3, 178, 166–8, 185–6, 217–8; Hodgson, *The World Turned Right Side Up*, 176–7; 'Cato Institute: "Libertarian" in a Corporate Way', Institute for Public Accuracy, http://www.accuracy.org/articles/cato; James Allen Smith, *The Idea Brokers: Think Tanks and the Rise of the New Policy Elite*. New York, 1991; 'William E. Simon', www.mediatransparency.org/people/willliam_Simon.htm; 'Biographical

Sketch', William E. Simon papers, Lafayette College Library, www2.lafayette.edu/
~library/special/simon/bio.html; 'Cato', www.disinfopedia.org.

24 Charles Murray, *Losing Ground: American Social Policy 1950–1980*. New York,
1984; Lawrence M. Mead, *Beyond Entitlement: The Social Obligation of Citizenship*.
New York, 1985; Bill Berkowitz, 'The Capital Research Center', Interhemispheric
Resource Center, 'Group Watch: Puebla Institute', Public Eye, www.publiceye.org/
research/Group_Watch/Entries-111.htm; William E. Simon, 'An American Institution',
Forward to Lee Edwards, 'The Power of Ideas: The Heritage Foundation at 25 Years',
www.heritage.org/heritage25/ideasfwd.html.

25 National Education Association, 'The Real Story'; 'David H. Koch', 'Cato',
www.disinfopedia.org; 'About Cato', www.cato.org.

26 'Interhemispheric Resource Center', 'Group Watch: Heritage Foundation', the Public
Eye, www.publiceye.org/research/Group_Watch/Entries-62.htm#P5202_1093295;
'The Council for National Policy', watch.pair.com/cnp.html; The Council for
National Policy, www.seekgod.ca/cnporganizations.htm; 'The Council for National
Policy', watch.pair.com/cnp.html; The Council for National Policy, www.seekgod.ca/
cnporganizations.htm; Joan Scott, 'The Campaign Against Political Correctness:
What's Really at Stake', Jeffrey Williams (ed), *PC Wars: Politics and Theory in the
Academy*. New York, 1995, 22–43, 23; James Neilson, 'The Great PC Scare: Tyrannies
of the Left, Rhetoric of the Right', *PC Wars*, 60–89, 60–1; Tom Lewis, '"Political
Correctness": A Class Issue', *PC Wars*, 90–108. Michael Berube and Cary Nelson (eds),
Higher Education under Fire: Politics, Economics and the Crisis of the Humanities.
New York, 1994; Lynne V. Cheney, *Telling the Truth: A Report on the State of the
Humanities*. Washington, 1992; Dinesh D'Souza, *Illiberal Education: The Politics of
Race and Sex on Campus*. New York, 1991; William J. Bennett, *To Reclaim a Legacy:
A Report on the Humanities in Higher Education*. Washington, 1984; Allan Bloom,
*The Closing of the American Mind: How Higher Education Has Failed Democracy and
Impoverished the Souls of Today's Students*. New York, 1987; Scott Henson and Tom
Philpott, 'The Right Declares a Culture War', *Humanist* March–April 1992; Roger
Kimball, *Tenured Radicals: How Politics Has Corrupted Our Higher Education*. New
York, 1990; Ellen Messer-Davidow, 'Manufacturing the Attack on Liberalized Higher
Education', *Social Text* 36, 1993, 40–80; Christopher Newfield and Ron Strickland
(eds), *After Political Correctness: The Humanities and Society in the 1990s*. Boulder,
1994; Arthur Schlesinger, *The Disunity of America*. Knoxville, 1991; Simon, 'An
American Institution'.

27 Dick Armey, *Policy Review*, Summer 1994, as quoted in 'Heritage Foundation',
www.disinfopedia.org.

FIVE: REVELATION: MARKETING MORALITY

1 Friedrich Hayek, 'Intellectuals and Socialism', *Chicago Law Review*, 16: 3, 1949,
417–33.
2 Adam Smith, *An Inquiry into the Nature and Causes of the Wealth of Nations*. Oxford,
1978.
3 Adam Smith, *Theory of Moral Sentiments*. Oxford, 1976.
4 See Richard Teichgraeber, *'Free Trade' and Moral Philosophy*. Durham, 1986, 1–28;
Christopher Berry, 'Adam Smith and the Virtues of Commerce', John Chapman and
William Galston (eds), *Virtue*. New York, 1992, 69–88.
5 Smith, *Theory of Moral Sentiments*, 86.
6 Smith, *An Inquiry into the Nature and Causes of the Wealth of Nations*, 610.
7 Smith, Introduction, Part II, 'Of Merit and Demerit', Part VI, 'Of the Character of
Virtue', *Theory of Moral Sentiments*.
8 Ibid., 121.
9 Milton Friedman, with the assistance of Rose D. Friedman, *Capitalism and Freedom*.
Chicago, 1962, 2.
10 Ibid., 3, 4, 200.

11 Milton Friedman and Rose Friedman, *Free to Choose: A Personal Statement*. London, 1990, reprint of 1980 edition, 5–6, 7, 127.
12 Ibid., 283, 284.
13 Friedman, *Capitalism and Freedom*, 2, 7, 13, 18.
14 James M. Buchanan and Gordon Tullock, *The Calculus of Consent: Logical Foundations of Constitutional Democracy*. Ann Arbor, 1962, vi, 303, 304.
15 Buchanan, *Ethics and Economic Progress*. Norman, 1994, 2, 3, 5, 27, 31, 51, 60.
16 Ibid., 79, 112.
17 Michael Novak, *A Theology of Radical Politics*. New York, 1969.
18 Novak, *In Praise of the Free Economy*. St Leonards, 1999.
19 Michael Novak, Interview by Paul Morris, American Enterprise Institute, Washington, DC, November 2003.
20 Novak, *In Praise of the Free Economy*, 76; Novak, *The Spirit of Democratic Capitalism*. Washington, 1982; Novak, *The Catholic Ethic and the Spirit of Capitalism*. New York, 1993.
21 Douglas Myers, 'A Tiger on Your Tail?'; Roger Kerr, 'The Challenge of the '90s: Labour Reform in Australasia', Australian Institute of Company Directors Western Australia Division, 19 February 1993, www.nsbr.org.nz/documents/speeches/; Richard Epstein, 'Economics and the Judges: The Case for Simple Rules and Boring Courts', 'Defining Social Welfare and Achieving it', www.leanz.org.nz; For more on Richard Epstein's influence see the NZBR website and the Law and Economics Association New Zealand (LEANZ) website, www.leanz.org.nz; 'Aid to Pacific Countries "Ruinous"' *Dom* 23 April 1991; 'Why Crime Beats Work', *NBR* 14 May 1993.
22 Robert A. Sirico, *Economics, Faith and Moral Responsibility*. Wellington, 1993; Vaughan Varwood, 'God's Work – Does Business Need Religion?', *Management Magazine* October 1993; Jenni McManus, 'Will No One Rid Me of This Turbulent Priest?', *Independent* 28 May 1993; editor, 'How State Coercion Turns Charity Cold', *Independent* 11 June 1993; Tom Frewen, 'Ye Shalt Drink bubbly, go Forth and Trickle', *NBR* 4 June 1993; Kerr, 'Read Your Catechism', *Independent* 26 February 1993; Epstein, 'No One Is Really A Moral Skeptic', *Religion and Liberty* 3:6, December 1993, 1, 6–7.
23 Lord Ralph Harris, Interview by Paul Morris, IEA, London; Robert Wheelan, Interview by Paul Morris, Civitas, London.
24 'Peruvian Writer to Lecture', *NBR* 13 August 1993; Julian L. Simon, 'Economic and Social Trends are Cause for Optimism, Not Gloom', *NBR* 25 November 1994 (an edited version of an article in *Policy*, the CIS journal); Wolfgang Kasper, 'East Asia Needs Us – But on Its Terms, Not Ours', *NBR* 2 December 1994; 'Hymns Sung to Market's Tune', *NBR* 24 February 1995.

SIX: TOWARDS THE PROSPEROUS LAND
1 Roger Douglas, *There's Got to Be a Better Way!*; Douglas, *Labour's Economic Policy: A Framework*. Wellington, 1982; Labour Party Policy Committee, *Labour's Economic Package*. Wellington, 1983; NZ Labour Party, *Manifesto, 1984*. Wellington, 1984.
2 Margaret Wilson, *Labour in Government 1984–1987*. Wellington, 1989.
3 Roger Douglas, Interview by Paul Morris.
4 Richard Prebble, Interview by Paul Morris, September 2002. Prebble, like Douglas, prided himself on not being a trained economist or specialist. He too claimed not to have read Adam Smith or Friedrich Hayek and denied understanding monetarism – 'I didn't follow all that monetarist theory'. 'What I knew about, what I understood,' he recollected, 'was sound money and that people wanted not to have to worry that their money would buy less than it did yesterday.'
5 Richard Lipsey and Alex Chrystal, *Positive Economics*. Oxford, 1995.
6 Economic Summit statement.
7 Douglas, Interview by Paul Morris.

8   Roger Kerr, 'Seven Deadly Economic Sins of the Twentieth Century', as quoted in Jonathan Boston, 'New Zealand's Welfare State in Transition', 4.

SEVEN: FROM DECENCY TO DEUTERONOMY: JIM'S GOSPEL, RUTH'S BOOK AND JENNY'S CODE
1   Edmund Bohan, *Burdon: A Man of Our Time*. Christchurch, 2004, 110, 112, 120–1, 125, 134, 143; Sir Ron Trotter, as quoted in Bohan, *Burdon*, 140; Robert Muldoon, as quoted in Bohan, *Burdon*, 174.
2   Philip Burdon, as quoted in Bohan, *Burdon*, 125, 141, 148, 147; 'Pay Equity Law Comes under Fresh Attack', *NBR* 22 August 1990; see also Jonathan Boston, Paul Dalziel, Susan St John, *Redesigning the Welfare State in New Zealand*; Jack H. Nagel, 'Social Choice in a Pluralitarian Democracy: The Politics of Market Liberalization in New Zealand', *British Journal of Political Science* 28:2, April 1998, 233–68; Andrew Sharp, *Leap into the Dark*; Jack Vowles and Peter Aimer (eds), *Voters' Vengeance: The 1990 Election in New Zealand and the Fate of the Fourth Labour Government*. Auckland, 1993; R. C. Mascarenhas, *Government and the Economy in Australia and New Zealand: The Politics of Economic Policy*. San Francisco, 1996; G. M. Kelly, 'Structural Change in New Zealand: Some Implications for the Labour Market Regime', *International Labour Review* 134:3, May–June 1995, 333–60; Brent McClintock, 'Whatever Happened to New Zealand? The Great Capitalist Restoration Reconsidered', *Journal of Economic Issues* 32:2, June 1998, 497–503; Graham Scott, *Public Management in New Zealand: Lessons and Challenges*. Wellington, 2001.
3   *Dom* 29 October 1990, as quoted in Bohan, *Burdon*, 152; Bohan, *Burdon*, 152, 153; Warwick Roger, 'The Rise and Rise of Young Mr English', *North & South* April 1999, 34–8, 40–2; Boston, 'New Zealand's Welfare State in Transition', 10–19; Dalziel and St John, 'The Role of Government', Boston and St John, 'Targeting Versus Universality: Social Assistance for All or Just for the Poor?', Pat Walsh and Peter Brosnan, 'Redesigning Industrial Relations: The Employment Contracts Act and Its Consequences', Toni Ashton, 'The Health Reforms: To Market and Back?', Laurence Murphy, 'Housing Policy', *Redesigning the Welfare State in New Zealand*.
4   *Post* 30 September 1991, as quoted in Mascarenhas, *Government and The Economy*, 102–3; David Barber, 'National Takes Axe to Welfare State', *NBR* 20 December 1990; Rodney Dickens, 'Families Come to Fore as Welfarism Crumbles', *NBR* 12 August 1991; Colin James, 'Jenny Shipley's Small-Town Values – Tale with a Moral', *NBR* 27 August 1993; Glenys Hopkinson, 'There's large writing on the wall for the public health system', *NBR* 31 January 1992; Bruce Jesson, *Fragments of Labour*, 69–72; James, 'Off They Go Into the Wild Blue Yonder', *NBR* 5 July 1991; Bohan, *Burdon*, 169–70, 171–4, 176, 177, 179; for this image of Richardson see, for example, the *Listener*; see also Boston and Dalziel, *The Decent Society*; Boston, John Martin, June Pallot and Pat Walsh (eds), *Public Management: The New Zealand Model*. Auckland, 1996; Brian Roper and Chris Rudd (eds) *State and Economy in New Zealand*. Auckland, 1993; Kelly, 'Structural Change in New Zealand'; Brian Easton, 'Economic and Other Ideas behind the New Zealand Reforms', *Oxford Review of Economic Policy* 10:3, October 1994, 78–95; Brian Silverstone, Alan Bollard and Ralph Lattimore (eds), *A Study of Economic Reform: The Case of New Zealand*. Amsterdam, 1996; Dalziel and Lattimore, *The New Zealand Macroeconomy: A Briefing on the Reforms*. Melbourne, 1996; Richard Le Heron and Eric Pawson (eds), *Changing Places: New Zealand in the Nineties*. Auckland, 1996.
5   Bohan, *Burdon*, 176; Miles Wallace, *Sunday News* 23 June 1991, as quoted in Bohan, *Burdon*, 173; Warren Berryman, *NBR* 20 September 1991, as quoted in Bohan, *Burdon*, 185–7; John Deeks, *Business and the Culture of the Enterprise Society*, as quoted in Vaughan Varwood, 'God's Work – Does Business Need Religion?'
6   New Zealand Catholic Bishops Conference, 'Employment Contracts Legislation: A Catholic Response' (1991), 'The Church in Jubilee' (1996), Chris Orsman and Peter Zwart (eds), *Church in the World: Statements on Social Issues 1979–1997 by New*

Zealand's Catholic Bishops. Wellington, 1997, 39–42, 230–9.

7   As quoted in Boston, 'Christianity in the Public Square: The Churches and Social Justice', Boston and Alan Cameron (eds), *Voices for Justice: Church, Law and State in New Zealand*. Palmerston North, 1994, 11–35; Richard Randerson, *Hearts and Minds: A Place for People in a Market Economy*. Wellington, 1992; Ruth Smithies and Helen Wilson (eds), *Making Choices: Social Justice for Our Times*. Wellington, 1993.

8   Roger Kerr, 'Moral Codes do not Ethical People Make', *Independent* 19 February 1993; 'Miracles Need to Be Funded', *Dom* 13 July 1993; 'Poor Pulpit Politics', *Dom* 14 July 1993; 'A Clerical View of Social Justice', *Post* 13 July 1993; Simon Upton, 'Churches Step into Politics', *Dom* 19 July 1993; Agnes-Mary Brooke, 'Muddled Thinking', *Dom* 11 August 1993; Michael Irwin, 'Don't Confuse Gospel with Ideologies', *Dom* 12 August 1993; John Terris, 'Churches Turn Back the Clock', *Dom* 14 August 1993; Lloyd Geering, 'Caesar's Things Belong to God, Too', *Dom* 22 July 1993; Petrus Simons, 'Social Justice and the Treasury Line', Boston and Cameron, *Voices for Justice*, 167–79; Harold Turner, 'DeepSight: Its Development', http://www.deepsight.org.

9   Michael Pusey, *Economic Rationalism in Canberra*, 21–2, 180, 231–3; see also Donald Horne (ed), *The Trouble with Economic Rationalism*. Newham, 1992; Peter Beilharz, *Transforming Labor: Labour Tradition and the Labor Decade in Australia*. Cambridge, 1994; Ray Broomhill (ed), *The Banana Republic? Australia's Current Economic Problems*. Sutherland, 1991; David Burchell, 'The Curious Career of Economic Rationalism: Government and Economy in the Current Policy Debate', *Australian New Zealand Journal of Sociology* 30:3, November 1994.

10 Stephen Bell, 'Globalisation, Neoliberalism and the Transformation of the Australian State', *Australian Journal of Political Science* 32:3, November 1997; John Hyde, 'Foreward', Michael Warby, 'Scapegoating and Moral Panic: Political Reality and Public Policy versus Anti-Rationalism', Helen Hughes, 'Australia and the World Environment – the Dynamics of International Competition and Wealth Creation', Chris James, Chris Jones and Andrew Norton (eds), *A Defence of Economic Rationalism*. St Leonard's, 1993, v–vi, 160–7, 162–5; David Thomson, 'Welfare States and the Problem of the Common', St Leonards, 1992.

11 Gabriel Moens, 'Affirmative Action: The New Discrimination', John C. Goodman and Alistair J. Nicholas, 'Voluntary Welfare', James Cox, 'Private Welfare', Gabriel Moens and Suri Ratnapala, 'The Illusions of Comparable Worth', Cathy Buchanan and Peter R. Hartley, 'Criminal Choice: The Economic Theory of Crime and Its Implications for Crime Control', Barry Maley, 'Marriage, Divorce and Family Justice', CIS Publications, List on back of David Popenoe, Norton and Barry Maley, *Shaping the Social Virtues: Taking Children Seriously*. St Leonard's, 1994; Popenoe, 'The Roots of Declining Social Virtue: Family, Community and the Need for a "Natural Communities Policy"', Norton, 'Reviewing Australia: The Modes and Morals of Australia in the '90s', Maley, 'Morals and Modernity', *Shaping the Social Virtues*, 5–35, 38–76, 77–109, 12, 29, 31, 39, 44, 71, 79–80, 83, 86, 95, 106, 107; Maley cited Jon Davies, 'From Household to Family to Individualism', *The Family: Is It Just Another Lifestyle Choice?* London, 1993; Charles Murray, 'Underclass: The Crisis Deepens', London, 1994; David Green, *Reinventing Civil Society*.

12 Gary R. Hawke, *Changing Politics? The Electoral Referendum 1993*. Wellington, 1993; Brian Easton, *The Whimpering of the State*; Bohan, *Burdon*, 207–15; Peter Shirtcliffe, 'Peter Shirtcliffe Answers His Critics', *Independent* 30 April 1993; Jenni McManus, 'Anti-MMP Ads Prey on Public Anxiety', *Independent* 9 July 1993; Gareth Morgan, 'Campaign Slogans Slay Debate, Doo Daa Doo Daa', *NBR* 5 November 1993; 'Peter and Janet Shirtcliffe Gracious in Defeat', *NBR* 12 November 1993.

13 Stephen Harris, 'Richardson Under Threat', *NBR* 26 November 1993; Bob Edlin, 'BRT Submission Advocates Labour Reform', *Independent* 23 September 1994; 'Maurice McTigue', biography, Mercatus Institute, George Mason University, Fairfax, Virginia; Alastair Thompson, 'Step Up Reform Say Employers', *NBR* 30 September 1994.

14 Robert Mannion, 'Libertarianz Brook No "Nanny-State" Nonsense', *Dom* 6 July 1996; Bohan, *Burdon*, 240–7.

15 Fred Argy, *Australia at the Crossroads: Radical Free Market or Progressive Liberalism.* St Leonard's, 1998, 185–96; Mascarenhas, *Government and the Economy*, 69.

16 Frances O'Sullivan, 'Morals and Money Mix', *NBR* 24 March 1995; James, 'The Gospel According to Michael Novak', *NBR* 24 March 1995; Alan Cocks, 'Democratic Capitalism's Three Spheres: Michael Novak Speaks to Alan Cocks', *Policy* Winter 1995; Geoff Chapple, 'Capitalism with Everything', *Listener* 8 April 1995; Margaret Clark, 'Role of the State a Pivotal Issue', *Post* 5 April 1995; James, 'Three Cheers for What? A Biblical Trip around some Difficult Posers', *NBR* 24 March 1995; Angela Ots, *Post* 25 March 1995; Frank Haden, 'Boffin Vouches for Voucher System', *Sunday Star-Times* 24 December 1995; Wolfgang Kasper, 'Kiwis Have a Better Chance to Succeed', *NBR* 8 March 1996; Richard Epstein, 'Safeguarding Liberty by Scrapping the Human Rights Act', *Independent* 26 July 1996; Robert Sirico, 'It's Time for Capitalism to Seize the Moral High Ground', *NBR* 26 August 1996; Green, *From Welfare State to Civil Society*, 1–2; Sirico, 'Defending the Indefensible Is Not State Business', *NBR* 16 February 1996.

17 Graeme Hunt, 'Welfare Rot Eats into Society's Fabric', *NBR* 4 April 1996; 'Welfarism's Evil Empire', *NBR* 16 August 1996; Kate Coughlan, 'Righting Society's Wrongs Can Be Unjust', *Post* 13 November 1996; Thomas Sowell, 'What is Justice?', *Independent* 15 November 1996; Graeme Thompson, 'Sowell Suspect', *Dom* 22 November 1996; Epstein, 'Human Rights and Anti-Discrimination Legislation', *NZBR*, Wellington, 1996; Sarah Boyd, 'Employers Step Up Efforts to Retain ECA', *Post* 20 March 1996; 'An Act for All Seasons', *NBR* 17 May 1996; Fiona Rotherman, 'Anniversary Conference Weighs Up ECA's Sins', *Independent* 17 May 1996; Epstein, 'The Role of the State in Education', *The Sir Ronald Trotter Lecture, 1995.* Wellington, 1996, 3–43, 11–12; Steve Evans, 'Michael Novak: Selling Capitalism or Claptrap?', *Independent* 24 March 1995.

18 Ian McAllister and Clive Bean, 'The Electoral Politics of Economic Reform in Australia: The 1998 Election', *Australian Journal of Political Science* 35:13, November 2000, 383–97; Argy, *Australia at the Crossroads*, 185–96; Mascarenhas, *Government and the Economy*, 69; Simon Kilroy, 'Waiting for Winston', *Dom* 14 October 1996; Michael Laws, 'Peters a Natural for the Finance Job', *Post* 15 November 1996; Chris Trotter, 'Are Peters' Politics Going against the Grain?', *Independent* 6 December 1996; 'Coalition: The Deal, Key Points', *Waikato Times* 11 December 1996, 'Peters Returns to Nat Roots', *Press* 11 December 1996; O'Sullivan, 'Jim Bolger and Winston Peters: This Two-legged Pony Can Run', *NBR* 13 December 1996.

19 Tim Duesevic, 'The Gradual Revolutionaries: Howard and Costello Have Refashioned Australian Society. Can Anyone Stop Them?', *Time International* 26 May 2003; Pusey, *The Experience of Middle Australia: The Dark Side of Economic Reform.* Sydney, 2003; Bob Catley, *Globalising Australian Capitalism.* Cambridge, 1996, 86; Frank Devine, 'Utopian Clerics on Yesterday's Bandwagon', *Australian* 30 November 1998; Friedrich Hayek, *The Fatal Conceit.*

20 Craig Young, 'The Building Blocks of Maxim', 24 March 2003, GayNZ.com, http://www.gaynz.com/features/maxim-2.asp; Lois Bryson, 'Transforming Australia's Welfare State – Social Policy under Labor', *Just Policy* 6 May 1996; Dennis Woodward, 'The Federal National Party of Australia', Brian Costar and Dennis Woodward (eds), *Country to National: Australian Rural Politics and Beyond.* Sydney, 1985; Samuel Gregg, 'The Moral Foundations of a Free Polity: Samuel Gregg Talks to Archbishop Dr. George Pell', *Policy* Autumn 1999; Eileen Disendorf, 'The New Right: Winning Friends in the Churches: Ideologies', *National Outlook* 8:9, October 1986, 19–21; Jim Jose, 'Drawing the Line: Sex Education and Homosexuality in South Australia, 1985', *Australian Journal of Politics and History* 45:2, June 1999, 197–213; Larry Galbraith, 'The Bogeyman We Had to Have – The Place of Fred Nile in Building a Strong, Vibrant and Politically Successful Gay Movement', *Outrage* November 1993,

18–23, 96.

21 Ruth Laugesen, 'Clothes Maketh or Breaketh', *Sunday Star-Times* 16 February 1997; James, 'A Match Made in Heaven or One Destined for Hell?', *NBR* 13 December 1996; Astrid Smeele, 'Public Enemy Number One Ready to Claim Political Throne', *Waikato Times* 4 November 1997; Brent Edwards, 'Anatomy of a Coup', *Post* 5 November 1997; Brent Edwards, 'PM Shipley's First Six Months at Helm', *Post* 2 June 1998; Nick Venter, 'Acrimony Takes Leaders to Brink', *Press* 14 August 1998.

22 Samuel Gregg, 'The Tragedy of Democracy: "Rights", Tolerance and Moral "Neutrality"', *Policy* Winter 2000; Tony Rutherford, 'The Flight from Virtue', *IPA Review* 49:1, 1996; Susan Windybank, 'Beyond the Welfare State: Susan Windybank talks to Charles Murray', *Policy* Spring 200l; Hyde, 'Reforming Economic Reform: It is About Fairness and Morality – So Reformers Should Say So', IPA *Review* March 1999; Padraic P. McGuinnes, 'Economic Freedom as a Good in Itself', IPA *Review* July 1997; Michael Warby, 'Moral Greed and the Politics of Insult', IPA *Review* September 1998; Samuel Gregg and Wolfgang Kasper, 'No Third Way: Hayek and The Recovery of Freedom', *Policy* Winter 1999; James L. Richardson, 'Economics: Hegemonic Discourse', *Quadrant* March 1997; Norton, 'Economic Rationalism: Realities in Conflict', *Quadrant* May 1997; Hyde, *Dry: In Defence of Economic Freedom*; 'The Good Offices of John Stone', *National Observer* Autumn 2003; Hyde, 'Reforming Economic Reform'.

23 Brash, 'New Zealand's Remarkable Reforms'; Steve Evans, 'Reserve Bank's Influence Runs around the Globe', *Dom* 4 June 1997; Mike Ross, 'Chopping off the Dead Hand of the State', *NBR* 14 August 1998.

24 John Goulter, 'Nun from Hell Swears Easy Benefits are Bad for Mums', *Post* 12 March 1997; 'Church in Doubt on "tough love" Nun', *Dom* 17 March 1997; Paul Morris, 'Fr Sirico Refused to Honour Agreement', *Post* 3 April 1998; Steve Evans, 'NZBR Knights Slog on Through Rough Country', *Dom* 26 March 1997; Tom Frewen, 'God is the Market and the Market is God', *NBR* 3 April 1998; Gareth Morgan, 'NZ on Road to Apartheid', *Post* 15 April 1998; Kenneth Minogue, *Waitangi, Morality and Reality*, Wellington, 1998; 'Grievance Culture Ignores Context', *NZH* 15 April 1998; Colin Robertson, 'Treaty "nullity" misconstrued', *Independent* 6 May 1998; 'American Scholar Questions Treaty', *Dom* 29 March 1999; Bob Edlin, 'NZBR Worried about Fiscal Discipline, Imprudence', *Independent* 17 February 1999.

25 Srikanta Chatterjee, Peter Conway, Paul Dalziel, Chris Eichbaum, Peter Harris, Bryan Philpott, Richard Shaw, *The New Politics: A Third Way for New Zealand*. Palmerston North, 1999; 'FPI Is a Think Tank, Not a Political Party', *Independent* 6 October 1999; Helen Clark, 'Implementing a Progressive Agenda After Fifteen Years of Neoliberalism: The New Zealand Experience', Address to London School of Economics by Rt Hon Helen Clark, Prime Minister of New Zealand, London, 21 February 2002; Robert H. Fagan and Michael Webber, *Global Restructuring: The Australian Experience*. Melbourne, 1994; Bob Catley, 'Australian Capitalism, 1972–2002: The Triumph of Liberalism', *Quadrant* 46:11, November 2002, 38–41; Francis G. Castles, Rolf Gerritsen, Jack Vowles (eds), *The Great Experiment: Labour Parties and Public Policy Transformation in Australia and New Zealand*. Sydney, 1996; Boston et al., *Left Turn: The New Zealand General Election of 1999*; Chris Trotter, 'Nats Regain Momentum: Shipley Seizes Helm', *Independent* 7 November 1997; Marion Fourcade-Gourinchas and Sarah L. Babb, 'The Rebirth of the Liberal Creed: Paths to Neoliberalism in Four Countries', *American Journal of Sociology*, 108:3, November 2002, 533–80; Tom Conley, 'The Domestic Politics of Globalization', *Australian Journal of Political Science* 36:2, July 2001, 223–40.

26 Trotter, '1998: The Year the Paradigm Shifted and Left the Gov't Behind', *Independent* 23 December 1998; 'Nanny State Seeks Moral Mandate' *NZH* 18 February 1998; James, 'Political Messages Hidden in Social Code', *NBR* 20 March 1998; Juli Malo, 'Code Words Will Affect US All', *Sunday News* 8 February 1998; Helen Bain, 'MPs Say Do as I Legislated, Not as I Do', *Dom* 24 February 1998; Ruth Laugesen, 'Shipley

Shapes Up', *Sunday Star-Times* 1 March 1998; Guyon Espiner, 'Fears "Big Sister" Time Survey Open to Abuse', *Post* 24 April 1998; 'Church Group Rejects Code', *Nelson Mail* 1 May 1998.

27 'D-day for Code', *Waikato Times* 28 October 1998; 'Stop Fiddling', *Nelson Mail* 3 November 1998; McManus, 'Business Abandoning Sinking Shipley', *Independent* 16 December 1998.

28 Brooke, 'Send Off the Clowns, Please', *Daily News* 3 August 1998; Graeme Speden, 'Shipley's Year of Three Governments – None of them Italian, She Says', *Independent* 23 December 1998; Kerr, 'Tired Old Policies in New Packaging', *Independent* 17 March 1999; O'Sullivan, 'Time to Rephrase the Teabreak, Add Passion', *NZH* 10 May 1999; 'NZBR Praises Government Policies', *Dom* 3 June 1999; 'Poor Not Poorer, Says NZBR', *Post* 11 June 1999; Epstein, 'Principles for a Free Society', Lecture given in Auckland, 23 March 1999, under the auspices of the Centre for Independent Studies, Wellington; Phil Love, 'Criticism of Megapay Just Envy – Shirtcliffe', *Post* 20 July 1999; 'NZBR Calls for Lower Taxes, More Asset Sales', *Waikato Times* 16 July 1999; Mike Ross, 'All Capitalists Have to Shake the "Invisible Hand"', *NBR* 23 July 1999; Pessimism Abounds, Says Myers', *Post* 11 August 1999; James Weir, 'Academic Weighs Up Results of Disarming the Unions', *Dom* 23 September 1999; 'NZ Needs More Labour Market Reforms, Says Kerr', *Dom* 19 October 1999; 'Voucher System for Schools Promoted', *Dom* 26 October 1999.

29 Anne Beston, 'Dinnergate: Shipley Fronts', *Waikato Times* 23 February 1999; Kevin Taylor, 'Successes Outnumber Mistakes', *Press* 3 October 1999; Chris Turver, 'Public Ridicule', *Dom* 11 June 1999; Kerr, 'The Rot Started Back in 1993', *Dom* 3 August 1999; Dean Bradford, 'Slow-Moving NZ Doesn't Need Braking', *Post* 29 September 1999; Victoria Main, 'Clark Victory Plan', *Press* 26 November 1999; 'Kiwis Turn Their Backs on Failed Reforms – Academic', *Post* 3 December 1999; 'National's Leader Has Earned Another Chance', *Post* 3 December 1999; Espiner, 'Slick Start as Winds of Change Begin to Blow', *Post* 4 December 1999; Venter, 'Politics' Winners and Losers', *Daily News* 20 December 1999.

EIGHT: SEXUALITY FOR SALE?

1 Laurence David Guy, 'Worlds in Collision: The Gay Debate in New Zealand, 1960–86', Ph.D. Thesis, University of Auckland, 2000, l24–5, 164–9, 171–5, 181, 189, 190, 193–5, 197–8; 'Homosexual Law Change Urged', *NZH* l0 January 1981, *Dom* l4 January 1981.

2 Barry Gustafson, *The First 50 Years: A History of the New Zealand National Party*. Auckland, 1986, 282; Margaret Wilson, *Labour in Government*, 8.

3 Women Who Want to Be Women later changed its name to Endeavour Forum and remain linked to the Eagle Forum led by Phyllis Schlafly; Guy, 'Worlds in Collision', 77–85, 131, 133, 141–4, 174; Mies Omen, Letter to the editor, *Challenge Weekly* 7 September 1994.

4 'Eyewitness News', 6 August 1985; Graeme Russell, Gay Task Force, to the Secretary, Broadcasting Corporation of New Zealand, 12 August 1985, Lou Sheldon and John Swann, Folder 8/2, Lesbian and Gay Archives of New Zealand (LAGANZ); Bernard Moran, 'New Zealand Now Prime Target', *New Zealand Tablet* 18 September 1985; Michael Fitzsimons, 'The HLR Bill, "Be on Guard" says Anti-Reformer', *Zealandia* 15 September 1985; Guy, 'Worlds in Collision', 255, 259–60; J. Weir, 'Sin is God's Territory'; Michael Fitzsimons, 'Sin for Sure but a Crime?', *Zealandia* 31 March 1985; Bill Logan, Gay Task Force, 8 July 1985; Paul Cameron, 'A Case against Homosexuality', *Human Life Review* 4:3, Summer 1978, 17–49; Institute for the Scientific Study of Sexuality, Folders 8/4/1, 8/4/2, LAGANZ; Guy, 309, 337–48; James Bacon, 'Social Effects of Homosexuality in New Zealand', Christchurch, 1985; Gay Task Force, 'Rebuttal of a Handbook of Homophobia: A Response to the Coalition of Concerned Citizens Social Effects of Homosexuality in New Zealand', LAGANZ.

5 Guy, 'Worlds in Collision', 55, 58–9, 60–1, 125; Francis Schaeffer, *A Christian*

Manifesto. Wheaton, 1982; John Adsett Evans, 'The New Christian Right in New Zealand', Bryan Gilling (ed), *'Be Ye Separate': Fundamentalism and the New Zealand Experience*. Hamilton, 1992, 69–106; Christopher Marshall, '"A Little Lower than the Angels": Human Rights in the Biblical Tradition', William Atkin and Katrine Evans (eds), *Human Rights and the Common Good: Christian Perspectives* Wellington, 1999, l4–76; Rousas John Rushdoony, *The Institutes of Biblical Law*. Nutley, 1973; Petition for God – For Family – For Country, Barry Reed, 'A Movement of History', Fran Wilde's Information Pack for Correspondents, Folder 7/49, loc. cit.; Notes on the Petition/Referendum regarding Homosexual Law Reform Pamphlet 729.75 Gay (copy 3) Lesbian & Gay Rights Resource Center, LAGANZ; P. G. Parkinson to Pastor Richard Flinn, 29 April 1985, P. Richard Flinn to P. G. Parkinson, 8 May 1985, 'Homosexuality and Law Reform: Freedom at Last?', Christchurch, 1985 Folder 8/6 Reformed Churches, NZ, R. Flinn, Gay Task Force, LAGANZ; Mike Steel, 'Anti-Gay Churchman Urges Death Penalty', *New Zealand Times* 19 May 1985.

6 Rex J. Adhar, *Worlds Colliding: Conservative Christians and the Law*. Aldershot, 2001, 221; based on an analysis of submissions to the Select Committee on the Homosexual Law Reform Bill that included 255 individuals and 50 institutions supporting the bill and 459 individuals and l40 institutions opposing the bill, out of a total of approximately 960 submissions, LAGANZ; based on analysis of LAGANZ materials and discussions with Phil Parkinson, formerly Lesbian and Gay Rights Resource Centre head and now archivist, LAGANZ, National Library, Wellington, and Alison Laurie; Janet Halley, 'The Politics of the Closet: Towards Equal Protection for Gay, Lesbian and Bisexual Identity', *UCLA Law Review* 36:5, June 1989, 915–76.

7 'Zeal in New Zealand', *Washington Post* 24 January 1985; Steve Lohr, 'New Zealand on Ship Ban; Issue of Pride', *New York Times* 10 February 1985; John Corry, 'Falwell in Debate on Nuclear Weapons', *New York Times* 20 June 1985; Seth Mydans, 'Lange Seems Delighted to be in the Center of Things', *New York Times* 29 September 1985; Mydans, 'By Making Waves, New Zealand Gets on the Map', *New York Times* 4 October 1985.

8 Rev. Michael Blair, Vicar of St Barnabas Church, Roseneath, to the Wellington Diocesan Synod 3 July 1985, 'Regarding the Homosexual Law Reform Bill', Folder 7/39, MS papers 0081, Box 4, LAGANZ; Christians for Homosexual Law Reform, 'Say Yes, Christians and the Homosexual Law Reform', Folder 7/46, loc. cit., LAGANZ; 'Cold Shoulder for US Pastor', *NZH* 7 August 1985; 'US Vicar in Bid to Stop Reform', *NZH* 5 August 1985.

9 Selwyn Dawson, 'God's Bullies', *Metro* July 1985, 170–6; Mydans, 'By Making Waves'.

10 Fran Wilde's Information Pack, LAGANZ; Lesbian & Gay Rights Resources Centre, Press Clippings Notebooks, 1984–1986, LAGANZ; Jane Clifton, 'Gay Rights: MPs Say Yes', *Dom* 10 July 1986; 'Will Attitudes Follow the Law?', *Post* 11 July 1986; 'Rights for a Minority', *Dom* 11 July 1986.

11 Based on Interviews with Katherine O'Regan and Phil Parkinson by Dolores Janiewski.

12 Based upon analysis of the Submissions and other materials contained in Submissions on Human Rights Bill, 1992, Katherine O'Regan papers, MS Papers 0082, Peter Northcote papers on Human Rights Act, MS 423, Boxes l–2, LAGANZ; Interview with Phil Parkinson.

13 David Bisman, 'Homosexuality and the "Free Market"', Papers attributed to David Bisman, Folder 7/38, Gay Task Force, MS papers 0081, Box 4, LAGANZ; see Dolores E. Janiewski, 'New Right Networks: The New Right as a Transnational Enterprise linking the United States, New Zealand and Australia', unpublished paper prepared for Networks in History Conference, Brisbane, 1 July 2002; Conversation with Phil Parkinson.

14 Jean Hardisty, *Mobilizing Resentment: Conservative Resurgence from the John Birch Society to the Promise Keeper*. Boston, 1998.

15 This can be confirmed by a Nexis search of the *Wall Street Journal*, *New York Times* and *Washington Post* for 'Monica Lewinsky' as compared to 'Enron' or the budget for the Iraq war.

NINE: EDUCATION FOR ENTERPRISE

1 *The Curriculum Review: Report of the Committee to Review the Curriculum for Schools*. Wellington, 1987, 67ff.; see also William Renwick, *Moving Target: Six Essays on Education Policy*. Wellington, 1986.

2 Roger Douglas, Interview by Paul Morris; Richard Prebble, Interview by Paul Morris.

3 Treasury, *Government Management: Brief to the Incoming Government*. Wellington, 1987.

4 Ibid., 166.

5 Ibid., 32, 33, 41, 114, 152, 262, 271. For an analysis of reaction and responses to proposals for reform, see Graeme and Susan Butterworth, *Reforming Education: The New Zealand Experience 1984–1996*. Palmerston North, 1998.

6 Gerald Grace, *Education: Commodity or Public Good?* Inaugural Lecture, Professor of Education, Victoria University of Wellington, Wellington, 5 September 1988, 4.

7 Ibid., 10.

8 Taskforce to Review Education Administration, *Administering for Excellence, Effective Administration in Education: Report of the Taskforce to Review Education Administration* (the Picot Report). Wellington, April 1988.

9 Cabinet Social Equity Committee Working Group, *The Report of the Cabinet Social Equity Committee Working Group on Post Compulsory Education and Training*. Wellington, July 1988; *Education to Be More*. Wellington, August 1988; the reports were followed by *Tomorrow's Schools*. Wellington, 1989; *Learning for Life: Education and Training Beyond the Age of Fifteen*. Wellington, 1989; *Learning for Life Two: Policy Decisions Learning for Life: Education and Training Beyond the Age of Fifteen*. Wellington, 1989; and *Before Five*. Wellington, 1989.

10 The Picot Report, 2, 21–5.2.26, 5.6.1.

11 Ibid., 62–63. This Parent Advocacy Council was to support parents in educational decision-making and to foster issues of wider or national concern. PAC was reviewed in April 1991 (*A Review of the Parent Advocacy Council*) and, after debates about contracting out and costs, was abolished in October 1991.

12 New Zealand Education Reform Implementation Process Team and Noel V. Lough, *Today's Schools: A Review of the Educational Reform Implementation Process* (the Lough Report). Wellington, 1990, 17–18.

13 See the Picot Report, chapter 7, on Maori equity, 7.22, 65.

14 *Tomorrow's Schools*, 26.

15 New Zealand Ministry of Education and Lockwood Smith, *Education Policy: Investing in People: Our Greatest Asset*. Wellington, 1991.

16 New Zealand Ministry of Education, *The New Zealand **Curriculum Framework** Te Anga Marautanga o Aotearoa*. Wellington, 1993.

17 NZBR, *Reforming Tertiary Education in New Zealand*. Wellington, 1988; NZBR, *Reforming Tertiary Education*. Wellington, 1991.

18 *Reforming Tertiary Education*, 1988.

19 *Reforming Tertiary Education*, 62; see also James D. Marshall (ed), *The Economics of Education*. Auckland, 1995.

20 New Zealand's Universities Review Committee, *New Zealand's Universities: Partners in National Development* (the Watt Report). Wellington, 1987.

21 Ibid., 47, 81.

22 See note 5, above, for details.

23 Gary R. Hawke, *Report on Postcompulsory Education and Training in New Zealand* (the Hawke Report). Wellington, 1988, 2.2.6.19–20.

24 The Hawke Report, Executive Summary, 6.

25 New Zealand Ministerial Consultative Group and Jeff Todd, *Funding Growth in Tertiary Education and Training: A Report of the Ministerial Consultative Group* (the Todd Report). Wellington, 1994, 159.
26 Ibid.
27 'Existing fee levels (already at the maximum of 20% of course costs proposed by [the Watt Report]) are causing hardship for many students leading to excessive withdrawals from courses and programmes. In 1993, 3,000 students withdrew from tertiary Education citing financial reasons.' The Todd Report, 158.
28 The Todd Report, 91.
29 New Zealand Treasury, *Briefing to the Incoming Government*. Wellington, 1996.
30 Ministry of Education memorandum, 1997b, 5.
31 New Zealand Ministry of Education, *A Future Tertiary Education Policy for New Zealand: Tertiary Education Review*. Wellington, 1997.
32 New Zealand Ministry of Education, *Tertiary Education in New Zealand: Policy Directions for the 21st Century*, November 1998. Wellington, 1998.
33 Ministry of Education, *Tertiary Education*. 1998, 17.
34 Ruth Butterworth and Nicholas Tarling, *A Shakeup Anyway: Government & the Universities in New Zealand in a Decade of Reform*. Auckland, 1994, 141.
35 Gary Hawke, 'Education Reform; The New Zealand Experience', Draft NZTC WP 20, 2003.

TEN: THE RESTORATION OF VIRTUE

1 This chapter is based on research undertaken by Andrew Gregg, Research Assistant, Royal Society of New Zealand Marsden Fund Research Project 'Marketing Morality: The Campaign to Remoralise New Zealand, 1984–1999', and his M.A. Thesis, 'Panic Attacks: The New Right, Media and Welfare Reform in New Zealand, 1987–1998', Victoria University of Wellington, 2004; Bert Walker's quote and Muldoon's critique are from Melanie Nolan, *Bread Winning: New Zealand Women and the State*. Christchurch, 2000, 282–7.
2 Graeme Hunt, 'Welfare Rot Eats into Society's Fabric', *NBR* 4 April 1996; Fritz W. Scharpf and Vivien A. Schmidt, 'Preface', Scharpf and Schmidt (eds), *Welfare and Work in the Open Economy, Vol II: Diverse Responses to Common Challenges*. Oxford, 2000; Phil Love, 'Social Policy Seen As Biggest Challenge', *Post* 26 February 1996; David Green, 'A Personal Duty to Help Others', *Dom* 27 March 1996.
3 For further discussion, see Alice O'Connor, *Poverty Knowledge: Social Science, Social Policy and the Poor in Twentieth-Century US History*. Princeton, 2001; and Alice O'Connor, 'Think Tanks and the War on Welfare', unpublished draft paper, presented at American Sociological Association Conference, Chicago, August 2002; Steve Lohr, 'New Zealand Tries Free-Market Stand', *New York Times* 10 June 1985; Love, 'Social Policy Seen As Biggest Challenge'.
4 Treasury, *Economic Management*; Treasury, *Government Management*; Jane Kelsey, *The New Zealand Experiment*, 46–62; on conservative think tanks, see James Smith, *The Idea Brokers: Think Tanks and the New Policy Elite*. New York, 1991, 22–3, 167–72; on Victorian virtues, see Gertrude Himmelfarb, *The De-Moralization of Society: From Victorian Virtues to Modern Values*. New York, 1995; and Joel Schwartz, *Fighting Poverty with Virtue: Moral Reform and America's Urban Poor, 1825–2000*. Bloomington, 2000.
5 On comparative welfare reform, see Julia S. O'Connor, Ann Shola Orloff and Sheila Shaver, *States, Markets, Families: Gender, Liberalism and Social Policy in Australia, Canada, Great Britain and the United States*. Cambridge, 1999, 140–1, 149, 152–3, 189–91; Sanford F. Schram, *After Welfare: The Culture of Postindustrial Social Policy*. New York, 2000, 52–8; and Herman Schwartz, 'Internationalization and Two Liberal Welfare States: Australia and New Zealand', Scharpf and Schmidt, *Welfare and Work in the Open Economy*, 69–130.
6 Schwartz, 'Internationalization and Two Liberal Welfare States', 75, 87, 88, 94–101;

see also Pat Walsh, 'The State Sector', *Reshaping the State*, 52–80; Robert Gregory, 'Reorganization of the Public Sector', Boston and Martin Holland (eds), *The Fourth Labour Government*, 111–33; Stephen Jennings and Robert Cameron, 'State-Owned Enterprise Reform in New Zealand', Alan Bollard and Robert Buckle (eds), *Economic Liberalisation in New Zealand*. Wellington, 1987, l21–52; Francis G. Castles, 'Changing Course in Economic Policy: The English-Speaking Nations in the 1980s', Francis G. Castles, *Families of Nations: Patterns of Public Policy in Western Democracies*. Aldershot, 1993, 3–34; Margaret McClure, *A Civilised Community: A History of Social Security in New Zealand, 1898–1998*. Auckland, 1998, 210–56; Geoffrey Rice, 'A Revolution in Social Policy, 1981–1991', Geoffrey W. Rice (ed), *The Oxford History of New Zealand*. Auckland, 1992, 482–97.

7   Murray, *Losing Ground*; Alex Waddan, *The Politics of Social Welfare: The Collapse of the Centre and the Rise of the Right*. Cheltenham, 1997; Schram, *After Welfare*, 32–58; Gary Bauer, 'The Family: Preserving America's Future', 1986, as quoted in Lou Cannon, *President Reagan: the Role of a Lifetime*. New York, 2000, 456–7; Heritage Foundation, *Mandate for Leadership* I and II. Washington, 1981, 1984; Mead, *Beyond Entitlement*.

8   Castles, 'Changing Course in Economic Policy'; O'Connor, Orloff and Shaver, *States, Markets, Families*; Lord Ralph Harris and Arthur Seldon, 'Over-ruled on Welfare', IEA, London, 1979; 'Charles Murray and the Underclass', IEA, London, 1996; Margaret Thatcher, *The Downing Street Years*. London, 1973, reprinted in Margaret Jones and Rodney Lowe (eds), *From Beveridge to Blair: The First Fifty Years of Britain's Welfare State, 1948–98*. Manchester, 2002, 28–30, 32–4, 53–4.

9   Treasury, 'Social Policy', *Government Management*, I, 121–86, 124–5; 187–311; 435–70.

10   *NBR* 16 October 1987.

11   Michael James, 'Introduction', Michael James (ed), *The Welfare State: Foundations and Alternatives: The Proceedings of CIS Conferences held in Wellington and Sydney, November 1987*. St Leonards, 1989, ix–xi, ix, x.

12   Janice Peterson, 'Ending Welfare as We Know It: The Symbolic Importance of Welfare Policy', *Journal of Economic Issues* 31:2, June 1997, 425–31; Evelyn Brodkin, 'The Making of an Enemy: How Welfare Policies Construct the Poor', *Law and Social Inquiry* 18, 1993, 647–70; Nancy Fraser and Linda Gordon, 'The Genealogy of Dependency: Tracing a Keyword in the US Welfare State', Nancy Fraser et al., *Critical Politics: From the Personal to the Global*. Melbourne, 1994, 77–109.

13   Daniel Moynihan, *The Politics of a Guaranteed Income*. New York, 1973, 17, as quoted in Fraser and Gordon, 'The Genealogy of Dependency', 77–8, 86; O'Connor, Orloff and Shaver, *States, Markets, Families*, 189–91; for a discussion of the 'medicalisation' of welfare, see Schram, *After Welfare*, 59–88.

14   For international comparisons of welfare systems see Gosta Esping-Andersen, *The Three Worlds of Welfare Capitalism*. Princeton, 1990.

15   The Royal Commission on Social Policy, *The April Report: Future Directions*, II. Wellington, 1988, 6–7, 11.

16   Alan Gibbs, 'The Welfare State Should Go the Way of SOEs', *NBR* 5 February 1988; O'Connor, Orloff and Shaver, *States, Markets, Families*, 191.

17   Stephen Harris, 'Welfare State Morally Bankrupt', *Dom* 11 November 1987; 'Welfare Pride and Prejudice', *NZH* 11 April 1988; 'Persuading People to Work', *Press* 12 January 1990; 'Working for a Benefit', *Press* 28 May 1990; David Wilson, 'The Benefits of Being Poor', *Press* 30 July 1990; K. Ross, 'Social Welfare Pays for Abortions', *Dom* 9 July 1990; E. Heath, Cartoon, *Dom* 16 October 1990; as quoted in Gregg, 'Panic Attacks', 58, 70–1, 77, 83, 81, 86.

18   Alan Woodfield, 'Private versus Public Provision of Social Welfare Services in New Zealand', Colin James, *The Welfare State*, 115–54, 128; David Band, Director, CIS Social Welfare Research Program, 'Unintended Consequences and Unthinkable Solutions', *The Welfare State*. 27–47, 29; Charles Murray, 'The American Experience

with the Welfare State', *The Welfare State*, 71–83, 83; Murray, *Losing Ground*; Ken Ovenden, 'The Prime of Ms Ruth Richardson', *North & South* May 1988; S. Cave, 'Ruth Rules', *Listener* 28 January 1989, 16; Anthony Hubbard, 'Right by Ruth', *Listener* 20 August 1990, Jane Clifton, 'Jobless Free Ride Over Says Nats', *Dom* 21 May 1990; Mike Munro, 'Nats Get Tough on Young Solo Parents', *Dom* 11 August 1990; Richard Long, 'Nats Aim to Encourage Solo Mothers to Work', *Dom* 10 October 1990; Simon Collins, 'Richard Proposes Redesign for Welfare', *NZH* 3 May 1990; Simon Upton, 'Social Welfare, Maoris – How National Differs', *Press* 24 July 1990; as quoted in Gregg, 'Panic Attacks', 61, 72, 74, 75.

19   Mike Ross, 'Welfare needs to go private', *NBR* 21 January 1991; Rodney Dickens, 'Families Come to Fore as Welfarism Crumbles', *NBR* 12 August 1991; James, 'Jenny Shipley's Small-Town Values – Tale with a Moral', *NBR* 27 August 1993; David Barber, 'National Takes Axe to Welfare State', *NBR* 20 December 1990; Richardson, 'Address to the Wellington Chamber of Commerce', 27 March 1991; Richardson, 'A State of the Nation Speech to the Lincoln and Hornby Rotary Clubs', 3 April, 1991, as quoted in Philippa Horrex, 'Industry, Thrift and Divine Reward: An examination of the ideology and theology of work in New Zealand (1840–1992)', Ph.D. Thesis, Religious Studies, Victoria University, 1999.

20   Submission of Social Justice Sector Council of the Anglican Diocese of Auckland to Finance Bill 1992; Hubbard, 'The Rev Stirrer', *Listener* 28 October 1998; Submission of Auckland Methodist Mission to Finance Bill, 1991; Smithies and Wilson (eds), *Making Choices*, as quoted in Gregg, 'Panic Attacks', 102, 106.

21   Smithies and Wilson, *Making Choices*, 32, 44, as quoted in Gregg, 'Panic Attacks', 106; Robert Sirico, 'Primetime TV', 25 May 1993; Robert Sirico, 'Economics, Faith and Moral Responsibility', as quoted in Gregg, 'Panic Attacks', 115.

22   Patrick Mooney, 'New Right's Charity Agenda', *Post* 12 April 1996; 'Welfare State Doesn't Work', *NBR* 12 April 1996.

23   Richard A. Epstein, 'The Role of the State in Education', *The Sir Ronald Trotter Lecture, 1995*. Wellington, 1996, 3–43, 11–12; see also Epstein, 'Principles for a Free Society', Lecture given in Auckland, 23 March 1999, under the auspices of the Centre for Independent Studies, Wellington; Gary S. Becker and Guity Nashat Becker, *The Economics of Life: From Baseball to Affirmative Action to Immigration, How Real-World Issues Affect Our Everyday Life*. New York, 1999; Gary S. Becker, *A Treatise on the Family*, 1981.

24   Green, *From Welfare State to Civil Society*; Anna Kominik, 'New Blueprint for Social Welfare', *Dom* 25 March 1996; Green, 'A Personal Duty to Help Others'; Karl Du Fresne, 'Provocative Attack on Welfare Spending', *Post* 2 April 1996.

25   Ian F. Grant, 'From Welfare State to Civil Society', *Management Magazine* November 1996.

26   'Response of a Civil Society', *Post* 3 April 1996; Hunt, 'Welfare Rot Eats into Society's Fabric'; Tom Cardy, 'Welfare Recipients Targeted', *Post* 2 April 1996; Rosemary McLeod, 'Let's Keep the Fallen Women in Line', *Dom* 28 March 1996; Michael Belgrave, 'Dark Satanic Mills No Jerusalem', *Post* 12 April 1996; E. J. Borich, 'Dark Side of Capitalism', *Post* 12 April 1996; Peter Nickless, 'The Welfare System is Not Destructive', *Post* 15 April 1996; Jocelyn Brooks, 'Society's Moral Obligation', *Post* 12 April 1996; Smithies, 'Soup Kitchens and Social Policies', *Dom* 10 April 1996; Chris Trotter, 'Guest Comment', *Independent* 19 April 1996.

27   Department of Social Welfare, *Strategic Directions: Post-Election Briefing Paper* Wellington, 1996, 14, as quoted in Gregg, 'Panic Attacks', 114.

28   Du Fresne, 'Deserted Pews in Mainstream Churches', *Post* 10 April 1996; Agnes-Mary Brooke, 'When Dream Time's Over', *Dom* 1 May 1996.

29   Brooke, 'When Dream Time's Over'; Ross, 'Unwritten Ethics Supply Vital Spark to Economy', *NBR* 28 June 1996; Cardy, 'Learning from the Wisconsin Changes', *Post* 12 March 1997; Ian Templeton, 'New Political Order Has a Few Shocks in Store', *Sunday Star-Times* 16 February 1997; Irving Kristol (fellow of the American Enterprise

Institute), 'Forget the Money, Welfare State's Crisis is Spiritual', *NBR* 21 February 1997.

30 'Tough Love', *Press* 20 March 1997; Cardy, 'DSW to Sell U Hutt Unit', *Post* 30 April 1997; Lawrence M. Mead, 'The New Paternalism: How Should Congress Respond?', *Public Welfare* 50:2, 1992, 14–17; Lawrence M. Mead, *The New Politics of Poverty: The Non-Working Poor in America*. New York, 1992; Lawrence Mead, Interview by Dolores Janiewski, New York University; Hubbard, 'Making the Welfare System Work', *Sunday Star-Times* 16 March 1997; Simon Kilroy, 'Welfare Revamp Leans on US Model', *Dom* 14 May 1998.

31 Lawrence M. Mead, 'Raising Work Levels among the Poor', 'Beyond Dependency', *Social Policy Journal of New Zealand/Te Puna Whakaaro* 8 March 1997, 1–28, 14; Charles Murray, 'Here's the Bad news on the Underclass', *Wall Street Journal* 8 March 1990; Mead, 'Raising Work Levels among the Poor', 17, 21, 23.

32 Steve Evans, 'Circling the Wagons for the Attack from the Left and Right', *Dom* 17 May 1997; 'Tough Love', *Press* 20 March 1987; 'Tough Love Must Replace Welfare', *NZH* 15 March 1997; Martin Hames, 'Hard-Bitten Old Nun Shows the Harm Done by Welfare', *NZH* 21 March 1997; Bill Berkowitz, 'Father Robert Sirico: Power Broker on the Rise', 3 July 2001, AlterNet, www.alternet.org.

33 Muriel Newman , 'Poor Welfare Performance Shows Need for Reform', *NBR* 6 March 1998.

34 Phillida Bunkle, 'How Market Theory Propels "Social Inequality" – a Theoretical Critique of the Market', Mike O'Brien and C. Briar (eds), *Beyond Poverty: Citizenship, Welfare and Well-Being in the 2lst Century*. Auckland, 1997, 28–9; Sue Bradford, 'Beyond Dependency – On Whose Terms?', 17–22; C. Briar, 'Poverty as the Result of Idleness? – The Example of Working Women's Poverty', 23–6; Anne Else, 'Is Growing Welfare Bill a Problem?', *NZH* 8 April 1997; C. Masters, 'Theme of Welfare Gathering Criticised', *NZH* 15 March 1997; as quoted in Gregg, 'Panic Attacks', 129–130.

35 Jo Myers, 'Cost of Social Welfare Conference "Crass"', *Evening Standard* 6 February 1997; Cardy, 'Learning from the Wisconsin Changes', *Post* 12 March 1997; Margaret Bazley, 'Welfare Dependency', *Dom* 21 April 1997.

36 'Only Real Jobs Will Cure Welfare Dependency', *Waikato Times* 21 March 1997; 'Breaking the Cycle of Dependency', *Post* 19 March 1997; 'Stop the Benefit Treadmill', *Dom* 24 March 1997; 'How Small-Minded, Not to Listen to Others' Opinions', *Daily News* 21 March 1997.

37 David Lange, 'Discrimination against Women Actively, Routinely Pursued', *Southland Times* 25 March 1997; 'Welfare Conference', *Southland Times* 24 March 1997; Annette King, 'Beneficiary Bashing is Not Welfare Reform', *Post* 10 July 1997; Evans, 'Circling the Wagons for the Attack from the Left and Right', *Dom* 17 May 1997; Trotter, 'Turning Back the Clock to Slums of 1911', *Dom* 11 April 1997; Sally Ansley, 'Where are the Voices of Dissent?', *Press* 11 April 1997; Kelsey, 'For Richer or Poorer', *Sunday Star-Times* 27 April 1997.

38 Helen Bain, 'Peters Hints at Benefit Cuts for Parental Neglect', *Dom* 3l May 1997; C. Daniels, 'Peters Wants Code for Beneficiaries', *Dom* 27 June 1997; James, 'Reaching for Slipper Future vs. Restoring Humpty Dumpty', *NBR* 20 February 1998; 'Code Aimed at All Parents – Sowry', *Dom* 2 July 1997; Jane Clifton, 'Code Blue', *Listener* 4 October 1997; Kim Hill, 'Focus on Politics', National Radio, 18 February 1998; James, 'Political Messages Hidden in Social Code', *NBR* 20 March 1998; P. Luke, 'Shipley to Shore: Social Code No Moral Crusade', *NBR* 21 February 1998; Neville Bennett, 'Plan to "Improve" Families Will Push against Tide of Society', *NBR* 27 February 1998; Patricia Herbert, 'Nanny State Seeks Moral Mandate', *NZH* 18 February 1998; William Low, 'Cracking Shipley's Code', *NZH* 5 March 1998; 'Shipley Wants Radical Work on Social Issues', *Dom* 4 April 1998; as quoted in Gregg, 'Panic Attacks', 137, 138, 139, 141, 143, 152.

39 'Many Beneficiaries to Blame – MP', *Dom* 29 September 1997; A. Laxon, 'ACT Takes Tough Line on Dole Handouts', *NZH* 29 September 1997; 'Expanding Welfare Futile',

Press 29 September 1997; 'Welfare System Anti-Marriage ACT', *Press* 10 October 1997; Gareth Morgan, 'Taxes, Queen Bees – and Drones', *NZH* 2 December 1997; James Cox, 'Adverse Consequences in Generous Welfare Benefits', *NZH* 12 February 1998; James Cox, *Towards Personal Independence and Prosperity: Income Support for Persons of Working Age*. Wellington, 1998; Michael James, 'More Commercial Approach Needed', *NZH* 11 November 1997; K. Taylor, 'Love, Guidance and a Swift Kick', *Press* 28 March 1998, 'Limit Code to Beneficiaries – Business Lobby', *Dom* 12 May 1998; as quoted in Gregg, 'Panic Attacks', 139–40, 151, 155, 159.

40 'The 1998 Hikoi of Hope', www.geocities.com/ubinz/Hikoi/; NZ Press Association, 'Anglicans say Hikoi of Hope initiatives are making progress', 14 April 1999; Ken Mackinnon, 'No Wonder Social Welfare System is Unable to Cope', *NZH* 24 September 1998; 'Bishop Puts Hikoi Back on the Road', *NZH* 18 November 1998; McLoughlin, 'People Power', *North & South* April 1998, 28; Gordon Campbell, 'Church v. State', *Listener* 29 August 1998; D. Gee, 'Anglicans on the March over Poverty', *Press* 14 May 1998; as quoted in Gregg, 'Panic Attacks', 152, 164–5.

Index